The New Middle Class in China

*Frontiers of Globalization Series*

Series Editor: Jan Nederveen Pieterse, Professor of Sociology, University of California, Santa Barbara, US.

*Titles include:*

Sashi Nair
SECRECY AND SAPPHIC MODERNISM
Writing *Romans à Clef* Between the Wars

Shanta Nair-Venugopal
THE GAZE OF THE WEST AND FRAMINGS OF THE EAST

Jan Neverdeen Pieterse and Boike Rehbein *(editors)*
GLOBALIZATION AND EMERGING SOCIETIES
Development and Inequality

Boike Rehbein *(editor)*
GLOBALIZATION AND INEQUALITY IN EMERGING SOCIETIES

Eileen Yuk-Ha Tsang
THE NEW MIDDLE CLASS IN CHINA
Consumption, Politics and the Market Economy

---

**Frontiers of Globalization Series**
**Series Standing Order: HBK: 978–0–230–28432–6 PBK: 978–0–230–28433–3**
*(outside North America only)*

You can receive future titles in this series as they are published by placing a standing order. Please contact your bookseller or, in case of difficulty, write to us at the address below with your name and address, the title of the series and the ISBN quoted above.

Customer Services Department, Macmillan Distribution Ltd, Houndmills, Basingstoke, Hampshire RG21 6XS, England

# The New Middle Class in China

## Consumption, Politics and the Market Economy

Eileen Yuk-Ha Tsang
*City University of Hong Kong, Hong Kong*

First published 2014 by
PALGRAVE MACMILLAN

Palgrave Macmillan in the UK is an imprint of Macmillan Publishers Limited, registered in England, company number 785998, of Houndmills, Basingstoke, Hampshire RG21 6XS.

Palgrave Macmillan in the US is a division of St Martin's Press LLC, 175 Fifth Avenue, New York, NY 10010.

Palgrave Macmillan is the global academic imprint of the above companies and has companies and representatives throughout the world.

Palgrave® and Macmillan® are registered trademarks in the United States, the United Kingdom, Europe and other countries

ISBN 978-0-230-35444-9

This book is printed on paper suitable for recycling and made from fully managed and sustained forest sources. Logging, pulping and manufacturing processes are expected to conform to the environmental regulations of the country of origin.

A catalogue record for this book is available from the British Library.

A catalog record for this book is available from the Library of Congress.

*For my parents*

# Contents

# List of Figure and Tables

**Figure**

**Tables**

# Preface

This is a story of my research journey. And like all research, it begins with the researcher and the interviewees.

A researcher's interest in a certain phenomenon goes quite a long way in shaping the initial conception of what the research study is about. How that interest is framed necessarily reflects a particular vantage point taken by the researcher and reflects his or her interests, destinations and motivations. Steier (1991: 1) has been enlightening in this respect: 'What I describe in my research is in no way existent apart from my involvement in it – it is not "out there"'.

Since around the 1990s, the 'Chinese new middle class' has attracted considerable attention. State socialist countries have undergone varying degrees of economic and political reform in recent years and these have undoubtedly aroused concerns over their formation and their reach and impact and their consequences for society. Highly visible are the growing numbers of the Chinese new middle class, who are seen to have an obvious enthusiasm in leading an affluent way of life by way of status symbols such as owning brand-named products and expensive automobiles.

My own interest for the purposes of this study is the growing groups of increasingly influential people who are viewed as the 'Chinese new middle class': regional party cadres, entrepreneurs and professionals in today's post-reform China.

Research is 'primarily about discovering new knowledge' (Gilbert 1993: 33; Kwong 2001) in an unknown territory. The research process involves, to a greater or lesser degree, a continual interaction of ideas and that interaction may drive the work in unexpected directions (Roberts 1981; Kwong 2001). On the first leg of my research journey, I had crude ideas of the direction and the terrain of the research landscape before me. My attention had been drawn to the ways of living and consumerist behaviour of newly rich groups in contemporary China in general and in Guangdong province in particular. However, I would not be able to plan too far ahead. I took my 'researcher self' in the research process as seriously as practicable. I wanted to research into something that I wanted to know and was going through myself. And this has motivated me to settle on my long research journey, despite the sometimes clear and present twists and turns in the research process, which should be regarded as 'mistakes' by design.

Over the past few years, I had surveyed the body of literature on a wide but related range of topics: the indigenisation of the middle class and the consumption patterns and lifestyles of the Chinese new middle class. Meanwhile, I kept close connections with various members of the Chinese new middle class whom I have interviewed. It transpired quite early on that my preliminary perspective rested on some research questions and assumptions.

One preliminary assumption is that cultural differences have been grossly amplified to the extent of reinforcing cultural stereotypes by some cultural sociologists. Culture and meanings are embodied in the way a person sees, thinks, interprets and values. The connection between theories and practice is far more complex than I had at first thought. I wanted to take the various theories and link them up one way or another with real-world class practices by means of interviewing the Chinese new middle class in Guangdong province: they should speak for themselves about their own lifestyles and consumption habits. The Chinese new middle class had sprung into existence in Chinese society and their sudden arrival appears to have important implications (albeit yet to be determined) for the new social stratification and social inequality in mainland China. Producing a description of the quality of lived experience is inadequate and insufficient. Increasingly obvious to me is this point: what is most important to our understanding is to describe the *meanings hidden behind* the lived experience and the value that they have to the actors. The product, therefore, is a constructed text of human actions, behaviours, intentions and experiences in the actors' life-world.

Theoretical frameworks and empirical data are of paramount importance to me since they provide a guiding thread to a more comprehensive framework to better understand the empirical setting of the development of China under the dual influence of economic reform and globalisation. Even so, my own experience as a researcher tells me that more concrete practices, unfettered access to fieldsites in Guangdong and the personal quality to get along well with people are usually more important in the field. These aspects are especially important in a place like China where conservatism and reserve are still the norm and many of the Chinese new middle class are wary of accepting the approach of a researcher to conduct in-depth interviews. Theories and practice are complementary partners (or at least they should be) to understand the peculiarities and idiosyncrasies of the Chinese new middle class in Guangdong province (Kwong 2001).

Having *rethought* the aims and focus of the study, I then went on to examine the methodological questions for the study. I picked up the 'story' metaphor from my in-depth interviews and participant observations of people's experiences and the meanings they made of those experiences. I decided to 'talk' to the Chinese new middle class and collect their 'stories' of how they became the rising stars of the reform era. The people of the Chinese new middle class narrated their private lives and revealed, to a greater or lesser degree, the various versions of the Chinese new middle class that they apparently subscribed or aspired to at different points in their careers and everyday lives. Based on those in-depth interviews, I as the participant researcher used my own reflections (Steier 1991), subject knowledge and analysis to interpret or reinterpret their meanings.

This book transcends the strictures of Western class theories in its theoretically-led empirical study of the Chinese new middle class who are distinguished by their socio-cultural rather than economic traits. Based upon qualitative interviews in Guangdong, Southern China, the study looks at entrepreneurs, professionals, and regional party cadres from various age groups. It highlights the complex networks amongst these different groups as well as the salient role that cadres play in the reproduction of class in post-reform China.

The study also explores generational differences and illuminates how the older generations are pragmatic and business-oriented in their consumption. For comparison, the younger generations are more flexible, individualistic and more preoccupied with personal gain. The author argues that, contrary to the arguments of Western stratification theorists, both generations of China's new echelon remain tepid towards the idea of political reform alongside market reforms. The conclusion is clear: despite being vanguards of consumption, they are laggards in politics.

# Acknowledgements

I would like to thank the many people who helped bring this book to fruition.

Thanks are due, first and foremost, to my interviewees, whose willingness to speak frankly was inspiring. Their recollections provide a remarkable source of insights about Chinese society. We began as strangers and are now friends. Their identities have been protected here. 'Uncle Wong' in particular deserves special thanks. He made it possible for me to have access to a wide range of influential people across China. He often went the extra mile to arrange transport and accommodation and generally facilitate logistical matters for me during the course of my fieldwork. I owe a great deal to him.

I would also like to thank Professor John Holmwood, who spent many hours in incisive conversation with me, listening to my ideas and suggesting how they might be presented more effectively. His no-nonsense approach to theoretical and practical research work continues to inspire. Thanks are also due to Mike McIlvain, Professors Jeff Wilkinson and Michael Joseph Igoe, and Dr. Pak K. Lee, and Dr. José Lingna Nafafé, for their words of encouragement and attentive listening. They have nourished me intellectually and emotionally and helped me to contemplate avenues of exploration that I would not otherwise have embarked upon. This work is in every respect a product of interpersonal interaction.

Finally, I am indebted to my parents for their support and forbearance. This book is dedicated to them.

# Introduction: China Engages a Middle-Class Society in the 21st Century?

> The everyday social and cultural practices seen in China today exhibit heterogeneity rather than homogeneity. Such a heterogeneity (fragmentation, if you will) challenges traditional concepts of class. Class should now be incorporated into the body of socio-cultural terminology because the case of China shows that lifestyles and consumption patterns play an important role in redefining the class boundary, as is shown by the features of the Chinese new middle class. The explanatory power of class structure in general Sociology is set to undergo a fundamental change because of the Chinese situation.
>
> (Author's own memorandum)

I started thinking about the Chinese new middle class (中国新中产阶层 *Zhongguo xinzhongchan jieceng*, literally, the new medium-asseted stratum) in the first decade of the 21st century. It was a reaction brought on by an acquaintance, who will go by the pseudonym of 'Uncle Wong'. His story provided the impetus for me to think more deeply about this 'class' of people in today's China.

Uncle Wong is a man of substance: he is about 40 years of age and a party cadre in Guangdong. I first met him in 2008 through an acquaintance in Guangdong. Since then we have become friends. He is a frequent visitor to Hong Kong, with a reputation for generosity and lavish spending. I often accompanied him whenever he came to Hong Kong on his many shopping or sightseeing trips. In many ways, Uncle Wong was the inspiration for my research into the lifestyle and consumption patterns of the new middle class in post-reform China.

The first time I met Uncle Wong, I thought he (the big spender I have come to know him to be) was simply practising conspicuous, hedonistic consumption in Hong Kong. He was buying a large amount of valuable jewellery: jade, gold, diamond-studded watches, and so on. That shopping spree alone apparently cost him RMB20,000 (US$2,928 or £2,022).[1]

What was most interesting to me as a social-science researcher was not the shopping spree itself but that he paid for his purchases in cash, rather than by using credit cards or cheques. This behaviour astonished me, though it should not have done so. Later, I found that Uncle Wong's behaviour is quite common among the rich in China today. I then became curious about the people like Uncle Wong – China's burgeoning new middle class, their attitudes and aspirations. I hold that their lifestyles serve as a guide to contemporary China and the very distinct path of change upon which it is now embarking.

The introduction of market reforms – beginning in small steps in the late 1970s, but accelerating from the 1990s onwards – and China's apparent move from an economic system of state planning to a market-based one is a familiar story. But before I begin my outline of this study, I will briefly delineate the situations of pre-reform China and post-reform China which are affecting the rise of the Chinese new middle class in the wake of the reforms.

## Pre-reform China at a glance

The Chinese Communist Party (CCP) under Mao Zedong took power in 1949 and immediately began a programme of revolutionary change. One of their first steps was the passage of a new marriage law (based on the Soviet model of the 1920s) that set a new course for women and children (Meisner 1999). From the 1950s to the late 1970s, the central government imposed authoritarian rule with all policies being buttressed by a command economy and controlled by strict planning guidelines. In 1958–61, the regime carried out the Great Leap Forward (*Dayuejin* 大跃进), a radical campaign aimed at fast-forwarding the country to an egalitarian and prosperous communist society. It abolished private ownership and established a new social formation called 'the rural people's commune' (*renmin gongshe* 人民公社). Class became heavily conditional on party political affiliation and observance. Property in private hands was confiscated and evenly distributed among the entire Chinese population. The central authorities directed industries according to strict central planning guidelines (Lü & Perry 1997; Pun 2005; Walder 1986, 1989).

The two most salient social institutions of Maoist China were the *hukou* ( 户口 'household registration') and *danwei* ( 单位 'work unit') systems, both of which continue in a modified form to this day. The *hukou* system classifies the entire population into two (and only two) categories: agricultural registrants are domiciled in rural areas and non-agricultural (urban) registrants in metropolitan areas. Introduced in the 1950s, it had become firmly entrenched by the early 1960s. The *hukou* is a nationwide system of household registration set up under the 1958 Regulations on *Hukou* Registration, issued by the National People's Congress (NPC), in a bid to safeguard progress towards collectivisation in rural areas and to control food shortages in urban areas. It was designed chiefly to control internal population movements. It created a legal domicile for every person and bound each person permanently to that domicile. At the same time, in many contexts the *hukou* could also refer to a family register since *hukou* was issued on a household basis and usually included details of births, deaths, marriages, divorces and the movement of all members in the family. The *hukou* also identified a person or household by administrative category (rural *vs.* urban). A dual household management thus began to take shape. It was a system that curtailed the geographical mobility of people and also accordingly denoted the salience of native-place identity in urban China (Lü & Perry 1997: 43).

The *danwei* system refers to the place of employment, especially in the context of state enterprises during the pre-reform period. The *danwei* was the first step and principal channel for the implementation of party policy in the Chinese socialist infrastructure. The work unit once held considerable sway over the life of an individual: workers were bound to their work units for life. The work unit was almost wholly self-contained and provided an individual with a full complement of goods and services for living, such as housing, healthcare, and education. The same system monitored the behaviour of each individual in respect of their compliance with party policy. Individuals had to obtain permission from their work units for activities such as travel, marriage, childbearing, or even where to have meals (Lü & Perry 1997; Walder 1986, 1995c). Job allocation, even for university graduates, was a norm in such a centrally planned economy such as China was then.

*Hukou* and *danwei* were the two prominent features of pre-reform China. Cadres who had the greatest access to political capital or power became the leading and dominant class with higher status in society. *Hukou* and *danwei* could capture relevant stratification features of the pre-reform system. From 1966 to 1976, the leadership under Mao carried out the Cultural Revolution (Meisner 1999; Andreas 2009), an even more radical campaign to reset the entire Chinese society on the road to socialist utopia. Capitalist assets and private ownership were banned. Many so-called intellectuals and 'political subversives' and 'educated' youth were sent to the backwaters of the country 'to learn from the peasants'. Paradoxically, the peasants and workers of that period are generally considered to be the best of their generation (Goldman 2005).

The Cultural Revolution started with a couple of 'big-character posters' on a university display board. It was quickly used to unleash brutal attacks on writers and the so-called 'counter-revolutionaries'. Huge rallies were organised to provoke the emotions of the more politically minded. Broadly speaking, Maoist China had been a strongly egalitarian, relatively classless yet impoverished society. The concept of a middle class was not present at this time because the Communist Party brought an end to the propertied classes such as landlords. Maoist China had no culture of consumption and no landholdings or private property. Political attachment to the party (i.e. political capital) was paramount. When Mao died in 1976, a series of politico-economic events took place that ultimately led to the dismantling of the radical Maoist socialism in China.

## Post-reform China at a glance

The utopian socialist class structure of society as constructed by the Maoists dissolved rapidly when Deng Xiaoping and his protégés launched economic reforms and modernisation drives in 1978. The Chinese working class, hitherto protected by state enterprises and collective communes, was forced to give up its 'iron rice bowl' (*tiefanwan* 铁饭碗 ) in the face of urban reforms (BBC 1999; Hughes 1998; Pun 2005; Walder 1989). 'Iron rice bowl' is a Chinese idiom referring to employment that offers very good or guaranteed job security, along with a steady income, benefits, and sometimes extra perks as well. In particular, it refers to the system of guaranteed lifetime employment in state enterprises. Job security and wage levels are related not to job performance but in relation to adherence to organisational rules or party doctrine. The term derives from the traditional porcelain rice bowl, which breaks when dropped. By contrast, an iron rice bowl can be dropped multiple times without fear of breakage, implying that employees in certain positions can make numerous non-political mistakes without being fired.

Initially, pragmatism assumed priority and ideology was put on the backburner. The open-door policy and economic reforms that was launched in 1978 effectively made modernisation and economic progress the official ideology of the country, though it was obviously not described in such terms. The reforms essentially put an end to most of the more damaging forms of command-and-control restraints in the Chinese economy as well as to life in general.

Enterprises were now able to transact a variety of contracts with local governments, which in turn supplied enterprises with production materials and so-called bureaucratic services (such as licensing, certification, and tax concessions). These practices provided the channels for local governments to exercise control over property rights, resource allocations, and various other bureaucratic processes, including investment and credit resources. With the loosening of central command, 'strong local officialdom and public enterprises with a thriving market economy' appeared under economic reforms (Lin 1995b: 304). Deng's dictum 'economics in command' had effectively supplanted Mao's dictum 'politics in command' (Goodman 1999: 6). Even in the earliest years of the reforms, China welcomed and encouraged foreign enterprises and investment. Many of today's Chinese new middle class used to work for state entities or collectively-owned enterprises back in the 1970s and 1980s before switching to foreign ventures or private enterprises.[2] Their stories of their working lives are shared later in the study.

Special Economic Zones and joint ventures with foreign businesses were set up to accelerate the rate of economic modernisation. The most celebrated reform in the industrial sector was the establishment of 'town and village enterprises' (TVEs). These TVEs were usually small-scale businesses such as grocery stores and other establishments that supplied or manufactured daily necessities (Kung & Lin 2007; Park & Shen 2003). Many TVEs were located in coastal provinces and were ubiquitous in many cities in Guangdong province, which was the location for my study and will be described in detail in a subsequent chapter.

One of the key policy measures in the liberalisation of economic activities in reform China was the dual-track price structure. Under this system the same commodity was priced differently between the planned and the marketed portions of the economy (Zang 2008a). Under the dual-track price structure, one way of profiting was to increase production using low-priced raw materials. However, the far simpler and more profitable way was to pocket the spread (i.e. price differences) between the state sector and the market. Pocketing the spread became extremely lucrative in the 1980s. It meant that the Chinese cadres purchased state-produced commodities (such as cooking oil, salt, and rice) at a cheaper state-controlled price, and sold them at a higher market price to buyers. It was a means for cadres to manipulate the ambiguous and incomplete institutional policies for profit-taking – and served as a 'breakout' point for the rise of the Chinese new middle class.

Economic liberalisation also took place in the management of land. Despite land and property reforms in China, urban land remains 'state-owned', that is, owned by the state through government administrative or economic units, and what is transacted is *land-use rights* only. During the reform years, cadres and ex-cadres of land-owning work units sold land-use rights to commercial property companies at a substantial profit. The result is a loose but active network of property dealers across different cities driving up the number of land transactions.

The post-reform land-leasing system has two prominent features. One is the privatisation of public housing and the commercialisation of the housing market. The other is the 'spacing of class'. In the former, the general trend has been a move away from *danwei*-based housing provision to a commercial housing regime. This is an uneven process, with both winners and losers, thereby creating class differentiation in urban China.[3] As with any state of affairs that has winners and losers, housing therefore is an important element in the production of a new middle class.

As for the 'spacing of class', this feature continues in many Chinese cities today: socioeconomic differences are increasingly inscribed on space, especially regionally and between 'rural' and 'urban' areas under the divisive *hukou* system of registration (Chadha & Husband 2006: 119). Chinese cities have relatively lower degrees of internal inequality for inhabitants when considered alongside comparable cities in the West or even in the developing world (Friedmann 1985) because resources are accumulated in a handful of privileged groups like the cadres, entrepreneurs, and professionals. The greatest inequalities seem to be regional and seem to follow directly from the operation of the *hukou* system. The making of urban communities and the making of the Chinese new middle class are becoming two inseparable processes (Chadha & Husband 2006: 496).

According to Bian *et al.* (2005) and W. W. Zhang (2000), there is currently an urban labour force of about 342 million. This includes about 6% who are classified as professional employees and a further 6% classified as entrepreneurs. About 12% of the labour force comprises illegal migrant workers, a further 12% are unemployed and about 25% form a 'floating' population. While many of the consequent inequalities are manifested between regions in China, there are significant inequalities within cities like Beijing, Shanghai and those that make up the Special Economic Zone of the Pearl River Delta in Guangdong province. However, it is not easy to make a precise assessment because the illegal migrant workers in these cities are those with rural *hukou* and will be classified accordingly in official data. An official report for 2004 from the Ministry of Labour and Social Security (MLSS) highlights a serious situation: 68% of all migrant workers in 40 cities across China did not receive one rest day per week, and 76% received no time off for statutory holidays (*fading jiaqi* 法定假期). With respect to pay, 48% were paid regularly, but 52% experienced occasional and even frequent non-payment of wages, while 54% were never paid overtime earnings (which the law required employers to do). As to employment protection, only one-eighth had employment contracts and only 15% had social security scheme coverage (Lee & Shen 2009: 120). Also revealed by the MLSS report, those terms included overtime payments, that monthly income of illegal migrants was about one quarter that of the 'official' earnings of white-collar workers, while 'legal' manual workers earn about one-third of the monthly earnings of white-collar workers. As will become clear, the new middle class has access to income considerably in excess of their official salaries.

One crucial institutional change that characterises post-reform China has been the partial dissolution of the *danwei* system in urban China. *Danwei*, in combination with *hukou*, has been effective in shaping social space and relationships (and therefore identity and class boundary) for the new middle class in urban China because *danwei* carries symbolic and functional meanings of power, knowledge and discipline in the party-state (Chen & Sun 2006). However, even since 1980, the urban *hukou* holder has still been tied to the *danwei* (work unit) from which the individual obtains a wide range of goods and services. Therefore, the *danwei*, *hukou* systems and *guanxi* (or systems of personal networks) in urban areas still have an important impact upon class relations in post-reform urban China.[4] While the *danwei* system has broken down in the countryside, it remains a significant factor in urban areas where members of a household still wants to retain an attachment to a *danwei* in order to enjoy the wider benefits that would accrue to the household.

Both the *hukou* system of household registration and the policy of lifelong employment serve to stabilise (or, strictly speaking, restrict) the residential mobility of the urban family. Public housing is based on the length of service, so older employees receive priority for larger, better-built accommodation plus the option to have their married children live with them. The work replacement policy (i.e. 'grandfathering options') allows retiring employees the chance to secure employment in the same work unit for their grown children. These two policies and others enable the state to keep adult children dependent on their parents, thereby putting senior citizens in a superior position in the family structure and so promote family togetherness (Sheng & Settles 2006). Urban *hukou* has an absolute meaning in terms of the intergenerational transfers of privileges from the old generation to the young generation. In today's China, I would predict an urban *hukou* is still very important to the Chinese new middle class, particularly for the children of the old generation. This has some kind of intergenerational transfers to their children. Their children can study in the so-called brand-name primary schools, as well as secondary schools, and universities. By contrast, a rural *hukou* won't have this kind of privileges since most of the brand-name primary schools, secondary schools, and universities have some kind of quotas for their students' enrolment.

Professionals and entrepreneurs who are not originally urban *hukou* holders are financially able to afford a *hukou* transfer. A common method for them to do so is through employment with an international company and pay cadres as much as RMB100,000[5] (US$14,631 or £10,004) to 'acquire' an urban *hukou*. Therefore, the most distinguishing feature of a member of the Chinese new middle class is having an urban *hukou* as opposed to one who does not (the peasant).

The economic reforms and thriving economy have caused many professionals, entrepreneurs and cadres to pour into the newly established industrial or development zones predominantly located in Guangdong province, the base for much of the global capital in search of a commercial foothold in the Chinese market (Pun 2005: 30). The burgeoning economy of China since the 1990s paved the way and offered a good chance for the cadres who worked in the state-owned enterprises (SOEs) to switch to doing business (*xiahai* 下海 'to dive into the sea') by the 1980s. The privileged position associated with the urban Chinese new middle class became progressively prominent throughout the reform years (Pun 2005: 30) and this is set to become even more pronounced in future. The *guanxi* circles that ex-state workers have developed during their tenure with their *danwei* remain usable and important even after their switch to the business world.

China is now practising 'socialism with Chinese characteristics', a full-blooded capitalism in disguise, driving the economic growth of the country. It comes with a large grey zone of interconnecting relationships built up by gift-giving, wining and dining, collective memories, traditional Chinese values and the need for self-improvement. Loopholes in the machinery of government and the relationship-oriented nature of Chinese society result in a burst of administrative grey areas that encourage *guanxi* networks to arise as a means for 'getting things done' (Zhang *et al.* 1999).

*Guanxi* is what oils the cogs of bureaucracy and the wheels of commerce, and is the single biggest factor in spurring economic growth in China. The newborn or born-again bourgeoisie in present-day China overlaps closely with the bureaucrats and is intertwined with kinship networks (Bian 1994; Lin 1999; Oi 1991; Ong 1999; Pye 1999), so *guanxi* networks are increasingly important to get ahead in post-reform China as the country heads towards a fuller capitalist society.

Economic reforms have brought a greater degree of prosperity for many people in China. Individuals can now run their lives flexibly and with maximum collaborative potential through different kinds of institutional changes and also long-standing interpersonal networks that operate on shared backgrounds, lifestyles and consumption habits (Chaney 1994, 1996; Latham *et al.* 2006). The appearance of the Chinese new middle class demonstrates the importance of class understood in the Weberian sense, education, market, political values and the ruling party in the country. In considering the rising new middle class in transitional China today, class analysis allows us to think of the special nature of the Chinese market situation within the context of 'socialism with Chinese characteristics'.

To sum up, the picture of class in post-reform China is also complicated by the operation of both the household registration system (*hukou*), which produces spatially distributed inequality among the population, and the work-unit system (*danwei*), which helps give rise to regionalism among bureaucrats. The singular supremacy of the ruling party preserves the continued importance and relevance of bureaucrats (cadres) in Chinese society. The operational ideology of the party requires the use of such 'professional revolutionaries' to implement policies and operations at all levels of government. Significant or even substantial loopholes in the machinery of government, especially with regard to the marketed portion of the economy, encourages interpersonal relationship networks (*guanxi*) to develop between bureaucrats and the people in the private sectors including entrepreneurs and professionals.

Ex-cadres who have strong ties and close affiliations to the government enable *guanxi* (关系) to fully utilise *hukou, danwei*, and land reform. They convert these advantages into material wealth inside their class boundary. The creation of a mixed socialist economy has not eroded the institutional foundations of a cadre-dominated social hierarchy. That domination is attributable in large measure to the household registration system that has been in operation since the late 1950s. Cadres are the tiebreakers (*jueshengfu* 决胜负) in issuing those business licences, so entrepreneurs and professionals are usually very willing to cooperate with them. Cadres can enrich themselves by giving and accepting 'gifts' in the course of exercising their official duties. This is an almost universal situation in Guangdong.[6]

## Defining the Chinese new middle class

The creation of a conceptual framework for identifying the Chinese new middle class requires the establishment of five standards as the basis for selecting both my samples and also the techniques necessary to deal with them (see Table I.1). The first standard is a minimum per capita income of RMB9,000 (£850) per month, applicable to Guangdong province only, based on the author's operationalisation between the official data and her empirical ethnographic data. This baseline is an average discovered through the analysis of official statistics (Guangdong Provincial Statistical Bureau 2005–2007), academic surveys (CASS 2002, 2007; Qiao & Jiang 2005), as well as popular perceptions in the media (*China Daily* 2005, 2008). They should have a certain amount of disposable income; most should have RMB300,000 or above. This is based on my own observations in Guangdong province. Owning a house or a car either by mortgage or outright ownership is the second standard. The third standard is based on qualifications obtained via a minimum level of post-secondary education (technical or non-technical). The young generation of the Chinese new middle class born after the 1950s tend to have a post-secondary education, but the generation born after the 1970s must possess at least a bachelor's degree. The fourth standard is a managerial-level position or managerial-type job. This can be in either the state or the private sector, and can be either technical or non-technical. The fifth standard is an urban *hukou* status.

Table I.1  Selection criteria for samples as the Chinese new middle class

| Criterion | Requirements |
| --- | --- |
| Income and disposable income | Minimum RMB9,000 (£850) a month, per capita; The disposable income should have at least RMB300,000. |
| Occupation | Specialist or skilled job, or work at managerial or comparable level, either in the state or private sectors. |
| Education | Minimum post-secondary level, preferably higher, in any field. |
| *Hukou* | Native belonging (urban household registration). |
| House/car | Owning a house and/or car either by mortgage or outright ownership. |

## Research questions and empirical study in South China

There are three research objectives to investigate the middle class in post-reform China. My first research objective was to apply Weberian, Neo-Weberian, and Bourdieuian approaches to explain the sociocultural trajectories of the new middle class. The second research objective was to give a full account of the role of the Chinese new middle class in modern China. The third research objective was to use in-depth interviews to learn more about class boundaries among different groupings within the Chinese new middle class, about cooperation within and between those groupings, and about their cultural and political identities. Based on these research objectives, I can then generate a series of research questions: What are the defining features of the new middle class? What sociocultural factors bind the class members together? How do they (re)produce themselves as a class? Why are *guanxi* relationships so important in their mutual interactions? Is the middle class politically apathetic or lethargic and if so, what are the reasons for this? What is the role played by the Chinese Communist Party in the class formation? Why does it allow or even promote the growth of the new class?

Why did I choose Guangdong province as my field site? It is an area that has experienced a high level of economic development since the onset of the economic reforms. In particular, the open-door policy initiated there in the early 1980s quickly became the cornerstone for accelerated growth. These and other policies provide the background for the researcher to choose Guangdong province as an exemplary site to study the new middle class. It is also significant that the Pearl River Delta region is close to Shenzhen and Zhuhai, two of the 'Special

Economic Zones' identified in the early stages of the reform period in 1980. Geographically targeted areas were specifically chosen by Deng Xiaoping to be the generators of new economic growth. These zones provided preferential economic conditions and labour market 'freedoms', especially for overseas firms. This explains the rapid exponential growth of the six cities selected in Guangdong province for my sites. These six cities are also urban areas that have attracted a huge influx of migrant workers, both legal and illegal. Even illegal migrants enjoy a high degree of *de facto* legitimacy, having been residents in many cities for ten years or more. In this way, it can be seen that residency status, or *hukou,* operates to stratify the labour market and create restrictions upon more competitive processes that might destabilise employment relations in today's urban China.

Since it was the objective of this study to provide inside and insightful information on the Chinese new middle class, it becomes, in effect, the work of an insider with Chinese characteristics (in keeping with the concept of a society based on 'socialism with Chinese characteristics'). Therefore, research ethics play a particularly important role in observing the Chinese new middle class. Collecting qualitative data in the field reveals the need to consider sociocultural practices when doing research as an 'insider', particularly with the cadres. *Guanxi*, which means social networks and personal connections, are keys to success when using in-depth interviews and other qualitative methods.

This field study, done in six cities in Guangdong province, shows that both a cultural sociological approach and a qualitative methodology with high local specificity are required when investigating the lifestyles, consumption patterns, cultural identity, and social networking of the Chinese new middle class. Therefore, this empirical study will use qualitative research techniques such as in-depth interviews, participant observation, and other ethnographic skills. For this study, I interviewed 59 members of the Chinese new middle class. They included 31 entrepreneurs, 11 cadres, and 17 professionals. Pseudonyms will be used and personal details or locations redacted to prevent identification of the interviewees.

Initially in the interview process I assumed the role of a part-time business woman (helping a family member to manage his business in Guangdong), and it was possible to piggyback on those introductions to establish networks with the new middle class. As time went on, and with more travel into mainland China, I built up a greater familiarity with the contacts. New contacts became friends, who in turn introduced other members of their circles to me. The researcher understands the tactics of *guanxi* networking for doing business in China. Treating contacts to a meal is the simplest way to return favours. All of the business partners, cadres, and professionals I interviewed later knew that I am a college teacher collecting data to write my research for publication.

Within each selected city in Guangdong, between three and five natives introduced me to potential candidates (professionals, entrepreneurs, and cadres) for conducting in-depth interviews. I used snowball sampling to enlarge the sample size. It quickly became apparent that snowball sampling was by far the most effective strategy in terms of time and disbursements. By using this qualitative research technique, many features unique to the Chinese new middle class were revealed. For example, some of them have overseas passports, and often have foreign bank accounts. These two features are just a sample of the advantages enjoyed by the Chinese new middle class.

Using a combination of formal and informal methods helped the interviewees to feel more at ease, encouraging them to be more open and to reveal the deepest aspects of their self-identities, their philosophies of life, their insecurities, imaginations, and personal outlooks on various issues. By socialising with the interviewees and taking the initiative to set up meetings or shopping excursions with them, I was able to get a more authentic picture of their inner world, and a deeper understanding of their professional and private lives.

## Overview of this book

This book examines the emergence of the new middle class in post-reform China. It argues that Western class categories cannot directly be applied to the Chinese situation and that the Chinese new middle class is distinguished more by sociocultural than by economic factors.

Class analysis as applicable to post-reform China differs from Western-based analytical models in that 'class' in China is more of a cultural term than an economic one. Institutional changes in urban China such as *hukou, danwei,* land and property reforms become important factors in shaping the sociocultural characteristics of the new middle class when combined with the social pre-eminence of cadres and the importance of *guanxi* networks. Class in the post-reform Chinese context involves sociocultural factors that revolve around lifestyles and consumption patterns that take their cues and momentum from changes in the economy. Sociocultural factors help the Chinese new middle class distinguish itself from the rest of the population by creating new class identities. The new class identities are built on a foundation that combines institutional structures of state, economic progress, ambiguities of state governance, the marketisation of the economy, and globalisation impacts on society at large via the economy, and traditional values and mores.

In the Chinese context consumerism is defined as a way of life geared towards possession and acquisition (Aldridge 2003). The Chinese new middle class is already in the throes of globally-oriented consumption as a direct result of general economic progress as well as of the market-isation and globalisation of the economy. The supremacy of a more prosperous and globalised economy is important to attempts by the Chinese new urban middle class to refashion themselves, accumulate their high standards of social distinction and tastes (Pun 2005). New forms and standards of social distinction arise from new modes of consumption. Consequently, these aspects mould new identities for the class and make social distinction inescapable from our examination (Pun 2003: 477).

Consumption is the easiest indicator for the new class to represent its status, its wealth and its social reputation in post-reform China. Consumption is deliberately used as a contrasting device to distinguish the present day from pre-reform times, when only production existed but no consumption. As Pun (2005: 491) puts it: 'Consumption is a desire machine – not the signified but, rather, a signifier that registers a structure of abundance in a society of mere fantasy'.

China's massive moves into the international arena play an important role in putting the idea of consumption within the idea of production (Pun 2005). Producing for consumption has become one of the more lucrative means of profit-making, particularly today when inflows of international capital into China are becoming ever more numerous. These developments are working to start a new chapter in the cultural globalisation of China. This explains why I include the thick description of the living styles and consumption of both the old and the young generation of the Chinese new middle class in Chapters 2 and 3. Consumption is an indicator of culture. This justifies that a sociocultural perspective to investigate the Chinese new middle class is appropriate and illustrative.

The everyday social and cultural practices in today's China exhibit heterogeneity rather than homogeneity. This heterogeneity (frag-mentation, if you will) challenges traditional concepts of class. Class should now be incorporated into the body of sociocultural terminology because the case of China shows that lifestyles and consumption patterns play important roles inside the class boundary of the Chinese new middle class. The explanatory power of class structure in general sociology is set to undergo a fundamental change because of the Chinese situation.

Based upon qualitative interviews, the study looks at entrepreneurs, professionals, and regional party cadres to show the networks among these different groups and the continuing significance of cadres. The study also considers generational differences. The old generation are pragmatic and business-oriented, rather than being personally oriented in their consumption. They also show stronger collective identities, but these are based on personal networks rather than on a sense of a common class location that they share with others outside their personal networks. In contrast, the young generation appear more flexible and hedonistic. They tend to be more individualistic, materialistic and oriented towards personal gain. In neither the old nor the young generation, however, is there much evidence that the Chinese middle class is taking on a political role in advocating political reform alongside market reforms as is often suggested by Western modernisation theorists. The middle-class people are in the vanguard of consumption but they are the laggards in politics.

Both the old generation and the young generation in this book are referred to as the Chinese new middle class. I investigate the connections between different aspects of social organisation, including the middle class, generation, and individualisation. Within the sociological enterprise, there are contrasting theoretical perspectives on the notion of individualisation which explain how people in industrial societies can no longer look to traditional and communal sources for security and personal identity. Instead, they develop personal strategies as a means of coping with the tensions of living in this uncertain age of globalisation and mass consumption. Since the 1990s, debates about the rapid individualisation of society in a de-centering of class as individualisation have become more prominent. Since the literature on individualisation is dominated by Western perspectives (Beck 1992; Yan 2009), it is timely to examine individualisation within the context of the Chinese new middle class. Asian peoples are generally described as *collectivist,* in contrast to their individualist counterparts in the West. Thus, in Asian societies, it is the traditional and communal bonds of the extended family, neighbourhood, and wider communities that are assumed to be the primary forces in shaping an individual's identity, choices and biography. In reality, however, matters are not so straightforward. We argue that to understand the Chinese new middle class (the old and the young generation), Western theories of class analysis and individualisation cannot be transposed and need to be adapted to the nuances of China. This book seeks to elaborate on the *dialectical* relationship between the Chinese new middle class, generation (the old and the young generation), and individualisation in China, in both empirical and theoretical terms.

## Structure of this book

The Introduction sets out the overall framework and major arguments and standpoints of this book. This part also gives concrete information about the reasons for selecting the sites in Guangdong province as opposed to any other location. Importantly, it explains how insider research and research ethics are done 'with Chinese characteristics' and why it does not follow the same procedures as are mandated in Western research sites.

Chapter 1 first depicts the background of class analysis in its original Western context. It will present arguments from the Marxist and neo-Marxist approaches and highlight their inherent problems with respect to the Chinese situation. The literature review will also show how and why Pierre Bourdieu's cultural sociology supports the claim that the Weberian/Neo-Weberian approach is more robust (that is, better suited) to depict a fuller, more accurate picture of the Chinese new middle class than is a neo-Marxian account. It also reviews the application of class analysis to post-reform China. More detailed information about class analysis in post-reform China will be introduced. At the same time, it will highlight how the Chinese new middle class is in fact socioculturally constituted in the context of Chinese society and has Chinese-specific characteristics as manifest in lifestyle and orientation to consumerism.

Chapters 2, 3, 4 and 5 form the core of this book, and present the findings about the Chinese new middle class. Chapter 2 focuses on the old generation of the Chinese new middle class and presents information about the class boundaries and culture of that particular subset of the new middle class in Guangdong. Excerpts from the interviews will be used to show the pragmatic and utilitarian inclination of the old generation towards consumption matters, collective memories, and other matters.

Chapter 3 discusses the consumer revolution taking place in post-reform China. It also explicates the lifestyles and consumption patterns of the young generation of the Chinese new middle class. I argue that there is an emerging sign of individualisation in post-reform China in the young generation, and in contrast to the old generation in the new Chinese middle class.

Chapter 4 is about institutional changes relating to *guanxi* networks in which cadres are still in collaboration with professionals and entrepreneurs in post-reform China. In fact, cadre-entrepreneurs are the dominant leaders of the Chinese new middle class. This chapter highlights the ambiguities and incompleteness of national and local official policies, and the networks that arise from them as a counterbalance.

Chapter 5 considers the orientation towards political development, cultural and moral values of the new middle class. The self-disclosure and insider information collected from the Chinese new middle class are the primary sources employed to elucidate the middle class's identity and their close relationship with local governments in a highly globalising China.

The last chapter is the conclusion. It provides an epilogue to offer readers a reflexive discussion of the study. While this final chapter marks the end of the book, it also marks a point of 'opening' out to critique and further research.

# 1
# (Re) Framing Class Theories: Class Analysis in Post-Reform China

> ...China's new middle class is a term without a single identi-
> fiable social interest or propensity to action. It encompasses not
> only the owners of capital, but also the managers and bureau-
> crats, as well as the professionals who service and support
> capitalist entrepreneurs and the modernizing state...
>
> (Robinson & Goodman 1996: 40)

The model of traditional class theories in the West is not completely appropriate for conducting a class analysis of contemporary Chinese society. I argue that Western class categories are not directly applicable to the Chinese situation and that the Chinese new middle class is distinguished more by sociocultural than by economic factors. The Chinese new middle class is more diversified and heterogeneous than it appeared at first. The cultural and social identification of the Chinese new middle class operates mainly through cultural practices and consumption patterns. *Hukou* creates spatially distributed inequality. *Danwei* continues to be significant in considering class and class distinction in urban China. Both *hukou* and *danwei* create differences in work situations by forming *guanxi* networks inside the boundaries of the new class. This explains why *hukou* and *danwei* manifest themselves in sociocultural rather than economic differences. Significant effects on the new class also come from institutional changes in the framework of property ownership and the dominant role of the cadre in society. Therefore, 'class' in the Chinese context is a relatively sociocultural term rather than solely an economic one.

In this chapter, I shall reframe the class analysis by reviewing how Western class theories are not applicable in the emerging Chinese new middle class in today's China. First, I shall examine the Marxist theory on class and how Marxist principles deal with questions about stratification orders within a modern society. Second, I will use cultural capital and 'party' (political determinism) from Weberian class analysis but I note that political determinism works in different ways in China from the way it does in the West: political affiliation/support for the CCP (China) *vs.* political parties competing for power in the public realm (West). I will also use 'economic class' from Weberian class analysis because it seems to work in a more refined (or less blunt) way than in Marxist class theory. Third, I will develop Weberian 'economic class' in terms of 'work situation' and 'market situation' drawing on the work of neo-Weberians such as John Goldthorpe (1980, 1982), whose seven-class scheme is more easily modifiable to the Chinese situation. Finally, I shall also seek to supplement the neo-Weberian approach with the approach adopted by Bourdieu and the work of other cultural sociologists to explain some of the lifestyle and consumption patterns of the Chinese new middle class.

The second part of this chapter will explain how the established theoretical models help to operationalise a conceptual framework of class for this study using concrete scenarios to depict the actual situation in today's China. The Chinese new middle class is emerging in ways that depart from the standard development pathways proposed by Western mainstream theories about the middle class. The political and economic realities of 'socialism with Chinese characteristics' are so unique that they have no direct parallel elsewhere, so they impart correspondingly unique characteristics to the Chinese new middle class. The advent of a new class in a modern, part-socialist/part-capitalist society like that of China is a sign that market, class and political intervention are important, but their forms are different from those in the West (Anagnost 2008).

I will begin by enumerating some special considerations that pertain to the Chinese case:

1. Generational stratification, family norms, value changes, parent–child relationships and marriage patterns detected in Chinese society today are markedly different from those in Western societies.
2. Occupational types in the Chinese case also tend to overlap one another or even encompass all possible categories, especially in the case of those categories associated with the new middle class. For example, a single individual may straddle two or even all three of what I shall argue as the primary categories of cadre, entrepreneur and professional.

3. Some institutional systems of China have no parallel in the West. For example, workers outside the *hukou* and *danwei* systems do not have the same or even comparable contractual positions as those inside them.
4. The culture and social identification of the Chinese new middle class operates mainly through cultural practices and consumption patterns. This is unlike the Western middle class, which operates through patterns of social stratification (Goodman 1999, 2008; Li 2010).

## The inapplicability of Western class analysis

Classical Marxist class theory is a theory that rests on notions of class antagonisms and struggles. It involves two dichotomous classes in a state of continual conflict because of one class exploiting the other. Class exists in society when there is an exploitation relationship in production, which, under capitalism, in Marxist theory is between the bourgeoisie and the working class. As capitalism progresses, the gulf widens between the bourgeoisie and the working class, and becomes ever deeper and more distinct with time. Marxist theory bases its argument on ownership and lack of ownership of property in the means of production as being the essential determinant of class relationships.

The class debate in the West is framed primarily in terms of a debate about Marx's theories. The Marxist analysis of class and society is best able to account for socioeconomic phenomena, but even here Marxist concepts break down when dealing with modern capitalist societies (Clark & Lipset 2004; Meiksins 1998; Migone 2007). The weakest point in Marxist thinking, even for the analysis of Western capitalist societies, is the conspicuous absence of intermediate classes between workers and bourgeois capitalists. In a capitalist society, according to the Marxist argument, the bourgeoisie consists of industrialists, financiers, landowners and merchants. They are in continual conflict with each other and they as a whole are in opposition against workers. The real-life problem for Marxist theory is that all societies around the world have undergone major transformations since the theory was first developed more than a hundred years ago. Class lines are relatively blurred in present-day China. The theory is unable to deal with groups like managers, civil servants, doctors, computer programmers and many others who are salaried but own no means of production, at least as defined in Marxist theory (Saunders 1990: 15). Neo-Marxists such as Nicos Poulantzas (1973, 1975, 1978, 1982) and even C. Wright Mills (1979, 1985a, 1985b, 1994, 1997) and Wright *et al.* (1999) tried to compensate for theoretical problems by reclassifying the modern middle class as the petty bourgeoisie of small business owners, independent farmers and white-collar salaried workers. The reclassified middle class is then situated between the financiers and industrialists on the one hand and the industrial workers on the other (Arbam 1989: 332), but the theory cannot escape the shrinking role of the latter and the declining significance of class polarisation, at least in terms of class structure.

The Marxist class theory, then, has quite deep-seated problems and reclassification sounds like a stopgap measure. Numerous studies have confirmed that no existing communist state has ever existed in pure communist, classless form (and that the only classless societies that have existed, in Marx's sense, are those of 'primitive' communism, not 'advanced' communism). Indeed, Marxist theory could not even offer a sustainable explanation of European feudal societies. In mediaeval Europe, the cleavages and conflicts in society were not between owners and non-owners of assets of production. They were mostly between the monarch and the nobility or the church, or between the crown and the burghers in townships that tried to assert autonomy from royal control, or just blood feuds (Saunders 1990: 12). We can see that the two concepts of exploitation and class structure are already too limited to explain feudal societies. The fact is that all societies are always progressing under various degrees or types of transformations. The Marxist theory uses class categories like property and means of ownership to classify class in society. That makes most Marxist-based class theories of decreasing relevance for examining modern-day class structures and class relationships.

If Marxist theory has lost its utility for analysing Western societies, it has even less appropriateness for explaining the new patterns of social stratification that are now emerging in China. The Chinese case introduces problems – it is a retrogressive transition, from state socialism to market socialism (capitalism). The Chinese transition complicates the Marxist analysis by including a trajectory not recognised by Marx. The class philosophy, historical materialism and the two-class dichotomy of Marxist theory are legacy conceptualisations for China watchers. Today's China is a mixture of socialism and capitalism with spatial characteristics. So, confronted with a problematic transition, Marxist theory, as a theory of transition, is generally implausible when applied to the Chinese new middle class in today's China.

## Weberian class analysis

Long-standing attempts by sociologists to understand modern capitalism in terms of class usually begin with Marxist theories but have moved in a Weberian direction because of complications presented by real-life situations. Max Weber's (1946, 1947, 1951) pioneering work in class analysis takes up the slack in Marxist thinking on two levels. On one level, Weberian class analysis breaks the Marxist materialist link between class and the economic/productive process by showing that people are also consumers of goods and services in the marketplace and not just sellers of labour (workers) or owners of capital (the capitalist elite) (Liechty 2003: 11).

Weber developed a typology of class, status and party as the key bases of social stratification. He considered them as important influences in people's lives, as opposed to the Marxist emphasis on property classes alone. That means that the Weberian approach looks at the underlying structure of class as differential sets of life chances for members. Differential demand in the marketplace for capital, commodities and labour represents differential property ownership and income opportunities, which in turn give rise to differential life chances. Differential life chances create differential demands for goods and services, and differential access to them. All these make Weberian class analysis more of a consumption-based model of class than a production-based one, or at least, allow a production-based account to be supplemented by a consumption-oriented one (Wallace & Wolf 2006; Ashley & Orenstein 2005).

If capital accounting predominates in modern Western capitalism, then Weber was right to make a distinction between property classes and acquisition classes. Property classes are established on the disparity of property holdings, whereas acquisition classes reflect the possession of skills that help secure resources in the market, thus enabling the Weberian approach to accommodate intermediate divisions. In Weberian thinking, then, social class or group formation rests on (1) ownership of the means of production, (2) economic or market position of an individual's skills and other marketable qualifications such as education (both of these are usually associated with the Weberian definition), (3) social prestige or honour (*status*) accorded to an individual by others, and (4) group belonging (*party*).

## Class

In Weberian thinking, classes derive their existence from economic situations associated with property holdings and positions in the labour market. Currently, neo-Weberian class conceptualisations articulate class positions primarily in terms of market and work situations.

Weberians agree with Marxists that all class divisions are based on property holding, but differ in two important respects. Class is (*a*) a set of people with a common, actual and specific component in their life chances, insofar as (*b*) the common life-chance component is represented exclusively as economic interests by possession of goods and income opportunities, and under the conditions of the commodity or labour market (Ashley & Orenstein 2005: 234).

Let us consider that for a moment. Based on property divisions, then, Weberians would identify the propertied classes as property-owning entrepreneurial groups and the petty bourgeoisie. Groups that are non-propertied but possess formal educational credentials are distinguished from manual workers (Breen & Rottman 1995: 28). As a set of people who share common life chances, the market provides the common condition for the decisive moment when a life chance appears to the individual. Weber said that the market distributes life chances in proportion to the resources that individuals bring to it (Weber 1946, 1947; Breen & Rottman 1995). There is a market variation in these resources (e.g. property owners *vs.* non-owners, skilled *vs.* unskilled) (Breen & Rottman 1995: 29). As Weber wrote:

> ...The factor that creates class is unambiguously economic interest with classes stratified according to their relations to the production and acquisition of goods... (cited in Raynor 1969: 8)

Therefore, class situation is now equivalent to market situation, so the redefinition now reckons that people come to the commodity, credit and labour markets in unequal fashion (Breen & Rottman 1995: 28). Class becomes redefined in terms of resources held by or resources accessible to individuals instead of the relative place of the individuals in the production process.

## Status

Status alludes to prestige or reputation differences between social groups. It also concerns the prestige and lifestyle of the individual and the social estimation attached to them, which means status distinctions could vary independently of class divisions. Social honour may be positive or negative. For example, doctors and lawyers are positively privileged status groups in modern capitalist society, but Jews were a pariah group in mediaeval Europe and banned from certain occupations and official positions.

The possession of wealth normally confers high status, though there are exceptions. Weber (1946, 1947) believed that members of a status group share a common claim to a certain level of social prestige based on lifestyle, education or occupation. Status situation could be a highly important factor in that it may have a direct bearing on class situation for individuals.

On the one hand, social status relates to individual or group lifestyle, education, training and socialisation as well as inherited or occupational prestige. On the other, class distinctions are linked in various ways with status distinctions. As such, property is not necessarily recognised as a status qualification, although in the long run it is and with extraordinary regularity (Weber 1946: 186–7; Liechty 2003: 14).

The Weberian analysis provides useful insights into how consumption and status could be related to the dynamics of middle-class cultural practices (Liechty 2003: 11). The rationale is that sociocultural processes in Weber's intermediate stratum (i.e. middle class) revolve around the wide range of cultural formations, lifestyles and status claims, and how they compete with one another within those stratums. For Weber, class is the position of an individual or a group in the market as a function both of production (capitalist *vs.* labour) and of capability to consume goods and services. This means the social order of the middle class is determined relatively less directly by its relationship to the means of production but relatively more by relationship to the market, status, lifestyle and consumption (Storey 1999; Pinches 1999).

Status is relatively underdeveloped in the Weberian approach, which usually sees it in terms of the transition from pre-capitalism to capitalism. It is useful to link Weberian/Neo-Weberian class analysis with the concepts from Bourdieu on the subject of sociocultural aspects of class formation in relation to field, taste and habitus, and then pick up the issue of political determinism of class positions. This chapter will discuss those links in detail later.

## Party

Weber defined a 'party' as an association of individuals who work together because they have common backgrounds, aims or interests. Basically, the Weberian interest in 'party' is concerned with how the formation of groups in 'civil society' relates to the political arena as they arise from the 'field', which is either in the economy (classes) or in society (status groups). Weber emphasised that party formation can also influence stratification independently of class and status. In short, 'party' in the Weberian sense is about the political representation of classes or status groups. The concept ultimately relates to the subject of political parties and their socioeconomic foundations, and, hence, the entire body of Western studies that examines the class basis of voting.

To what extent is the Weberian concept of party relevant to post-reform China? The mutual operation of market economic mechanisms and a single-party domination lead to the development of a not-so-completely-capitalist economy and a not-so-completely-transparent government (Zhang 2007: 426, 431). Class and status positions in China are politically determined through institutional structures operated by the Communist Party (such as *hukou* and *danwei*), but also conditional on Confucianism and traditional Chinese cultural norms. However, to develop the Weberian idea of 'party' further would give us the link to party cadres, a group in the Chinese new middle class that does not exist as a stratification entity in Western societies (Lu 2002). The political orientations of the Chinese new middle class would need to be expressed in terms of different tendencies or even factions within the Chinese Communist Party rather than on the idea of voting intentions that Western studies tend to indicate. Therefore, the concept of party fits in quite nicely with the continuing importance of political determinism in the Chinese new middle class in addition to that of market and work situations.

## Neo-Weberian class model: John Goldthorpe

The original Weberian class model is multidimensional, emphasising status, class and party as life chances in property- and labour-related economic situations. Neo-Weberians extend the model further and set class within market and work situations, and that is the current Weberian/Neo-Weberian approach today. Broadly speaking, intermediate classes are considered as 'fractions' (factions) between the two polarised classes, as argued by Poulantzas and E. O. Wright from a Marxist perspective. However, in the neo-Weberian position such as that propounded by John Goldthorpe (1980, 1982), the expanded scheme of seven class categories does not need a primary framing of intermediate classes 'within' the core, 'polar' classes. The Goldthorpe model seems to be able to provide a more robust form of class analysis to explain the concrete situations observed in this study, and this chapter later will set out the reasons why it follows the Goldthorpe model (Goldthorpe *et al.* 1968).

Goldthorpe's studies (1980, 1982) are particularly relevant in our search to understand the Chinese new middle class because his class framework is primarily divided into those who exercise 'delegated authority or specialised knowledge and expertise' (Goldthorpe 1980, 1982) and those who do not. The authority factor is the one most likely to give rise to differences in working conditions and market capacity, even if status and party tend to be residual terms for Goldthorpe.

Goldthorpe's initial approach to class is grounded in David Lockwood's concepts of market situation and work situation, both defined in terms of production units and employment relations in labour markets (Scott 1994: 93). Market situation refers to an occupation and its income source and level, associated conditions of employment, the degree of economic security and the extent of economic advancement. It also refers to the categories of occupations whose members are known and have connections with each other in the job market. Work situation refers to where an occupation is located in the systems of authority and control within the production process (Goldthorpe 1980: 40). Individuals of the same class have the common market and work situations.

Educational credentials and marketable skills are the primary class classifiers in Goldthorpe's seven-class scheme. His scheme is concerned with the relationships between class structures, mainly work and market situations, which determine class stratification and social mobility in society. Cultural capital, even at the most basic level that Goldthorpe conceptualised it, is applicable to developments seen in Chinese society today. It also allows the Goldthorpean analysis with respect to work and market situations to be applicable to the case of the Chinese new middle class. Based on this line of reasoning, I could use a modified version of the Goldthorpean classification (Bian *et al.* 2005) to explain the Chinese case (see Table 1.1). The Chinese new middle class would then be in classes I, II and III in the modified scheme.

Goldthorpe (1982: 171) suggests that the class formation process itself could be a crucial intervening variable in the reproduction of social classes. There are two aspects: demographic identity and sociocultural identity. As defined here, demographic identity is the ability of, and extent to which, individuals occupy the same class from generation to generation. Sociocultural identity is the ability and extent of individuals to share distinctive lifestyles and patterns of preferred associations of a class. The degree of relationship between class and distinctive lifestyles is sometimes called sociocultural continuity (Lau 2002). Class formation at its normative level is how extensively individuals in the same class positions share common values and beliefs, and it shows the degree of class cohesiveness and homogeneity (Lau 2002).

Table 1.1 Modified Goldthorpean class scheme for the Chinese new middle class

| Class | Original classification | Modified classification | Features (modified) |
|---|---|---|---|
| I | Upper service class | Upper class of professionals, administrators and managers | Holds supervisory positions above the level of 'section chief' in the public sector (government/party agencies, industrial enterprises) or in the private sector (industrial or other profit-making enterprises). |
| II | Lower service class | Middle level of professionals and managers | Holds specialised secondary or post-secondary education and **either** (*a*) white-collar, non-routine, non-supervisory positions higher than a 'section chief' **or** (*b*) white-collar office employees performing routine tasks. |
| III | Routine non-manual employees | Private owners and the self-employed | **Either** (*a*) those who employ others and also have substantial capital assets, **or** (*b*) service or production workers who do not employ others and have a small amount of capital assets (*geihu* 个体户). |
| IV | Petty bourgeoisie | Skilled manual labourers or production workers | Blue-collar manual labourers directly involved in production. |
| V | Lower-grade technicians | Semi-skilled or routine manual/ non-manual labourers | Skilled or unskilled employees who provide direct services, including retail cleaners, repairers, cooks, janitors and drivers. |
| VI | Skilled manual workers | Migrant workers | Those deemed to be the majority in the lower/lowest rungs of society. |
| VII | Semi-skilled or unskilled workers | Peasant | – |

*Source*: Modified from Bian *et al.* (2005).

Class and the distinctive lifestyles of a class are interdependent and form core concepts in the Goldthorpean analysis of modern stratification. The main weakness of this model is that it does not incorporate political capital, a factor that would otherwise explain the membership of regional cadres in the Chinese new middle class. What has been observed of the Chinese new middle class generally concurs with the Goldthorpean conceptual framework, especially with respect to distinctive lifestyles. Even discounting the absence of political capital in the theory, the Goldthorpe model still allows us to develop it further with inputs from Bourdieu and other cultural sociologists such as Mike Featherstone (1991) to operationalise an alternative to the more usual Weberian/neo-Weberian method.

## Bourdieu and the sociology of culture

Economic progress has helped to foster a new consumer society in post-reform China based on mass markets in production and consumption. As mentioned earlier, the rise of a new middle class reflects a realignment of social order: this reflects a need to construct new social identities (i.e. new classes) focusing more on goods and property than on the work they do (Liechty 2003: 15). Consumption has emerged as one of the many defining characteristics of middle-class cultural life.

Bourdieu provides the latest version of conceptualisations on class that help bring work and market situations from Weber into a cultur-ally-oriented analysis. His culturally reflective conceptualisations have now replaced the traditional 'materialist' concept of class (Bourdieu & Wacquant 1992; Bourdieu 1977, 1984, 1986, 1989; Bourdieu & Wacquant 1992; Bourdieu *et al.* 1999; Jacksons 2008; Webb *et al.* 2002). In Bour-dieu's theory, cultural distinctions are the foundations of class distinc-tions, and taste, and as a deeply ideological category, functions as a marker of class (Bourdieu 1977, 1989; Bourdieu & Wacquant 1992; Acciaioli 1981; Jacksons 2008; Webb *et al.* 2002). His theory draws a basic distinction between the bourgeoisie and the intellectuals among the dominant classes in a given society (Bourdieu 1977, 1979, 1984, 1986, 1989). The bourgeoisie has higher economic capital but lower cultural capital, whereas the intellectual has the reverse. (Young generations within the bourgeoisie, however, tend to have higher levels of economic and cultural capital.) Tastes within these two groups are different. The bourgeoisie tends towards the baroque and flamboyant goods, whereas the intellectual shows a preference for aesthetic modernism.

Bourdieu's theory, although drawing on Marxian rhetoric, opposes the Marxist view that society is analysable purely in terms of classes and class-determined interests and ideologies. Income differentials signify class differences under very specific societal conditions, but the extent of class structuring in modern societies is determined by more than just income differentials (Bourdieu 1977, 1979, 1982, 1989; Bourdieu

& Wacquant 1992). Therefore, the bourgeoisie draws its power and profits from the economy, and its functioning depends as much on the production of *consumer needs* as on the production of the goods themselves.

Bourdieu's theories on cultural capital, tastes, habitus and cultural practices have become influential indicators in the investigation of middle classes anywhere. He is perhaps a more comprehensive sociologist mainly because of his detailed descriptions of daily practices. For Bourdieu (1989), class formation is deeply rooted in the formation of habitus. Habitus can be defined as 'a system of durably acquired schemes of perception, thought and action, engendered by objective conditions but tending to persist even after an alteration of those conditions' (Bourdieu & Passeron 1979: 12). Habitus is an embodied internalisation of objective social relations, which is a generative grammar of practices (Bourdieu 1977, 1982, 1986, 1989). In other words, habitus is a set of subjective dispositions that reflect a class-based social grammar of taste, knowledge and behaviour permanently inscribed in each developing person (Bourdieu 1977, 1989; Bourdieu *et al.* 1999). Habitus forms a vital part of the everyday life of individuals, thereby giving rise to lifestyles for each social group.

Bourdieu sees the habitus as the key to class reproduction because perception, thought and action are what actually generate the regular, repeated practices that constitute social life. In that sense, habitus is 'the product of social conditionings' (Acciaioli 1981: 116) and links actual behaviour to class structure (Acciaioli 1981: 86). Bourdieu's (1977, 1989) concept of class habitus indicates that cultural capital is the pivotal determinant of values, instincts and lifestyles. Cultural capital comes in various institutionalised forms, but most readily as education and skills. Bourdieu (1989) and Bourdieu & Wacquant (1992) emphasise the leading function of education to predispose an individual or group to engage in certain cultural practices. The inference is that education brings out differential cultural patterns. A dominant economic class able to access superior culture (e.g. good taste) legitimises its position of superordination relative to other classes. Education enables the class to progressively capture the means of cultural reproduction as a way of increasing its chance of social reproduction (Bourdieu 1977, 1989). In short, education is a crucial capital to maintain high social status from generation to generation.

If education is important in influencing cultural practices (Bourdieu 1984), then it is education in Western societies that ultimately assists in the reproduction of differentiated cultural patterns (Bourdieu & Wacquant 1992). The level of education is already a measure of the competitive position of an individual in society. If education influences cultural practices and if that, in turn, influences social positions, then education seems attractive, not for what it offers educationally, but for what it could give socially. The class habitus theory tells me that I could predict a low likelihood of friendships between (say) professionals and manual workers because they differ sharply in terms of their cultural capital. The more cultural similarities there are between people, the more likely it is that they will become close associates (Silver 1990; Zang 2006). Real life bears this out: professionals are mostly university graduates trained in critical thinking and they develop a tendency to exchange views only with their equivalents (Zhang, W. 2000).

Bourdieu's concept of habitus (along with his concept of fields) provides a useful way to understand what culture is and how it shapes local interaction at the individual and group levels right through to the institutional or state level. Habitus guides individuals in social life by supplying them with an implicit grasp of 'the rules of the game'. Class habitus therefore indicates that people follow instincts when making important life decisions like friendship choices. Bourdieu's line of thinking closely aligns with the idea that prospering groups like the Chinese new middle class possess a distinctive habitus and taste in everyday life because of its higher-than-average cultural capital.

As a deeply ideological category, taste is an important indicator of class (Bourdieu 1977, 1979, 1989; Bourdieu & Wacquant 1992). Bourdieu points out that:

> Taste is the practical operator in the transmutation of things into distinct and distinctive signs, of continuous distributions into discontinuous oppositions; it raises the difference inscribed into the physical order to bodies to the symbolic order of significant distinction. It transforms objectively classified practice, in which a class condition signifies itself (through taste), into classifying practice, that is, into a symbolic expression of class position... (Bourdieu 1984: 174).

Bourdieu believes that taste is one of the main battlefields of the cultural reproduction and legitimisation of power (Bourdieu & Passeron 1979). Certain constellations of taste, consumption preferences and lifestyle practices are confined to certain social groupings (Bourdieu 1989). This implies that certain goods could be used in certain ways as instruments for making social distinctions. For example, Bourdieu

(1989) describes how the French upper class prefers rich courses, desserts, vintage champagnes and truffles. Since each social group has a different habitus, it follows that different taste structures would emerge from different social groupings (Bourdieu 1977, 1982, 1986, 1989; Bourdieu & Passeron 1979; Calhoun 2007). In other words, different 'objective conditions' are internalised via habitus as expressed in tastes. For example, taste in food is based on knowledge of the proper methods of preparation and presentation, as well as on the 'correct' foodstuffs for a well-balanced diet.

Bourdieu distinguishes three kinds of taste. Pure or legitimate taste is the first kind and it is the taste whose cultural objects are legitimate. It is the kind of taste usually found in parts of the dominant class with the highest educational capital. The second kind is average taste: that which is directed to less-valuable and more common objects. Popular or vulgar taste is the third kind and refers to the value that has been inflated by its proliferation, for instance, pop music. Demarcation lines in taste run from the good to the bad and to the 'barbarian'.

From a practical standpoint, Bourdieu's concept of taste means that a more highly educated person with more pure or legitimate tastes can legitimise his or her status in society. The more highly educated a person is, the more they are able to distinguish themselves from the status of those less well equipped. The implication from Bourdieu is that taste is a means of power, an instrument for domination that could be used by the dominant class to distinguish itself from other classes that are represented by other taste categories.

The taste that a person shows in goods is an indicator of his or her social class in a commodity-oriented (i.e. consumption) culture (Featherstone 1991: 88). That makes consumption culture the 'field' to create, preserve and replicate social differentiation and social disparities (Bourdieu 1977, 1989; Bourdieu & Wacquant 1992). If, as already mentioned, a dominant class uses education to nurture its culture and to preserve its class position, then that is saying that education shapes taste, consumption behaviour, and social differentiation and class boundaries, which in turn shape the characteristics of the consumption culture. This is the way that Bourdieu interprets class in cultural terms (lifestyle and consumption patterns), which is similar to how Featherstone (1991) interprets it except that the latter focuses on consumption rather than production.

Consumption of commodities in Featherstone's interpretation (1991) is effectively a means of self-expression and source of identity for an individual. If the identity of the individual consumer is expressed through the consumption of commodities, and if an item (commodity) has a symbolic value beyond its material value, then consumption of commodities is actually a consumption of values. If consumption of values is captured by such terms as 'taste', 'fashion' and 'lifestyle', the implication is that consumption itself is being commodified: the value of a commodity is judged in terms of symbolism in addition to exchange, production and utility. In other words, consumption itself is reflexively consumed. If consumption is differentiated into individualised tastes, the family or the community ceases to be the principal unit of consumption. This suggests the formation of status acts through the sharing of symbols in lifestyle and consumption patterns. Therefore, taste, fashion and lifestyle could be used in place of class and political affiliation as terms to show social differentiation. If Featherstone is right (and he seems to be in the Chinese case), the shared structures of class positions would help people coalesce into social groups like the Chinese new middle class and, once formed into them, goes on to help them look for economic interests to maintain social status.

Applying Bourdieu's concepts to post-reform China, we can see the appearance of a new logic. The Chinese economy requires hedonism (consumption based on credit and gratification) at the expense of an aesthetic ethos (production and accumulation based on sobriety, abstinence, calculation, saving) (Bourdieu 1986: 310). Two major implications follow from this. The first is that the factors influencing or determining class positions are even more complex than at first sight. The second is that income differentials are no longer the sole indicator in examining the lifestyles and consumption behaviour in advanced industrial societies (Bourdieu 1977, 1982, 1986, 1989). In the Chinese case, a new economy needs new flexibility in values, and the new middle class is the initiator of such values (Bourdieu 1977, 1982, 1986, 1989).

## A class analysis of today's China

China since the 1980s has experienced institutional changes that further render traditional class theories problematic for use in China. *Hukou* (household registration) has no parallel in the West. It restricts access to the city for individuals and so creates *spatially* distributed inequality. Spatial distribution of equality is politically determined in China whereas it is economically determined in the West.

The *danwei* (work unit) essentially provides workplace-linked benefits in state-sector employment. Its continued, albeit abridged, operation in urban China gives rise to differences in work situations because *danwei* provides the political affiliation of the Chinese new middle class to get along with. If they have the same *danwei* or the same affiliation, they are acquaintances and most likely they have the same types of collective memories. Both *hukou* and *danwei* create differences in market and work situations, thus encouraging social networks (*guanxi*) to emerge across the different groupings associated with the Chinese new middle class.

The dichotomy between the state and private sectors of the economy plus the structures of land and property acquisition and ownership both serve to maintain a cadre-dominated social hierarchy. That in turn highlights the importance of political capital in an otherwise market-oriented economy. Kraus (1981) observes that the new middle class in China appears to be stratified in two modes. The first is 'stratification by class designation'. This includes some capitalists and landowners as well as intermediate designations of the petty bourgeoisie. The second is 'stratification by occupational rank', which emphasises income and educational levels. By adding in *danwei* and *hukou*, land reforms, *guanxi* and cultural values, it is clear that that the Chinese new middle class strives to utilise their own advantages in the development path of Chinese society.

The relevance of class analysis in post-reform China is also different from that of post-Soviet Russia (Gerber & Hout 2004; Sitnikov 2000). The Russian analysis has no objection to the idea that the country makes a transition from communism to capitalism. Accordingly, it draws on class categories in understanding that transition. This derives from the displacement of the communist party by political liberalisation alongside economic liberalisation. In China, however, it is unclear if the country is actually undergoing the same sort of transition. There is considerable dissension within China studies (and even in general Political Science and Sociology). We have to caution that we do not know for sure what the transition is in the Chinese case. The continuing existence of the *danwei* and the specific nature of the reforms in land and property rights are illustrative of the politico-administrative and social ambiguities in China today. They underline the fact that the Chinese transition is at variance with other post-communist countries. They also underscore the continuing influence of party cadres in Chinese society and the reason for the Chinese new middle class to have collaborations with cadres in many areas of life. There is a pro-capitalist tradition taking root in China.

## Political capital and other capitals in the context of communist societies

While China is now undergoing a transformation from a command economy to a market economy, habitus forms a vital part of the everyday life of individuals, thereby giving rise to lifestyles for each social group. The rise of a hybrid élite of entrepreneurs and 'cadre-entrepreneurs' (Nee 1989, 1991, 1996) is particularly peculiar and prominent in post-reform China. An implication is that political affiliation is an important base of class stratification. Since the 1980s, cadres have been capitalising on entrepreneurial pathways in both the public and private sectors of the country's mixed socialist economy. These entrepreneurial pathways are structurally located in social networks. Djilas (1957) depicted a new class based on the privileges of the bureaucratic officials. He pointed out that, even in communist countries, society simply ends up creating a new class: the political bureaucracy. People in that political class have the power and privileges that enable them to control the rest of the population (Wallace 2006). The new class, the political bureaucrats, adopt a variety of measures to exert control over property ownership. The state property of the communist system is controlled by the bureaucracy of the party and the state, which therefore becomes the *de facto* owner. By virtue of its exercise of control over state property, then, the party bureaucracy assumes the role of the new ruling and exploiting class. Djilas (1957: 39), in describing the new class, said:

> The new class may be said to be made up of those who have special privileges and economic preference because of the administrative monopoly they hold.

For Djilas (1957), the core of the new class is made up of those who occupy political-bureaucratic positions in the party apparatus, i.e. the full-time party officials. The party itself tends to decline in importance, as the new class becomes a bureaucratic class. The bases for their formation of the new class would appear to be the penetration and domination of the party by those who possess higher educational achievement. Djilas (1957) claimed that the emergence of the new class was the result of bureaucratisation, which formed a party of professional revolutionaries. It was from this group of revolutionaries that the new class emerged. It established its power in a party system. The party bureaucrats are at the core of the new class, heading a much larger apparatus of power. It gradually consolidated its position through the establishment of strict authoritarian control over recruitment to its highest levels.

In addition, Szelenyi *et al.* (1998) argues that the new class includes professionals who possess cultural capital such as higher educational credentials and professional knowledge. An understanding of the notions of political capital and cultural capital are both important to analyse such groups in the transitional countries in Eastern Europe like Hungary. First of all, political capital is important since only those who joined the communist party had a chance to climb to the top of the political hierarchy. According to Szelenyi *et al.* (1998), ascending to the top echelon, it required not only the possession of human capital (specific skills and technical knowledge), but also mastery of the new hegemonic symbolic code of Marxism-Leninism. Secondly, in post-communist social structure, cultural capital becomes primary. Szelenyi *et al.* (1998) claims that those who were successful in the labour-intensive industries would benefit from the transition to capitalism during the late communist period. The coalition that governs post-communist societies comprise technocrats and managers, many of whom held senior positions in the former communist institutions or were former dissident intellectuals who contributed to the fall of communist regimes in the late 1980s (Szelenyi *et al.* 1998: 33). Cultural capital dominates the social structure of post-communist societies.

China shares more or less the similar situation depicted by Djilas in socialist countries and by Szelenyi in relation to Eastern Europe. But what is different in China's case is that it is not from capitalism to socialism but rather from socialism to capitalism. China has never gone through the transition from capitalism to socialism as it was experienced in Eastern Europe. China will move through the trajectories of capitalism in the 21st century but Eastern Europe has been going through the trajectories of capitalism since the 19th century. Whether or not it is capitalism it is still problematic and unknown to us. This makes class analysis in post-reform China much more complicated and intriguing. The existing importance of political capital and the revaluation of cultural and economic capital have taken place to meet the imperatives of a market economy. The main winners in the transformation are the highly educated people and political bureaucrats. People who possess political capital, such as the political bureaucrats, and cultural capital, such as the well-educated professionals and intellectual elites, play key roles in transitional countries in Eastern Europe such as Hungary. Being in possession of both cultural capital and political capital, they are able to convert their former political capital into valuable post-communist resources. Overall, Szelenyi's major argument is that the technocratic factions of the former communist ruling elite could be viewed as the big winners in the post-communist transition. They move rapidly towards a confrontation with the communist bureaucracy. People who have both political and cultural capital become the most upwardly mobile groups in post-communist society.

Cadres use political capital as the means of establishing useful relationships in political, economic and social fronts. However, no sooner had the opening-up and marketisation policies begun in 1978 than many cadres came to realise that political capital alone is not enough to survive in a decentralising system. Cadres could have a more favourable footing in society if they also possess economic capital, in the forms of organisational assets, bureaucratic access, professional skills, or entrepreneurial abilities. They could further affirm their footing by extending attachments to cultural and social capitals. Already with access to official political networks by virtue of their existing or former job positions, cadres readily extend themselves into other social networks. Political capital therefore becomes a channel to accumulate social capital.

## *Hukou* and its effects on the Chinese new middle class

The *hukou* system of household registration in China was implemented nationwide in 1958 at around the same time as the launch of the Great Leap Forward campaign. It became widespread in China very quickly, becoming entrenched in society by the early 1960s. The system performs three main functions: (1) resource allocation and subsidisation for urban dwellers, (2) internal migration control, and (3) management of 'targeted' people such as political subversives (Wang 2004: 116).

As stated in the introduction, the *hukou* system is distinct in that it classifies the entire population into two (and only two) categories. Agricultural registrants are domiciled in rural areas. Non-agricultural (i.e. urban) registrants are confined to metropolitan areas (though it should be noted that the rural designation is largely a regional designation and includes large urban conurbations within it). *Hukou* holders, rural and urban, are integral part of *their households* with a *specified legal residence* (domicile) that is registered with the public security apparatus. The *hukou* classification (which the government calls 'status') could not be changed easily, even today (Lee & Yang 2007). Registrants receive essential services and welfare relief. (The same condition differentiates non-locals from locals. Non-locals receive fewer benefits than locals do.)

In pre-reform times, *hukou* made the free movement of people practically impossible, especially that of rural people into urban areas. No one could come into cities without prior official permission. The official party rhetoric was that *hukou* was about breaking down urban/rural barriers (Chan 2009; Chan & Buckingham 2008). *Hukou* rigidified the divisions between rural and urban societies. Urban residents were issued ration coupons to buy food and other goods at subsidised prices, and these entitlements were linked to domicile. (Rural residents were responsible for their own food provisions.) For the urbanites, ration coupons were valid for use only in their own neighbourhoods or at specified places. People living or working outside of their authorised domiciles did not qualify for rations, housing, healthcare, jobs, or other essentials. A rural *hukou* holder would have found it nearly impossible to survive in urban areas. The only channel in the old days for rural-to-urban migration was *nong zhuan fei* ( 农转非 ), a bureaucratic conversion programme tightly controlled by quotas (Lee & Yang 2007: 13). It does much to explain the very low growth of urban populations in China from the late 1950s to the late 1980s.

Thirty years of market-oriented reforms have wrought many institutional and economic changes on society (Bian *et al.* 2005). *Hukou* has laxly been enforced, which made for freer population movement. The *hukou* system is still in place today, albeit in a trimmed-down form, and effective in regulating rural-to-urban migration. Given that urban areas are growing economically at a very fast pace, internal migration control is important in maintaining social and economic order. Today, the main difference between the two *hukou* statuses is in medical insurance coverage and employment eligibility (Chan 2009; Pun 2005; Wang 2004). The latter is an important factor in determining class in terms of 'market situation'. Migrants from 'rural' to 'urban' designated areas without an urban *hukou* are restricted to the casual labour market.

The socialist market economy is an uneasy blend of planned and market effects. An example of such a blending can be seen in *lanyin* ( 蓝印 , 'blue-stamped') type of *hukou*. This relatively new *hukou* was instituted in 1992 and became quite widespread throughout the 1990s (Fan 2002; Chan 2009). It provides a migrant with the right of abode in city areas and with a particular set of welfare provisions. Qualification for the *lanyin hukou* essentially boils down to the applicants making a large investment or the purchase of an expensive home, in addition to the usual criteria like age, education and skills. Most rural migrants are ineligible for this type of *hukou* and basically cannot afford one.

*Hukou* therefore distinguishes each and every individual and household with a different social identity. By classifying people into one or other category, the system leads to the formation and segregation of different social classes. Urban *hukou* households qualify for relatively better benefits than rural *hukou*. *Hukou* therefore works to create differences in class positions (rural *vs.* urban proletariat) based on geographical location. This is a spatially distributed inequality (Saunders 1984; Otis 2003). In Western societies, spatial distribution of inequality is bound up in differential distribution of specific occupations across regions (Saunders 1984). In post-reform China, however, individuals of the same occupation (in class terms) may be rewarded differently in different regions because of the operation of *hukou*. An urban *hukou* automatically differentiates it from a rural *hukou*, so creating a system segregated between the two types of status, albeit incompletely, as I shall show.

Since the *hukou* status is government-regulated rather than market-driven, the rural-registered worker most resembles the classical Marxist proletariat, rather than a *lumpen proletariat*. It is a paradox in the Marxist or even the Weberian approach to class, in that a political designation of their status rather than the operation of the market define their economic position.

Even today the *hukou* system has major repercussions for the physical and social mobility of individuals, including their access to essential services. People, and their children, with no *hukou* in the area in which they live would face enormous difficulties in accessing jobs, education, healthcare, and welfare relief. The level and type of differential access in turn deepens social stratification. The system is not absolute, in the sense that there is a market for the purchase of *hukou*. Those without a *hukou* (for example, children born in breach of the 'one child policy'), or those with rural registration seeking to convert it to urban registration need to pay considerable sums of money for a *hukou*, whether rural or urban (the latter, are especially costly). Of course, the ability to pay is also an aspect of stratification. Essentially, then, *hukou* is part of how the spatial inequality operates, and it needs to be approached in those terms, since it is the main mechanism determining the flow of migrant workers and the terms on which migration takes place, whether legal or illegal. Indeed, most of the very considerable number of illegal migrant workers in the Pearl River Delta area are individuals (frequently from the same area) with rural *hukou*.[1] In this way, *hukou* provides one of the most helpful means for sociologists to distinguish members of the Chinese new middle class from the rest of the population. Rural and migrant workers do not have sufficient resources to buy an urban domicile, and urbanites have no need to purchase an (inferior backward) rural residency. Given that it was very difficult for a rural household to reclassify itself as an urban one, it stands to reason that the majority of the China middle class must have had an urban *hukou* to begin with.

The process of obtaining or converting a *hukou* status is gruelling and time-consuming, and it is usually unsuccessful. Yet an urban *hukou* is not entirely closed off to outsiders. It could be acquired by way of inheritance or naturalisation through marriage or birth, university admission, or economic contribution. Reforms in marriage and inheritance laws contribute to internal migration but in new ways. After 1998, children of rural–urban or cross-regional cooperatives are given a choice of taking up either their fathers' or mothers' *hukou*. This was not previously the case (Wang 2004: 123). In addition, by education one can be granted a temporary urban *hukou* upon admission to a university or a state-accredited educational institution (Wang 2004). After graduation, and if given an urban job, the graduate could automatically be given an urban *hukou* in the same location as his or her job, or one nearest to their original domicile (Wang 2004). So, skilful workers can quite easily get transitional ('blue-stamped') or even permanent urban *hukou*. In this way, the Chinese meritocracy is granted the privilege of mobility (Wang 2004).

Economic contribution is another route. Today, it is possible to buy an urban *hukou* in any city in China. Predictably, professionals and entrepreneurs are the main beneficiaries of this development. Two tracks apply: either make a large-enough job-creating investment or make a high-priced real-estate purchase in a desired locale (Chan 2009). Guangdong province has a third track: one can get an urban *hukou* if their actual tax payments reach a threshold, usually around RMB80,000 (US$11,708 or £8,088 p.a.) per annum (Chan 2009). Of course, buying a *hukou* is not an outright buy-and-sell transaction in the commercial sense of the word.

Around 11.5% of the population of Guangdong province in 2006 is classified as belonging to the middle class (Guangdong Provincial Statistical Bureau 2006), although there are varied interpretations of the total number of the Chinese new middle class in China today. This is not a particularly high figure but it does show that only the new middle class has the material advantages to pay for household registration. It is through following this pattern and route that the Chinese new middle class forms its own social distinction in society. Indeed, some localities have tried to attract talents such as Olympic medallists or scientists or high-profile industrialists with offers of as many as three local urban *hukou*. This kind of talent scouting causes an internal brain drain in China,[2] whereby highly educated professionals flock to desirable metropolitan areas such as Guangdong. In this connection, I can see that a mixed economy, together with the continued running of the household registration system, preserves the institutional foundations of a cadre-dominated social hierarchy.

If rural workers are truly representative of the ongoing situation, then migrant workers on the whole are on even lower rungs of the social and job ladders. The low level of education (cultural capital) among migrant workers (who were mostly peasants) is the main reason for this state of affairs. The reality is that migrant workers are part of a floating population because their *hukou* are institutionally (and therefore politically) linked by the system to their original domiciles rather than current locations in urban areas. Again, this segregates migrant workers as a distinct but significant subset of the whole community. The inference of all this is that *hukou* is still relevant and influential for the educated, the rich and the powerful. New measures enacted for the system since the 1980s have provided further and varying degrees of *de facto* mobility for the privileged few.

## *Danwei* and how it creates differences in the work situations of *guanxi*

The economic reforms since the 1980s have altered (and are still altering) the role of *danwei*. This leads to a general decline in the influence of *danwei* on modern Chinese life. *Danwei* refers to a place of employment, especially in the context of state-owned enterprises during pre-reform times. Today, *danwei* has been officially dismantled in rural China but it continues to operate in urban areas. Ultimately, *danwei* is the assortment of welfare benefits associated with the Weberian 'market situation' of some forms of employment.

*Danwei* is significant in stratification terms because it often provides the institutional framework for relationship (*guanxi*) networks to form inside a particular class boundary. In that sense, *danwei* is one of the major institutional factors that contribute directly to the emergence of the Chinese new middle class. *Danwei* creates differences in work situations in three main ways: (1) as a geographical distribution of occupations, (2) as the milieu that gives rise to new forms of central-local relations, and (3) as the surroundings that facilitate the formation of *guanxi* inside class boundaries (Wu 2002).

First, as a geographical distribution of occupations, a *danwei* is clearly a place of employment, in the context of state enterprises. It is the first step of a multilayered hierarchy that links employment with the political machinery of the party-state. In pre-reform times, workers were bound to their *danwei* for life. Each *danwei* was an almost self-sufficient, self-sustaining entity, providing members with housing, schooling, healthcare, commodities, and other essentials. *Danwei* once helped to create a quiescent, compliant population based on ethnic origin, guilds, and patron–client relations.

In post-reform times, though, decentralisation and marketisation of the state economy are putting work units in competition with one another in a more open market. Work units today find it increasingly hard to provide their members with various services and welfare. People today are able to have careers in non-state organisations or to set up their own businesses. That further decreases the dependence on work units. *Danwei* is not the sole source of resources for people anymore. People now generally have wider connections and they can survive without *danwei* patronage or protection. Rising unemployment also shifts the balance of relationships between the state and society. However, *danwei* continues to affect class relations in urban areas in that it also sets up segregation between migrant workers and the new middle class. The segregation is expressed in occupation, income, and welfare provision by virtue of *danwei* connections with work and market situations. The spatialisation of inequality endowed in *danwei* directly contributes to *guanxi* networks. The inference is that the build-up of *danwei* also becomes an internal differentiation within the Chinese new middle class, since not all members of that class are actually covered by it. Cadres and some managers operate within *danwei*, but private entrepreneurs do not.

Second, as the milieu that gives rise to new forms of central–local relations, the *danwei* is largely the place where most of the changes in national land policy occur in practice (we will return to this below). The reason for this is that the central government has delegated quite a large portion of the responsibilities for economic management to local authorities. In turn, local authorities have greater leeway to upgrade, downgrade, or otherwise modify the responsibilities of the *danwei* under their jurisdiction. In short, the decentralisation of state power to localities fosters localism (Wu 2002: 1090), which creates a new kind of central–local relationship in a marketised economy. This ultimately leads to great divisions, unseen in pre-reform Chinese society, between the emerging elites (such as the bureaucratic business class) and the popular classes in rural and urban areas (Lee 2005). The new central–local relationship is a mixture of power conflicts, negotiations, and collaboration. Localism's effects on the 'great divisions' as well as the Chinese new middle class is obvious. On the whole, it is mutually accommodating because harmony is in everybody's best interests (Lin 1999, 2000). The reason for that is that there are *danwei* relations between different factions of the new middle class and these factions straddle the central and local sides of the relationship. Third, as a facilitative background for *danwei* inside class boundaries, this is best explained by reference to how economic entities are formed and operate in China today. State enterprises often set up sideline companies and subcontract the work to *de facto* private operators. Because of the potential for higher income in the private sector, many state employees are motivated enough to leave the 'iron rice bowl' (*tiefanwan* 铁饭碗; Hughes 1998) – the cradle-to-grave security of the *danwei* system. The more resourced cadres use their already well-established networks in the local *danwei* communities as a springboard into the tumultuous seas of the market economy. Some have the best of both worlds: if a family member works in a *danwei* (state sector), the household could enjoy 'one family, two systems'. One member gets a higher income from the private sector while another family member receives the job security, housing, and other benefits from the *danwei* for the rest of the household. It is not unusual to find full-time professionals in the state sector having part-time jobs outside, and use the part-time jobs mainly to extend business networks. For others, the non-state sector work is the sole source of economic benefits (Wu 2002: 1076).

During much of the reform period, there has been a state-approved drive to corporatise state enterprises into a system of shareholding ownership, especially the ones that could be floated on international stock markets. Many state entities in the manufacturing, financial, and public-utility sectors have been divested of their most profitable parts as shareholding companies, which are then used to form new consortia with non-state entities. This means that managers and officials are effectively running twin businesses in concert for private advantage. One way is for them to (mis)appropriate materials for funds from the state entity and use that in their outside companies (Ding 2000a, 2000b). Another way is for the officials (especially if they are in charge of the corporatisation of their state enterprises) to simply designate themselves as the major shareholders of the new companies. There are documented cases of such officers acting to reduce or even remove pensions and other benefits of workers (Ding 1999).

## The importance of cadre-entrepreneurship

Those ex-cadres who have close affiliations with the state enjoy the greatest advantages in post-reform China. *Hukou* and *danwei* are significantly important for the cadres or ex-cadres to collaborate with entrepreneurs and professionals in post-reform China. The operational ideology of the party requires the use of such 'professional revolutionaries' to implement policies and operation at all levels of government. Significant or even substantial loopholes in the machinery of government especially with regard to the marketised portion of the economy encourage interpersonal relationship networks (*guanxi*) to develop between bureaucrats and the elites in the private sectors including entrepreneurs and professionals.

The emerging cadre-entrepreneurs are probably even more able to obtain lower transaction costs in trade across boundaries of the redistributive (i.e. state) and private economies. They are already involved on both sides of the economy and have more ready access to resources and marketing outlets than do the general entrepreneurial rank-and-file or regular cadres. Their jobs already give them special dispensation and advantage, and it is not challenging for them to avail themselves of that advantage for self-interest in the face of decentralisation. This is the argument advanced by Nee (1991, 1996) that the real winners of the economic reforms were former cadres, who could hit the ground running because they know the ropes of government and have the drive to run a business.

## Land, property restructuring, and reform

Class analysis in the Chinese context also involves implicit assumptions about the changes in property ownership in China and how those changes differ from Western forms. Given that private property ownership and collective ownership coexist in China, cadres have quite a large degree of decision-making influence in, among others, land-related matters. Therefore it is highly relevant to examine how cadres fit into Chinese class analysis.

The state is still the sole owner of all urban land in China. As a matter of ideology and public policy, the state ownership of land exists via administrative or economic units directly run by the government. The fundamental breakthrough in Chinese socialist land policy is in the progressive commercialisation of land-use rights since the beginning of the reforms. That has led to a rapid expansion of the Chinese real-estate market since the 1980s (Smart & Li 2006: 495).

In common with Western usage, land in China is classified as either freehold or leasehold. Freehold is absolute and defines the enduring ownership of a property (in the Chinese land context, the land itself and any structures built on it). Leasehold is property held under a lease for a fixed period of time; after that the land and any structures built upon it would return to the leaseholder. However, there may be some compensation for the structures. The difference between China and Western countries is that leases in China rest with the Chinese government. So those leases ultimately revert to the state, at least in principle.[3]

Decentralisation over the state control of land can be traced back to the City Planning Law of the People's Republic of China (中华人民共和国城市规划法) promulgated on 26 December 1989. That statute delegates (rather than devolves) to local government the responsibility for urban planning, general enforcement of development control and land-related administrative matters such as the issue of construction and land-use permits. Even projects undertaken by a central government unit must obtain prior land-use permission from a local government in order for funding to be obtained. Additionally, land-lease certificates are required from the local branch of the national Land Administration Bureau (地政局) (Wu 2002: 1080). The City Planning Law caused the commoditisation of urban land-use to explode from the 1990s.

What is the government approach to land-use? The Property Law of the People's Republic of China (中华人民共和国物权法), promulgated on 16 March 2007, provides that local government is the legally recognised leaseholder and grantor of leases. The purchaser is given time-limited rights to use the land for a price paid but no rights of land conversion. Rights to land conversion rest with local authorities or the central government. Both types of rights revert in time to the state (central or local government).

Let us take a brief legal detour. The statutory interpretation of 'leases' in the PRC Property Law appears to relate to the broader meaning of property ownership, as opposed to the more restricted meaning of a lessor (landlord) allowing a lessee (tenant) to take possession of the land in return for a rent (tenancy). The purchaser (grantee) is given *time-limited rights* to use the land for *a specified purpose* for valuable consideration (i.e. price and fees paid for the land). The problem here, legally speaking, is that it is not entirely clear whether the leases actually relate to property ownership or to tenancy since time-delimited rights conveyed in this legal manner could be interpreted in either way, or even both simultaneously. This is exactly the kind of institutional ambiguity that provides opportunistic loopholes for groups such as the Chinese new middle class to exploit for their own self-gain.

The result is that local government is now the maker and breaker of land contracts because the law effectively makes the local government both the lessor and the supervisor of land contracts (Wu 2002: 1079).

This kind of land decentralisation leads to a high level of regionalism in post-reform China because what has become commercialised is the *income derived from granting leasehold rights*. The income-generating potential therefore leads to increasing privatisation and commercialisation of the housing market in many areas of China (especially in Guangdong province). Increasing commercialisation of housing in turn leads to a buoyant black market in land transactions.

Since the 1980s, the privatisation and commercialisation of housing have become apparent in Guangdong province. Two distinct, prominent features become apparent when considering the post-reform land-leasing system. The first is the privatisation of public housing and the commercialisation of the housing market. The second is 'spatialisation of class'. In the first, the general trend of change is a shift from the *danwei*-based housing provision to a more commercialised housing regime. This shift is an uneven process and creates winners and losers. As with any zero-sum situation, housing therefore becomes an important element of social engineering in the making of a new middle class. With regard to the second, spatialisation of class is still going on in Chinese cities today because socioeconomic differences in China are becoming increasingly dependent on space (Chadha & Husband 2006: 119).

Given the spread of economic decentralisation since the 1980s, it has become increasingly easy for land-use rights to be converted into a money-making commodity and differential rents have begun to emerge. Various state-owned units that owned land – the 'socialist landmasters' – went along for the ride and established property companies for profit-taking. Officials and ex-officials of *danwei* that owned land sold land-use rights at sizeable profit to property developers or agencies in the state and private sectors. This resulted in a loose but active network of landbrokers appearing in many cities across China, driving up the number of land transactions.

The government invented various methods to convert industrial and residential land into commercial usage, but it was (and still is) common to see factory relocations and the exchange of land taking place directly between end users. For example, in Guangdong province, peasants often sell their landholdings in the suburbs directly to private property developers for the building of commercial complexes or villas. Many members of the Chinese new middle class have substantial resources and *guanxi* networks that enable them to buy lower-priced property or to be allocated housing units from their past employment with *danwei* – an association that continues after many switched over to the business world. We will return to the issue of land reform in China in Chapter 4.

The thriving black market in land is a serious issue in Guangdong. Outside of the formal land system, there is a highly competitive black market in land. The Chinese land market is composed mostly of private land developers. Since the supply of land has always been restricted in some way in China, land developers often earn huge profits from land speculation. Land speculation has long been a lucrative, if sometimes wild, business in China.

The land system of China operates in roughly the same way as its system of materials allocation. Economic reforms have brought marketisation over production materials, resulting in a relaxation of state control over them. State enterprises are allowed to buy production materials directly from the open market and sell surpluses to it after fulfilling state quotas. We can see this situation most commonly in government hospitals and property companies. The marketised portion of the dual-track price structure had grown so much and so efficient in practical terms that the state eventually abandoned its system of materials allocation (Wu 2002: 1007). Likewise in the land system, market decentralisation has introduced market mechanisms into the development and use of urban infrastructure. However, local governments are often unmotivated to take part in land and property reforms that benefit only the central government but offer no gains at the local level (Wu 2002). In an effort to control operational costs, the central government now requires local governments to contract out certain important local-level public services to the private sector. Similar to the way the land-lease system works, certain infrastructural developments then become more attractive to local governments. In such a way, it stimulates the tax base for the central government and benefits local governments with all sorts of extra revenue.

It is the localisation of the land system that offers loopholes for the black market. The City Planning Bureau (市规划局 *shi guihua ju*) that operates at the district government level is responsible for enforcing land-use regulations. But the overall complexities of land development in China makes land-use enforcement easier said than done. Illegal land conversions and black markets often involve individuals and companies that are well connected to the government (Wu 2002: 1078). Land speculators are especially willing to be cooperative with cadres because they know that only cadres have the actual power to release land and validate land contracts.

Often, the cadres are involved in land speculation and other related 'extra legal functions' for their own private interest. The Chinese property market reached its most recent peak in 2007, when dealers were bidding an average of RMB1 million (US$146,316 or £99,796) for a building or a plot of land. This is more or less the same problem as is experienced in big metropolitan cities like Beijing and Shanghai (Wu 2002). In Guangdong, as much as one-third of the price might go straight into the pockets of cadres. The most common way is for cadres to buy potentially lucrative plots of land in advance at below-market prices under the names of their family members or nominee organisations and resell the plots directly to buyers for hefty profit. Transactions would be initiated and settled entirely through 'informal' channels such as behind-the-scenes negotiations rather than formal open tenders or auctions.

In such a way, the localisation of the land system and the black markets attached to it reinforce the continuing pivotal role of cadres in post-reform China. Cadres cannot be expected to conduct the proper enforcement of the system because other cadres also figure in the black market as active speculators or accessories. More details about the collaboration among professionals, entrepreneurs, and cadres will be found in Chapter 4.

## Generational stratification and individualisation in post-reform China

There are interesting discussions about intergenerational relationships, but not in relation to the stratification between generations. If the institutional arrangements in China mean that the Chinese new middle class differs from the Western counterpart, then age and generational differences plus special features of the Chinese parent–child relationship also play their parts. Let us first turn to age and generational differences in terms of the cultural values, mentalities, and ideologies of generations and age cohorts. That different generations have different mindsets is self-evident and self-explanatory. Individuals born at different times have different life experiences. That in turn shapes and drives different attitudes, expectations, values, and beliefs. Different cohorts may in fact embrace divergent cultures with possibly contradictory beliefs and expectations. These may be reinforced or altered by contacts with different groups (Louis 1980; Martin 1992).

The old generations of Chinese are recognisable by their traditionalist values. As China's current life expectancy is about 75 years, then any individual born in the 1930s or thereafter would have had direct experience of the entire gamut of historical events that happened in the first four decades of the People's Republic. Table 1.2 shows the milestone events experienced by the old generations. By contrast, the young generations grew up in an atmosphere of little or no significant turmoil, and are therefore more apt to accept Western cultures and Westernised lifestyles than the old generations would be.

Table 1.2    Milestone events in the People's Republic of China

| Year | Milestone events |
| --- | --- |
| 1949 | Communist victory over Nationalists in civil war, driving the Nationalists to the island of Formosa (now Taiwan) to continue the existence of the Republic of China. Founding of the People's Republic of China. Reconstitutes the capital to Peking (Beijing) from Nanking (Nanjing). New marriage and family laws (based on Soviet laws of 1920s) implemented nationwide. |
| 1950–53 | Korean War: Chinese land forces mobilised to the Korean peninsula to aid defence of the Democratic People's Republic of Korea against US-led UN forces. |
| 1958 | Great Leap Forward begins, forming communes in the countryside to prove China's self-reliance to the world. *Hukou* system implemented nationwide to control internal movement of people. |
| ca. 1959–61 | Three years of famine associated with the Great Leap Forward. Causes 24 million to 30 million deaths. *Hukou* system entrenched by 1961. |
| 1966–76 | Cultural Revolution begins, causing nationwide political and social mayhem for ten years (1966–76). Mao used the Cultural Revolution to assert control, consolidating the personality cult surrounding him. Tens of thousands died, many committed suicide and the lives of millions ruined. |
| ca. 1967–75 | The 'Down to the Countryside' Movement sends millions of youths to the countryside 'to learn from the peasants' in an effort to alleviate urban unemployment and boost rural development. Education became disrupted or non-existent for many, creating the 'lost generation'. Secondary-school graduates at start of the movement lost the chance for university education when universities nationwide were shut down. University graduates at start of the campaign became the last graduating batch until the next batch at least ten years later. |
| 1971 | Lin Biao (林彪), the coup leader, escapes and dies in a mysterious plane crash in Mongolia on the way to the USSR. |
| 1976 | Death of Mao. Cultural Revolution ends. Arrest of the Gang of Four. Party struggle for leadership ends with Hua Guofeng (华国锋) becoming Mao's successor. |
| 1977 | Universities reopen. University entrance examinations reinstituted. First batch of students to enter universities and graduate in 1980–85 became the country's first batch of university-educated elites since the Cultural Revolution ended. |

Table 1.2   Milestone events in the People's Republic of China – *continued*

| Year | Milestone events |
| --- | --- |
| 1978 | Deng Xiaoping (邓小平) becomes paramount leader. 'Open-door' policy initiates economic reforms and liberalisation measures in incremental stages. The Third Plenum of the Eleventh CCP Congress adopts measures to promote national economic development. The Party announces that class struggle had come to an end, replacing it with economic advancement. |
| 1980s | Economic reforms implemented nationwide in incremental, geographically specified stages. 'Extra legal' activities surface across China in the state and nascent market sectors as a result of ambiguities or incompleteness in reform policies or administrative operation. |
| 1989 | Tiananmen Square protests in Beijing against widespread corruption in the bureaucracy and a prevailing winner-takes-all attitude in society produced by over attention to economic performance and under attention to social welfare. |

*Sources*: Bernstein (1977), Hung & Chiu (2003), with author's modifications.

If age and generational differences give a special facet to the Chinese new middle class, then the Chinese parent–child relationship gives a highly interesting point for sociologists to consider.

The first feature to identify is reduction in family size and its impact on the parent–child relationship. Broadly speaking, the nuclear family is replacing the extended, patriarchal family in urban China. Average family size throughout China is in decline. The average family size recorded in the first post-war census of 1953 was 4.33 persons. This then climbed to 4.43 in the second census of 1964 due to the absence of birth control in the 1950s as well as the baby boom of the 1960s. By the third census of 1982, the average family size had dipped to 4.41. In the census of 2000, average family size dropped further to 3.44 persons (State Bureau of Statistics 2010).

Despite increased Western influences and reductions in family size, intergenerational reciprocity is still strongly operative in the Chinese family (Ji 2003; Yuan 1987). Intergenerational reciprocity is the mutual dependence of the old and young generations on one another. What is interesting sociologically in this respect is that the vast majority of urban youngsters and young adults in China today are their family's only off-spring. The primary cause is the 'one-child policy' implemented in urban

China, which makes post-reform China unique in terms of the socialist trajectories of social development of populations.

Parent–child relationships in Chinese families are relatively unlike those now typical in the West. Mainland Chinese parents today tend to plan and do everything for their sole children, even to the point of finding jobs or accommodation for them. They will spend an enormous amount of time, effort, and money on their children to ensure that their children succeed and improve the social status of the family in a competitive and increasingly unequal society (Stockman 2000: 12; Stockman 1994). In return, the offspring tend to regard older folks as a source of daily help and a kind of trickle-down welfare shield. In fact, traditional Chinese mores and norms that anchor family life (such as filial piety and individual self-restraint for the greater good) seem only minimally diluted by politicisation, industrialisation and modernisation. In China, the state provides several types of welfare assistance to older people with children. Older people may qualify for temporary housing for their married children (34% of recipients), financial relief for non-co-resident (live-out) children (30%) and help with housework and childcare for co-resident (live-in) children (25%). (These figures here count only material relief benefits and exclude non-material, i.e. psychological, benefits (Sheng & Settles 2006).)

In the Chinese family even in post-reform times, parents are paramount in playing an instrumental and functional role as opposed to an equal-standing one. Some parents of the Chinese new middle class try to avoid being harsh, authoritarian, or patriarchal. Others might arrange for quality time with the children in order to get to know their offspring a little better. Still others might go as far as to learn to become friends or partners with their children. By and large in China today, however, Chinese parents almost never play a friendly, supportive role akin to that of their Western counterparts. Instead of a high degree of intimacy, as is generally seen in Western families, the average mainland Chinese parent maintains a domineering stance – to be a parent and nothing else. Indeed, quite a few of the old generation of the Chinese new middle class (10 out of 35), especially born between 1948 and 1960, do not even know what kind of parent–child relationship in the Western family milieu would be. This departure from the general Western patterns of parenthood makes the Chinese new middle class sociologically distinctive.

The second identifiable feature is the pattern of marriages. The marriage patterns of the young generations are profoundly different from those of their parents of the old generations (Moore 2005: 375;

Liu 2003). In traditional China, women always got married earlier than comparable to Western European women. Now, in post-reform China, more women have opportunities to receive an education. Some even go on to study for higher degrees. With better education, they show great potential in career or further study. With job satisfaction in their careers, they are likely to postpone their marriage. The well-educated women of the young generations are likely to challenge patriarchal power in terms of choosing a mate, marriage negotiation, and family life (Shirk 1984; Yan 2006: 106; Shu 2004), but economic liberation and reform seems to have no direct impact on changes in gender norms in today's China. Most of the traditional norms, such as the women being regarded as subordinate in the workplace, remain intact. They bear the double burden of both work and family, which is still internalised in post-reform China (Stockman 1994).

The last identifiable feature between the old generations and the young generations of the Chinese new middle class is individualisation. While research into China's new middle class remains at an embryonic stage, there is a conspicuous hiatus surrounding the various paths of individualisation embodied by the disparate generations that comprise this group. Through the development of a much-needed theoretically-led empirical expatiation of the emerging Chinese new middle milieu, their culture, careers and consumption, I examine the critical role that individualisation plays in the formation and reproduction of class in post-reform China. The spirit of capitalism that exists in post-reform China is clearly an indirect form of governance wielded by state authorities to yield results that are politically expedient. It is therefore the requisite precondition of human agency in capitalist development that is the locomotive that individualises the Chinese new middle class. In the relatively under-theorised literature on individualisation in China by Yunxiang Yan which makes no distinctions between the individualisation trajectories of the peasant and urban middle classes, capitalism's role as a system of governance and conduit of individualisation is unrecognised. Yan (2010: 507) expatiates on the contrast between the West and the situation in China:

> ...[I]ndividualization in Western Europe started in an affluent society under political democracy where individual rights and freedom were legally protected and material needs were no longer the primary goal of social progress. In contrast, individualization in China started in an economy of shortage, widespread poverty, and a totalitarian political regime where individual rights and freedoms were

suppressed for the sake of national survival and satisfaction of material needs.

Here, it is claimed that, in contrast to Western Europe, wealth, suffrage and the liberal imagination were not the antecedents to individualisation in China. Yan's claim may, however, be applicable solely to the peasant class. As far as the new middle class is concerned, we maintain that the advent of wealth and higher standards of living wrought by capitalism precipitate the individualisation of the senescent and young generations that comprise this group that will most likely be different to the minutiae of the *Agraria*.

Yan is nevertheless correct when he states that the distinguishing hallmark of individualisation in China is the state management of individualisation. By this, he refers to the state's right to peremptorily censure and enforce individualisation when doing so would be instrumental to the *summum bonum* of the organised collective community. Individuals who choose pathways preferred by the government, and who exert their self-autonomy only within clear and distinct socio-political boundaries, are rewarded both politically and economically (2009: 289). Thus, as the much-discussed fustian consumption choices of China's new middle echelon equate to 'digits in the economy', the party-state's manipulation of capitalism and free markets to satisfy the material desires of its middle class polity is, in reality, a state apparatus that manages the rise of the individual in a manner that will not attenuate the hegemony of the Leninist regime.

The rapprochement between individualisation and collectivisation in the lives of the new middle class is therefore buttressed by its desires to secure the *reproduction* of its elite status through political means. The pervasive lethargy towards democratic reform exemplified by this group can also be explained by Beverley Skeggs' (2004: 66) observation that the reconstitution, progression and progressive nature of the world's new middle classes is 'predicated on holding in place – fixing – that which must signify stagnation and immobility'. As the economic revolution gained momentum during the 1980s and 1990s, material possessions and consumption replaced political symbols as the key measures of one's social status (Yan 2009: 208). A mandate was therefore provided for a flourishing advertising industry (Hung *et al*. 2007: 839) to cultivate the desires of a new middle class that aspires to be distinguished from the common milieu.

The defining characteristics of the different groups that comprise China's emerging new class may remain somewhat inchoate. Nevertheless, consumption and a cultivated taste for designer accoutrements are the pre-requisites that one must exemplify to be admitted to this echelon (Smart and Smart 2003; Smart and Li 2006). Moreover, the predilections of the young generations to 'consume' a Western education (Gladney 2000) and to conspicuously flaunt their status by purchasing luxury 'mansions' and expensive cars (Hubacek *et al.* 2007) are emblematic of a self-conscious mentality and anxiety about the future of their class status. Accordingly, consumption is not simply an act of consumerism itself, but also reflects a hedonistic desire to experience leisure or plea-sure through consumerism. Farrer (2000: 244) is right in deducing that the ubiquity of a culture of leisure in a marketised economy punctuates a shift from a culture of production to a culture of consumption. The pleasure-seeking habits and self-consciousness of the members of the Chinese middle class suggest they remain enamoured with Western modernity's individualised lifestyles of consumerism and consumption that will be at tension with the hegemony of their ascribed identities and collectivist values.

This study finds that the young generations (born after 1970, including cadres, professionals and entrepreneurs) progressively capture the means of cultural reproduction as a way of securing its own social reproduc-tion (Bourdieu 1984, 1996). On the other side, the young generation is flexible enough to improve their competitiveness in the increasingly globalising China. They are quite anxious and uncertain about their life chances in the future. They tend to be more individualistic, materialistic and oriented to personal gain like most of the Western countries. How-ever, on the other hand, they are unlikely to practice the form of indi-vidualisation happened in some Western countries. I will return to this issue in Chapter 3.

## Summary

Using a sociocultural approach, which draws on neo-Weberian and Bourdieuian frameworks, I define the meaning of the Chinese new middle class by using the indicators of educational level, occupation, monthly household income, social networks, and consumption pat-terns. The Chinese new middle class tends to have the same consumption patterns and lifestyles. These sociocultural particularities are conducive to the emergence of the Chinese new middle class. Consumption is the easiest indicator for the new middle class to present its status, its wealth and its social reputation. Massive moves by China into the international arena play an important role in putting the idea of consumption within the idea of production (Pun 2005). New forms and standards of social distinction arise from new modes of consumption. Consequently, these aspects mould new identities for the class making social distinction inescapable (Pun 2003: 477). Consumption will be China's engine of economic growth. Since the late 1980s, consumption and asset possession have gradually replaced political symbols as the path towards defining one's social status and drawing class boundaries.

It appears that consumerism carries more sociopolitical meanings in China than in some truly capitalist societies. In Chapters 2 and 3, I am going to evaluate the consumption patterns of the old generations as well as the young generations of the Chinese new middle class. Consumerism, in a broad term, is the icon and indicator of everyday life practices. Not only is consumerism the symbol, status, and prestige of everyday life practice, but it is also a form of capital to change one's life chances and intergenerational mobility over generations.

# 2
# Class Boundaries of the Old Generation of the Chinese New Middle Class

> Every Tuesday, my friends and I meet up at the Lucky Restaurant to have dinner. It's a regular gathering and it's been our habit for the last six years. It provides the opportunity to catch up on things like the latest news, economic conditions and even the latest ways to earn extra money. No matter how busy I am, I always make time to attend. As we face the same issues and experiences, drink the same brand [Xiaohutuxin 小葫涂仙] and smoke the same brand of cigarettes [Hongtashan 红塔山], I feel really relaxed and comfortable. This type of get-together reinforces our friendship. It provides the topics [*huati* 话题] for us to discuss. It also provides a sense of a shared class background [*zijiren* 自己人] appropriate to the discussion of business matters.
>
> **(Uncle Yuen, 56, entrepreneur)**

Uncle Yuen's conversation seems to sum up an important element of class boundary and class membership. Common acquaintances act as a connecting thread to promote a 'common identity' and give them a greater sense of awareness within the new middle-class boundary. The ethnographic information collected in this study indicates that the common practices of the Chinese new middle class create a distinctly modern cultural space. This study classifies the Chinese new middle class into four broad cohorts according to the birth dates of the interviewees. These are the old generation (the first cohort was born between 1940 and 1958; and the second cohort was born between 1959 and 1969) and the young generation (the third was born in the 1970s and the fourth cohort was born in the 1980s).

Why should we classify the new middle class into old and young generations? Social institutional theory (see Inglehart 1977, 1990), historic generation cohort theory (see Inglehart & Norris 2003) and the concept of collective memory (for details see Belk 1988, 1991; Lipsitz 1990) all suggest that the behaviours and mentalities of different cohorts are shaped by social changes as well as by their peer groups. Each cohort will have different thoughts and ideologies based on their experience and perceptions of historical events.

Many events in the modern history of China have had a considerable influence on the life courses of the different generations of the Chinese new middle class (Mayer & Muller 1986; Mayer & Schoepflin 1989). Over the years, China has seen many national social changes take place: marriage law reform, legal schooling age, one-child policy, entitlements to state welfare services, compulsory social insurance, provisions of social services for age-specific target groups, economic liberalisation, and others (Meisner 1999). The direct impact of these modes of state action is to create a 'society-wide universalisation of the welfare-state-type life-course patterns' (Mayer & Muller 1986: 233). But the Chinese collectivist type of welfare state has been substantially disrupted by market reforms after the 1980s. This chapter focuses on the lifestyle and consumption patterns of the old generation of the Chinese new middle class. It also analyses the factors that influence those features of the old generation.

This chapter will focus on the old generation of the Chinese new middle class and initially presents information about the class boundaries and culture of that particular subset of the new middle class in Guangdong. Then excerpts from interviews will be used to show the pragmatic and utilitarian inclination of this old generation towards consumption matters, collective memories, and other aspects. Finally, the chapter critically analyses why the old generation practices both pragmatic and conspicuous consumption in a paradoxical post-reform China.

## The old generation of the Chinese new middle class

The old generation of the Chinese new middle class can be subdivided into two cohorts. The first cohort is now in their fifties and early sixties, born in the period 1948–58 (ages 50–60 in 2008), and occupies 22% of the research sample (13 out of N = 59). It is this generation that has first-hand experience of the hardship following the civil war between the Kuomintang and the Communists and the later political upheavals of the Great Leap Forward (GLF) and the Cultural Revolution which ended in 1976.[1] They are not particularly well-educated because of the disruptions caused to their education by the Cultural Revolution. They spent their childhood years in hardship when the country was in a state of internal political turbulence as a result of the GLF and the Cultural Revolution (Zhou & Hou 1999; Zhou & Pei 1997; Zhou & Brandon 1997; Deng & Treiman 1997).

The second cohort of the old generation is the post-war baby-boomers now in their forties and early fifties, born in the period 1959–69 (and therefore aged 39–49 in 2008). They account for 37% of the research sample (22 out of N = 59). This cohort is the first to experience the launch of the country's opening-up policy in 1978 and the first beneficiaries of the economic reforms when the country was most in need of a versatile élite for economic growth (Hewitt 2007). They lived through widespread economic changes of the early and middle reform years and had various experiences of the 1989 Tiananmen Square protests.

The first and second cohorts of the old generation occupy about 59% (i.e. 35 out of N = 59)[2] of the research sample. They are generally seen as the lucky ones when compared with the 'lost generation' of *xiagang gongren* (下岗工人 laid-off/redundant workers) when many Chinese state enterprises closed down in the mid-1990s because of economic streamlining measures. They did not suffer from the so-called destratification of social status (Parish 1984; Davis 1992a: 1062–1085; Bian 2002a: 105).

The young generation of the Chinese new middle class covers those people born in the 1970s and those born in the 1980s and beyond. The first cohort are now in their thirties, born in 1970–79 (aged 29–38 in 2008), and occupies 32% of the research sample (19 out of N = 59). The second cohort are in their twenties, born after the 1980s, and 9% of the research sample (i.e. 5 out of N = 59). The young generation accounts for about 41% of the research sample (i.e. 24 out of N = 59). Of this total of 24 individuals, 11 are single. These people have no significant privation or politically inspired negative experience in their childhood and their upbringing has been less restrictive than that of the old generation. They entered the workforce at the height of urban modernisation and globalised economic growth in the 1990s. Their employment is mostly contractual in nature (so covered by the labour contract system implemented in 1986) and based substantially on qualifications and performance. Both of these in many respects symbolised the dismantling of the 'iron rice bowl' of employment which had been prevalent in state enterprises up to that time (Hung & Chiu 2003: 224).

The old generation covers people born in the 1940s and 1950s (the first cohort of the old generation) and those born in the 1960s (the second cohort of the old generation). On the whole, they are characterised by their pragmatic frame of mind (not following a fixed set of ideas) in their way of life and their utilitarian consumption habits. As we shall see, this is in marked contrast to the conspicuous consumerism of the young generation that followed them (Smart & Smart 2003; Smart & Li 2006). The old generation can generally be characterised by their industriousness and their diligence in relation to saving. Typically, they are not well-educated owing to missed or denied educational opportunities as a result of the outbreak of the Cultural Revolution. Indeed, that political upheaval accounts for the fairly strong financial background but weak education of some of this generation of the Chinese new middle class since their fears about the uncertainties of the future cause them to save rather than consume.

## Factors encouraging pragmatic consumption

What causes the old generation to have more down-to-earth attitudes? Three major factors, identified from our research sample, encourage pragmatic and utilitarian consumption in the older new middle class.

1. The collective memory of the Cultural Revolution and the effects associated with it on the formative years of the people.
2. The continuing influence of traditional Confucian values and mores on modern life.
3. The constant need for self-improvement to uphold personal competitiveness in the face of rapidly changing economic and social environments. This self-improvement also covers gearing oneself to extending business connections.

Collective memory is a form of nostalgia that contributes to social identity (Chan 2003; Lee 2000; Yang 2003). For the old generation in my sample it can be delineated into two major time blocs that were characterised by negative experiences. The first time bloc is the Maoist period, especially the Cultural Revolution in the 1960s and 1970s. Here, the negative experiences are the poverty in childhood or early adulthood and the disillusionment around missed or denied educational opportunities. The second time bloc is the more liberal reformism of the 1980s and 1990s. Here, the negative experiences are those of the trials and tribulations of entering into the world of commercial business and involvement in 'extra legal' activities such as smuggling or illegal emigration/immigration.

## Collective memories

'Collective memory' refers to the shared experience of some major historical trajectories in life histories held by people born in the same age cohorts (Yang 2003; Chan 2003). A collective memory helps individuals to construct and maintain an identity in two ways, by (a) first making links between past experiences and their current meanings and (b) then stimulating them to articulate in narratives these links from their generational experience to moral critiques of the present (Bruner 1987; Josselson & Lieblich 1999).

In the Chinese context, collective memory tends to contrast a 'Past' viewed as containing meanings and purposes against a 'Present' dominated by economic inequality and instrumental rationality (Yang 2003). For many of the older Chinese new middle class, the unimaginable tumult and hardships they experienced during the Cultural Revolution is the most vivid, and the most clearly remembered past (Chan 2003: 82). The ghost of the Cultural Revolution is their signature collective memory, a memory and identity that evolved for them through a process of construction and negotiation over the years (Chan 2003: 85). Then there is the collective memory of working in state organisations/enterprises, and also the experience of transitioning to the private sector and possible involvement in 'smuggling' (a word that has a broader meaning to the Chinese in that it covers many 'extra legal' activities).

The first collective memory, nostalgia and identity derived directly from the Cultural Revolution. I can see the forces of this collective memory at play in the older new middle class. They have a certain nostalgia for Maoist times, and this is something of a general social sentiment of theirs (Lee 2000). In that idealised version of Maoist China, there was no pain and no worry even while they tell you that the past was not an unequivocal bliss (Lee 2000: 228). The romanticisation of past events and their childhood is sometimes heightened by tragic stories (Lee 2000: 225). Although the older new middle class might be nostalgic for Maoist times, nearly all of them are negative in discussing their experiences and their assessment of the regime during the Cultural Revolution under Mao Zedong. In the ten years that the Cultural Revolution lasted, the party suppressed all ideological dissent and human initiative. Various political campaigns brought about the wanton destruction of capital and manufacturing assets (not to mention cultural and intellectual assets) that led to an eventual near-collapse of the general economy by the mid-1970s.

It was the Red Guards (*hongweibing* 红卫兵) who, in the name of 'struggle' (*pidou* 批斗), set in motion the mayhem that led to much of the misery of those times.

> I still remember how the Red Guards forced me to inform on my family, reveal that my grandfather and grandmother had connections with the Kuomintang and betray other Kuomintang comrades. Perspiring and intensely uncomfortable, I was assaulted by memories of the past. My heart was filled with unimaginable sadness. I needed to change my surname to Lam and forename to Sam after the outbreak of the Cultural Revolution. **(Uncle Sam, 49, entrepreneur)**

Many point out that everyone was hungry and poor during this period. If anyone had been able to buy a chicken during the Cultural Revolution, they would have been unable to eat it because they would have been branded as counter-revolutionaries on suspicion of hoarding 'capitalist' seeds for the chicken. They yearned for peace and better times, but the future looked very bleak.

The Cultural Revolution is a source of painful memories for most people. Uncle Wah was about 18 years old when the Cultural Revolution broke out. He had been sent to the countryside to learn from the peasants. He says,

> We were the intelligentsia at that time even though I was only a senior secondary graduate. We wrote many *shanghen wenxue* (伤痕文字, trauma stories) about our harsh childhood. This process, called *yiku sitian* [益苦思甜 'trying to come up sweet'] has helped me deal with my emotions. I don't want to recall the painful memories of my childhood. This is why I needed to work hard in the early years of 1980s and seize every chance to enrich myself. Life was full of ups and downs. We didn't know what would happen, right? **(Uncle Wah, 50, professional)**

Close relationships are derived from collective consensus and understandings as a result of shared lifestyles and consumption practices by reason of belonging to the same age cohorts. Being in the same age cohort means the chances of their gathering together also increase. The sharing of memories and experiences causes people to have similar habits in lifestyle and consumption that they could share with one another. Shared lifestyle and consumption practices help to develop and reinforce deep and close relationships between those people.

The second collective memory is the nostalgia and identity derived from the experience of an impoverished childhood. Poverty is a common thread in the nostalgia of the older new middle class. Even by the mid-1970s no one in China was particularly rich. Everyone was equally poor. The experience of privations in childhood is a driving force in their current values of industriousness, thriftiness, and ambition. So when members of the older new middle class meet and gather together, they reminisce about past experiences of poverty and hardship.

> My home had fluorescent lamps. We were poor. We always went to our neighbours, who had electric lighting, to watch television in black and white. I remembered we were enthralled by soap operas. If anyone owned a bicycle or a television set, it was incredible – and made me feel envious. If you had a handkerchief, *baixie* [白鞋 white shoes, i.e. plimsolls], a bicycle, or a colorful fashion item made of *di que liang* [的确凉 Dacron], you were considered a rich and powerful person in China in the 1960s. The most common teasing in my childhood was "if you have clothes made of Dacron, then it will be easy for you to find a good and beautiful wife [上的下的, 左手一的的, 右手一个亲爱的 *shang-de xia-de, zuo-shou yi de-de, you-shou yi-ge qin-ai de*]. When we think of past memories, we always bring this up. It really made me laugh and was so unforgettable that I'd mention it frequently in gatherings with my friends. It made a strong impression on me during my childhood. **(Uncle Fong, 48, entrepreneur)**

Here is how the proverb works (according to the interviewee): De 的 is an abbreviated, highly colloquial nickname at the time for Dacron (*di que liang* 的确凉), the polyester-like fabric material. *Shang-de* (上的 *of the top*) means the upper part of the body, which the expression alludes to your ability to buy and wear clothes made of Dacron. Similarly, *xia-de* (下的 *of the bottom*) alludes to wearing Dacron trousers (or slacks, since skirts were not worn because of connotations of bourgeoisie decadence!). *Zuo-shou yi de-de* (左手一的的 literally, left hand [with] one of those) alludes to carrying the best things in life in your left hand as well as your ability or wherewithal to buy clothes made of Dacron.

*You-shou yi-ge qin-ai de* (右手一个亲爱的, [on the] right hand a loved one) alludes to the strong possibility of getting a good-looking and

good wife if you were one of the lucky few who had Dacron handker-
chiefs, Dacron clothes, bicycles and radio sets.

This is often repeated in any get-togethers of the old generation of
the new middle class, and it always elicits great laughter among them.
Their recounting of past experiences brings on in them feelings of
emotional attachment, deep love, unforgettable memories of joy and
suffering, melancholy thoughts of things past and reminiscences in
tears (Yang 2003).

Emotional traumas affect not only individuals, but also wider communities or even the entire nation. Emotional trauma is essentially a
social event (Muhlhahn 2004: 109). When we recount unpleasant things
from our past, we bring about feelings of warmth and connections
with others who share similar recollections. When people discuss their
past, they have feelings of adoration and apotheosis. It is the apotheosis of the self that becomes very important as a strategy in maintaining
individual identity under conditions of rapid change in general society
(Yang 2003). This is the social meaning of having the same sentiments
and being a member of the same group – *zijiren* (自己人 'one of our
own').

Recollecting the past creates the same feelings, especially in the older
new middle class. Those cohorts of the Chinese new middle class who
have experienced the whole history of the People's Republic are more
able to form and sustain close relationships with their peers because of
their shared experiences. Collective memory is the thread that stitches
different individuals into a cohesive group. Such a collective experience of the older new middle class can be referred to as the totality of
individual memories, articulated in the narrative, and contributing
to the collective nostalgia of their childhood. Radical changes in the
cultural terrain of modern-day Chinese life do not threaten or even destabilise the identities of these older members of the Chinese new
middle class because the internal anchor is the collective memory.

The third collective memory is the nostalgia and identity derived
from working in state-owned enterprises (SOEs). A lot of the older new
middle class started working at around 16 years of age due to the inter-
ruption caused by the Cultural Revolution. Many have been unable
to advance much beyond mid-secondary school, much less go on to
a university. The lack of education and the history of childhood
privations they experienced encourage many of them to live frugally.
The better-educated older group form the core of the Chinese new
middle class in terms of forming and contributing to the shared lifestyle and consumption patterns of that class. Lack of education, of

course, provides a built-in exclusionary imperative. A better job equals higher earnings and improved career advancement, both of which combined together equalled higher status in the social hierarchy of Maoist China up to the Cultural Revolution.

People of the older new middle class who experienced higher education in the late 1960s and early 1970s were the elite of society at the time. They were allocated to work in the state sector, usually in the larger, better-paying state enterprises in low-level positions such as clerks or even non-skilled workers. Many stayed in these positions for more than ten years. By virtue of long employment, quite a few have risen through the ranks into management. A few become highly influential bureaucrats. Working in the state-owned enterprises builds up their experience and sometimes provided opportunities to gain technical knowledge. Both in turn opened up vistas to accumulate economic assets following the market reforms, which in turn allows for the development of certain lifestyles that could be shared with others who have gone through the same sort of pathways.

As these people worked their way up to the top, many extended their networks into the private sector and professional bodies in the reform years. In other words, the possession of a component of cultural capital (i.e. educational credentials) guaranteed employment in the state sector in the old days after they graduated from senior high school. Higher education allowed former cadres in state organisations/enterprises to shift their career paths from the public to the private sector.

Most of the old generation have experienced a harsh past but a sweeter present. It can be very painful indeed to become impoverished again after having lived in better times. One big unknown is whether or not China will ever again be in social or political turmoil. The future, of course, is never certain. To be sure, the common experience of a bitter past moves these people to save up for contingencies and for their children. Even the rich are prudent with their money and in spending.

The fourth collective memory for the old generation is the nostalgia and identity derived from transitioning to the private sector. The road to success in the business world can be a tortuous one and fraught with pitfalls. Since the 1980s, the Chinese new middle class as a whole has been the most successful of all of the sections of the Chinese populace in adapting to an improved commercial climate, especially in Guangdong. Adapting to new conditions and making favourable use of the winds of change happening in the economy shows a high ability to achieve successful outcomes – or at least to avoid unsuccessful ones. The older new middle class has the ability to make practical adjustments to achieve reasonably successful outcomes within the framework of ambiguous/incomplete institutional policies.

Soon after the economic reforms and market mechanism started to take hold in the early 1980s, Guangdong was the first province to take off economically and the investment climate there became more and more attractive. The entrepreneurs who emerged in Chinese society because of the economic reforms at the time are widely regarded as opportunists whose business acumen and astute insights helped them to adapt to the new and favourable investment environment in Guangdong in a pragmatic way (Heberer 2007). Some of the old generation started out as small, self-employed shopkeepers who ran small street businesses such as grocery stores. Others had been street vendors because they could not afford to pay rent on any business property. These people mostly sold perishable or non-durable commodities such as groceries or perishable garments – anything considered to be daily necessities for the majority of people. Uncle Fong, one of the interviewees, ran a meat shop because his father, uncle and aunt had been butchers in the 1980s. He wisely adapted to the favourable investment climate in Guangdong:

> In the 1980s, I acquired food tickets and sold them at higher prices. I made profits from these transactions. I remember that I could earn RMB20 or even RMB30 [£2.50] a day. These lucrative profits inspired me and helped me acquire a larger house. You have to try many times to succeed, though. Life was hard at the time. I was in debt to my parents, relatives and friends. I still remember clearly how hard those times were. **(Uncle Fong, 48, entrepreneur)**

Ration coupons (*liang piao* 粮票) were a feature of urban life in Maoist times. They were issued to people by their work units or workplaces because in those days even people with money were unable to buy food or other necessities without the coupons. Rural domiciliaries had no need for ration coupons since they were self-sufficient in provisions. Today, many of the older new middle class have become quite rich, but the memories of these hard times stay with them and very much shape the way they conduct business today.

The fifth collective memory of nostalgia and identity are derived from extra legal activities (smuggling) and being a stowaway. In Maoist times, some topics were taboo or plainly too dangerous for any discourse even behind closed doors between like-minded people. Once-taboo topics, such as about smuggling (*zousi* 走私) or stowing away (*toudu* 偷渡),[3] can now be discussed fairly openly. These two practices were prevalent in China during the 1980s and 1990s. The reason for the relatively greater openness in discussing these taboo topics today lies in the way some people have become prosperous during the reform years: collusion with corrupt officials 'in the restraint of trade' (the World Trade Organisation euphemism for market cornering) or conducting illegal or illicit manoeuvres in times of market chaos.

The moment that any one of these taboo activities is made known to others during a gathering, many will describe having 'warm feelings' and mutual understanding with their friends and associates.

> When I was a worker in a collectively owned factory, the workload was heavy and the working hours long, from 8 am to 10 pm. I couldn't stand the long hours. In the late 1970s, I stowed away to Hong Kong five times in a row. The police didn't catch me the first four times, but the fifth time they caught me in Shataukok [the cross-border town between Hong Kong and Shenzhen]. The unpleasantness of prison scared and shocked me. I never forgot this experience. **(Uncle Moss, 48, entrepreneur)**

China was rife with smuggling between the late 1970s and the early 1990s. It was very lucrative, but also risky, as Uncle Moss's experience of arrest indicates. It was also an activity that could only be undertaken for a short period of time. However, those of the new middle class who became involved in this line of business sometimes recalled that part of their lives with great sentimental nostalgia.

> In the 1980s I wanted to fulfil my dream of making money, so I stowed away five times to Hong Kong. Unfortunately, this dream failed. Hong Kong already provided a huge mix of goods like sunglasses, trousers, jeans, blouses, T-shirts, digital watches and different types of foodstuffs. These goods were very cheap and even we could afford to buy them. Although our business was small-scale, we were profitable and aggressive. *I could make RMB40 [£4] a day* and this income was high when compared with working in the collectives, *which paid only RMB60 [£5] a month* in the late Seventies [*author's emphasis*]. When we went home we were singing. I remember we were happy doing this business. **(Uncle Chris, 49, entrepreneur)**

Although smuggling and stowing away to Hong Kong had always been illegal in China, the Police Bureau on the Chinese side paid little attention to stopping such activities. In fact the (then) Royal Hong Kong Police Force and the British garrison carried out much of the crime fighting during the 1970s and early 1980s. Smuggling and stowing away (which by the 1980s took the form of smuggling illegal immigrants into Hong Kong) turned out to be short-lived lines of making money since the Chinese authorities began to tighten up border policing after 1982.

A collective memory among ex-smugglers and ex-stowaways provides some sort of social lubricant allowing them to seek partners in more conventional, more legal lines of business and in *guanxi* networks with people with similar collective sentiments and shared understandings. As the business climate throughout the country became more positive towards the late 1980s and 1990s, their involvement in mainstream business helped their rise and success in Guangdong province.

Smuggling continues even to this day. Those who are still involved in it have close, inside connections with the government that permit them to carry out those activities. This may account in part for the widespread corruption among cadres in Guangdong.

> I got help [from some officers]. They seemed to have close connections with the district offices in Guangdong. Their help made my smuggling business smoother and *more lucrative in the post-reform era* [*author's emphasis*]. (**Uncle Ho, 49, entrepreneur**)

A common acquaintance acts as a connecting thread to infuse a common identity among people and draws them into a single circle of 'insideness' (Wank 1999: 164) within the new middle class circle. In the broader sense, the new middle class may be drawn together by the same accent, speaking the same tongue,[4] kinship ties, blood relationships and even the same surname. The past shared experience provides a lubricant for the old generation to define a class boundary and membership because they have similar topics and discourses to share. The same group can be formed by subtle and even minuscule cultural understanding (such as tastes and understandings). All of these things are elements of culture and form the sociocultural practices of the everyday life of the new middle class.

## Confucian values, self-improvement, and class boundary

There are other reasons to explain why some of the old generation are quite frugal in their consumption patterns. One of these factors might be considered to be the continued influence of Confucian values.

Given that most of the older new middle class had impoverished child-hoods, the majority of that old generation (30 out of 35) are very prag-matic in nature and outlook, and purchase only what is necessary to achieve their present success. The characteristics of the old generation seems to be characterised by the phrase 'income of the new middle class, consumption of the common people'. Confucian values exist in the minds of many of the old generation. This explains why they prefer frugal lifestyles. Quintessential Confucian values such as sin-cerity, integrity, compassion, and righteousness are still preserved in the minds of the old generation. These values have a way of working into the pragmatic/utilitarian approaches and handiwork of the old new middle class in both their private and business lives. It is not unusual for some of them making RMB100,000 (US$14,631 or £10,004) a month to bargain with shopkeepers by the roadside or keep leftovers from a meal for the next.

> I won't buy any famous brands even if I'm more than able to afford them. I pick up my leftovers when I dine out. It doesn't mean I'm mean, but it's the Confucian values I'm used to. I don't want to waste anything. Most of my friends are very conservative in the amount they consume. We buy what we need; we're not buying for pleasure, though we have money. (**Aunt Monica, 60, cadre**)

Industriousness and thrift have brought riches to the old new middle class, to restrain in consumption is something of a mantra of their prac-tical approach to life. They generally lead a life of relative simplicity and thrift. They have no overriding desire to buy branded merchandise, at least not for themselves. In fact, they can be characterised by 'little want and little waste' – down-to-earth in taste, pragmatic and utilitar-ian in direction. Even the more affluent members do not employ chauffeurs. On business trips, they travel not in first class but in economy.

However, they feel the need to upgrade themselves so that they have more marketable skills. The more contact they have with the 'outside world', the greater is the social impact on the old generation. A number of ideological beliefs and values normally associated with modernisation are making inroads into the picture of present-day life in China, such as initiative, competition and the pursuit of excellence. They are keen on overall change coming from economic progress and globalisation. Accord-ing to my in-depth interviews, the consensus of opinion from them is that it is impossible for China to keep the national economy running at a growth rate of 10% year after year. The idea that everyone everywhere is blessed with limitless opportunities and long-lasting materialism is less and less realistic as time goes by. Even financially secure members of the second generation of the Chinese new middle class now find it necessary to learn to be adaptable when they face the challenges of cultural pluralism that is integral to economic progress and globalisation.

> I am studying for a part-time MBA at a local university even though I already have a degree. If I want to get promoted and not get fired, I need to upgrade myself and pursue a higher qualification. Even though social networking is still very important in government bureaus, we face a threat from newly recruited young university graduates. They're very assertive, efficient, and relatively low paid. This poses a great threat to me. Even though I've worked in our department for more than fifteen years, I still face this threat... **(Uncle Leung, 48, cadre)**

> I started to work as a salesman at a small railway station in Hunan Province. I didn't want to stay at the station for ever so I taught myself accounting. Later I passed all my examinations and got promoted in Guangzhou. Though I'm quite experienced, I still believe earning a degree will be good for my career. So I went to Zhongshan University and earned my MBA. I must upgrade myself all the time... **(Uncle Fang, 49, cadre)**

Those who have suffered in some way from structural transformation in the economy no longer believe that work skills are the only survival tools necessary to cope with the future. Consequently, these people are much more ready and willing than others to upgrade their education to avoid being marginalised in society. The old generation are just afraid of future challenges if they are outdated or even phased out because of obsolete skills and social networks.

Uncle Fong, a rich and successful entrepreneur, relays his worries about the era of globalisation:

> I don't want to look back. If you are rich and enjoy life now, you don't want to revisit the economic bitterness and hardships of your previous life. I bought detached houses, apartments, commercial buildings and shops. I only graduated senior high school. Society has changed dramatically over the years. You don't know what will happen tomorrow. I don't spend lavishly, but will purchase well-

known brands in the presence of my business partners. You cannot cope with future challenges if you are outdated or don't have marketable skills. **(Uncle Fong, 48, entrepreneur)**

Social class boundaries are defined by (a) the associations between individuals or families, (b) the nature and extent of those associations over time, and (c) the particular class positions of those associations (Scott 1994: 934). Uncle Fong's remarks above illustrate why the older new middle class is so pragmatic and utilitarian in lifestyle and consumption. This will be particularly important if the old generation do not have higher educational credentials. These people always tend to take a backseat instead of a vocal stance in advocating for their causes. They have a high degree of anxiety that their educational credentials are insufficient. They fear they may be phased out because of their obsolete skills and outdated social networks in a rapidly globalising world. In a way, they are a somewhat calculating lot, always taking a cautiously watchful attitude to changes, and are often willing to wait until conditions are almost completely right before acting.

Based on Scott's (1994) indications, it is not hard to see why it is quite easy for the older new middle class to communicate, cooperate, and share in social and business affairs. Shared lifestyles, consumption patterns, and tastes help the older new middle class to demarcate the parameters of its membership. People who classify themselves as members of the new middle class will regard other similar individuals as *zijiren* ('one of our own') – an 'in-group' categorisation. Those who do not (yet) possess this kind of lifestyle or consumption stay outside that class boundary.

## Major features of consumption of the old generation

Our interviewees from the old generation are on average in their mid-forties today. They are generally regarded as industrious in work and diligent in saving money. Their fairly strong final standing in fact owes a great deal to their experience of political upheavals in the past. Their shared set of collective memories from childhood makes them advocates for practicality in all matters of life. They practice what they preach, lead relatively simple lives, and buy down-to-earth, reasonably priced goods that last.

The old generation of the Chinese new middle class tends to take part in entertainment activities as a group, especially with those who have similar backgrounds or lifestyles. They have more or less the same sociocultural factors such as shared consumption patterns and lifestyles to enter the new middle class circle. Entertainment activities are not used for the purposes of entertainment per se. Rather, it is a good way to seek more business partners with their former workmates in state enterprises and village mates.

## Entertainment activities

Entertainment activities can reveal much about the lifestyles, consumerism and attitudes of people. Karaoke lounges, bars, nightclubs, massage parlours, and lychee orchards are major venues for the old generation to gather together and relax with their friends or business associates. Other activities include playing chess or mahjong, having dim sum meals, or Chinese banquets and other different social gatherings.

> Owing to the nature of my job I have to go to karaoke lounges and nightclubs frequently. If professionals and entrepreneurs regard you as influential and you can help them, they will frequently seek help from you. Many entrepreneurs and professionals try hard to please me so that I give them favours when they register their 'special businesses.' I always attend their meetings; they give me gifts and throw banquets. This is not secret but a common practice here [Guangdong]. Going to karaoke becomes part of my job and is also my leisure activity. (**Uncle Fang, 49, cadre**)

The karaoke lounge is an important location in the entertainment activities of the older new middle class. Gatherings at karaoke are not simply for singsongs: singing and eating provide only symbolic meanings. In fact, going to karaoke is a group activity that offers them a space to share and reminisce, and sometimes to discuss business. Participants are joined and bonded together by shared personal histories and they communicate with one another within that framework. The karaoke is the main forum of social practices in the lifestyle of the old generation.

The massage parlour is another common venue. These establishments have grown in number and popularity in Guangdong since 1997. They are fairly affordable establishments and a typical four-hour session at an average massage parlour costs around RMB100 (US$15 or £10). Many are fitted with private rooms, large meeting rooms or clubhouses, licensed bar, indoor swimming pool, gymnasium, or even squash courts. The massage parlour provides enhanced privacy to discuss business.

Older members of the new middle class tend to have more sedate pastimes. Playing a couple of rounds of chess or mahjong with friends and acquaintances is a form of 'appreciation' of (that is, getting a 'handle' on) the other side in doing business. Mahjong is in the blood of all Chinese people in Guangdong and is a great way to enhance sentiments and connectedness with both friends and business people.

Other older members are content with visiting flower gardens or lychee orchards or just going to hotels for entertainment activities. Indeed, some of these people tend to live near these places and invite a fairly close circle of acquaintances to join them for visits. The invitees, of course, pay *lian* (臉 'face') to the inviter and feel obliged to attend.

> I invite business partners and friends to my lychee orchard. While they're very busy they usually come because they trust and respect me. Gathering all my friends together in this way is a good way to find new business partners and network. **(Uncle Hui, 60, cadre)**

> A major part of doing business here is holding 'face parties'. This develops social capital since we are introduced to potential business customers with the help of someone we know and trust. If there are influential entrepreneurs or people who have close relationships with government, I must attend. **(Uncle Fang, 49, cadre)**

In 2008 I was cordially invited to go to a lychee orchard with Uncle Wong. Thirty to 40 dishes were served to the guests at this meeting. The dinner offered a great variety of dishes, as many as you could ask for, vegetables, fish, meat, seafood, desserts, rice, noodles, congee, soup, fruits, and beverages, which were all served in a way of Chinese buffet. The Chinese new middle class talked about precious jewels, for example, diamond, jade, gold and silver accessories. What were the best gifts for cadres? They were luxury cars like Mercedes-Benz, houses, shares, funds, and land investment. They also considered other business opportunities[5] arising from the World Expo to be held in Shanghai in 2010. This manifested their middle-class lifestyles. I found that I hardly joined in their conversations.

It is observed that for the old generation there are symbolic meanings for lychee orchards. The lychee orchard serves as a source of arts for the old generation to meet in this special location. The lychee orchard is a commercial business but it serves not only as a commodity for the old generation. It also serves as a holiday resort to have tea, reunion, gathering with their potential friends who later may become business partners. The lychee orchard is a classic symbol of refinement and a statement of civilisation. But it also serves as a kind of symbol of the Chinese new middle class.

In terms of business engagements, the old generation look on entertainment activities with a certain degree of pragmatism, even if they sometimes do not relish attending such functions. They know that entertaining for business helps to extend opportunities or serve customers. They are also useful gateways for building careers or political capital or for extending general social networks.

The tactical objectives are risk minimisation, transaction cost reduction, supply assurance, and cost control of time and money spent in gathering information. To entertain people also allows business people to display their personal side. Personality is very important to the old generation in business. It is not too surprising to find the older new middle class often entertain or are entertained in nightclub banquets until the early hours of the morning. In business, perceptions of trustworthiness always play a significant role (Wank 1999: 275).

## Tobacco and liquor

Smoking and the passing around of cigarettes among smokers has become another ritual among Chinese business people. Since many of the old generation share common tastes in terms of lifestyle and consumption, people are probably going to 'use' smoking and drinking to seek mutual collaboration within the middle-class boundary. The old generation state that this is a courtesy and an ice-breaker in socialising with different kinds of people if you know the ways to smoke and drink. In China, handing out cigarettes to greet friends plays a similar role to shaking hands or giving a hug to friends in the West. Mutual collaboration helps to improve sentiments, cohesion and trustworthiness when doing business.

> Every Tuesday at 7:00, my friends and I go to the Lucky Restaurant to meet for dinner. We share our childhood experiences. Also, these get-togethers help me express my feelings, including unhappiness and frustration with family or business matters. No matter how busy I am, I attend our gatherings and definitely won't miss any of them.
> **(Uncle Chung, 56, entrepreneur)**

Indeed, business partners are often entertained in the company of ex-schoolmates and other close friends. The older new middle class love to see their ex-classmates at any opportunity. So gatherings are precious moments to catch up and gossip without the overt pressure of using those gatherings to make money. When former cadres went into business in the early 1990s, many of their ex-classmates, villagers, and comrades who worked with them in various state entities became their business partners. At these gatherings of the older new middle classes, the same discourses are shared between the participants, lubricated by drinks, and stoked by cigarettes of popular brands like Xiaohutuxin (小葫涂仙), Wuliangye (五粮液)[6] and Hongtashan (红塔山).[7]

The old generation has no particular reason for mentioning those brands of drinks and cigarettes other than the fact that whenever the brands *are* mentioned they tend to evoke certain common feelings among participants. In gatherings, the drinking and smoking of the same brands is used for enhancing credentials and perceptions of trustworthiness. People would willingly spend RMB1,000 (US$146 or £99) on a bottle of Remy Martin X.O. cognac and a further RMB1,500 (US$219 or £149) on a karaoke or bowling gathering. The older new middle class often sees this kind of high spending as 'assets' that are crucial in the world of commerce.

Sharing the same brand of consumables in social gatherings helps to lighten the load of possible friction in business and ameliorate the search for a mutually equitable resolution. In other words, if you are willing to spend serious money on drinks, you are in effect sending a message to the other side that you are prepared to bend over backwards to please them because you are honourable and upstanding (Davis 2000a: 275).

These gatherings contribute to the enhancement of same-class sentiments, and provide a convivial ambience to lubricate later business discussions. In short, these gatherings provide a peaceful and harmonious atmosphere to discuss business. Shared practices suggest an undercurrent of shared sentiments and worldviews in the old generation of professionals, entrepreneurs, and cadres.

> In our meetings in karaoke lounges, bars and nightclubs, if you give me a cigarette, I will give you back a cigarette of the same brand. No one really thinks it's important, but it creates a sentiment [*ganqing* 感情] [of friendship] between us and it becomes easier to discuss things. (**Uncle Yuen, 56, entrepreneur**)

Shared sentiments and worldviews imply solidarity with like-minded individuals or at least a willingness to be in cohesion with them.

Solidarity or willingness to pull together in turn reinforces a sense of togetherness in the same group.

As stated earlier, the old generation has lived through the same historical developments in China. Some have roughly the same collective memory of their upbringing. Drinking and smoking the same brands during entertainment activities paints a picture of mutual goodwill and respect for one another's worldview. Cadres play influential roles in today's China. The reason for seeing entertainment activities as a power-building exercise is that 20 years of economic reforms have given cadres a larger and wider range of authority, particularly in the regulatory structure over business licensing and taxation (for more details see Chapter 4). The first benefit of a close relationship is the ability to discuss problems more frankly. The second benefit is to act as a framework to let nostalgic feelings surface and to reinforce any sense of solidarity among parties to the relationship.

The general measures of justice and regulatory oversight in China continue to be administered haphazardly, with sizeable pockets of inertia or corruption, or both. Close personal ties developed in this or any other manner go a long way to help reduce the hazards of administrative or legal harassment that can occur from confrontations with some regulatory agencies.

Shared consumption patterns in terms of smoking and drinking habits produce a set of common activities and practices which promotes a sense of sociability. This is valuable in the cold, hard-headed world of business and serves as the warmth of connectedness and increases understanding and harmonies, thereby promoting collaborative strategies in business for the older new middle class.

Some administratively mediated commodities could only be available even within officially recognised channels through the development of good relationships with officials. The business people therefore try to build warm human relationships with powerful or knowledgeable people in or around the administrative apparatus. The continued haphazard nature of the overall administrative structure but the increase in the authority of cadres means that economic survival is in many ways conditional on having the right kind of 'business intelligence' network, as it were. By doing apparently commonplace things such as smoking the same cigarettes and drinking the same brands of alcohol together, the older new middle class is making use of these practices 'to condition' others into developing close relationships that could be used for economic objectives.

## The cultural politics of food and eating

Chinese cuisine is among the best in the world, and eating out offers an ideal condition for transforming informal socialising into active economic or political networking. The cultural politics of food and eating of the old generation can be regarded as pragmatic and utilitarian. Around half of the entrepreneurs (20 out of 31) and cadres of the old generation in this study state that they prefer to dine out for business. Their choice of venue would be upmarket restaurants, hotels, and coffeehouses because those types of establishments tend to meet the practical needs of business transactions. The majority of the professionals (8 out of 17) say they prefer to dine out at some Western fast-food shops like McDonalds, Starbucks, Pacific Coffee, or other Western cafes. Going to Western venues shows a new adaptation of the old generation of the Chinese new middle class in a highly globalising world (Held & McGrew 2002, 2003).

The pragmatic food consumption patterns of the old generation have several essential aspects. The general rule is, the more important the occasion, or if it is business-related, the more expensively they eat. They will patronise more moderately priced and decorated establishments when dining out with their relatives, friends, or neighbours. At any other time, it is dinner at home. In other words, the older new middle class dines according to the objective situation.

Normally, food consumption for the older new middle class is a 'no-frills' affair.

> I don't always go to very luxurious restaurants, which I regard as rather gratuitous, and only when it's necessary for my job. Dining with clients is an inevitable part of my life. I like to go to elegant rather than luxury restaurants. My character is like that of many Cantonese people – that is, practical. **(Uncle Chan, 60, professional and cadre)**

Another interviewee echoes this point:

> A business dinner party can double as a social engagement and typically costs RMB7,000 (US$1,025 or £708) or RMB8,000 (US$1,171 or £809) each time. I don't mean to show off. I don't have a sense of superiority. I prefer to spend money on buying houses or cars. If I gambled away RMB10,000 [US$1,463 or £999] betting on football, I'd forget about this the next day. This is a common attitude for

many people of the Chinese new middle class. **(Uncle Fong, 48, entrepreneur)**

The old generation are more accustomed to having lunch or dinner in fast-food shops or restaurants if they have no business appointments. Their food and eating patterns are rather plain and simple whether dining out or at home. Food-related social attitudes and behaviour are becoming increasingly apparent in present-day China. The old generation of the Chinese new middle class also seems to like to patronise restaurants, fast-food shops and other places and settings that are popular in a globalising China.

In addition, the preference for buying food in large-scale street markets (but not supermarkets) is widespread among the older generation of the new middle class. They consider foods in street markets to be fresher, with a variety of choice and much cheaper than in supermarkets.

Dining out in upscale Chinese restaurants is also widespread among this group.

If I have no meetings with clients, I'll stay home for lunch and dinner. I don't really care about the aesthetics of food and eating in a luxurious way. For example, there's no need for me to eat luxury foods like oysters, shrimps and other seafood every day. I'm not concerned about what to eat and how to eat it, but follow my own tastes. If you've spent your childhood in poverty, you can't even identify what different tastes like sweet, bitter, sour, or salty are. So you won't insist on what to eat and how to eat. In my own situation, I think even vegetables and rice will make a very good meal. **(Uncle Victor, 50, entrepreneur)**

The old generation is flexible and pragmatic, and for them consumption is more to nurture cordiality and trust-building. Situations like doing business require rapport between the parties. The old generation knows it is important to draw upon and also show their internal reservoir of personal credibility. Credibility comes from the judicious disclosure of personal biographies, recollections and worldviews, preferably in a socially acceptable setting. The exchange of gifts solidifies that credibility. In other words, they must engage in frank and cordial conversations with their business collaborators to help induce the 'appropriate' emotional response suitable for business. Trustworthiness, friendliness, and friendship for the older new middle class are made to work *for business*, not just *in business*. Therefore, eating out (and its attendant gift-giving) is the socially acceptable setting to oil the wheels of commerce and set the stage for making money.

Many anthropologists like Lévi-Strauss and Mary Douglas (Douglas & Isherwood 1996; Watson *et al.* 2005) have tried to link food (and eating) with other dimensions of a given culture. Mary Douglas tried to decipher the social codes contained in meals and to analyse different metaphors of food. However, there is no concrete food stratification to be found just simply by looking at the restaurants and fast-food shops that the Chinese new middle class frequent. Rather, social boundaries blur. In Guangdong at least, food consumption patterns among the older new middle class do not appear to be particularly extravagant or luxurious. They prefer to buy durable goods instead of consuming extravagantly and luxuriously.

In terms of food, the old generation of professionals display some differences from their counterparts of entrepreneurs and cadres. They dine out at some Western buffets or go to Starbucks or McDonald's but this is nearly always for the purpose of doing business. They will also go to some cheap restaurants. The professionals of the old generation as a whole are not epicurean devotees of sensory pleasure when it comes to food consumption (Jussaume 2001; Ritzer 2001). They don't have particular patterns for meals. But they do quite highly emphasise the importance of hygiene and nutrition. The professionals of the old generation select food more for nutrition and fitness than for mere sustenance (Watson 2007) or even narcissism. Even so, they would almost never eat in food stalls, only in visibly sanitary and air-conditioned restaurants. Interior décor is as important to them as the food itself, for surroundings can make you healthy or ill. For them, hygiene and nutritional value supersede low prices.

## Consumption in fashion and travel practice

Most people in Guangdong (the old generation of the new middle class included) are not particularly mindful of how they dress relative to the rest of China. This is partly because Cantonese culture towards fashion is markedly different from that encountered in Shanghai, Nanjing, or places up north.[8]

The Northern Chinese sometimes remind us of the French: it is not uncommon to see them dressed stylishly as they shop for groceries in supermarkets or even communal street markets ('wet markets'). Down south in Guangdong, the order of the day for most people is simply T-shirt and jeans. Perhaps the subtropical climate is a factor. Even so, the Cantonese new middle class will still dress up for important occasions, and in ways that play up status and identity. Therefore, I can surmise that the pattern of fashion consumption in a place like Guangdong is essentially pragmatic and utilitarian. As a matter of habit and preference, the old generation generally wear high-quality, branded casual wear such as Adidas, Nike, and Puma. They also prefer to buy from department stores and only very reluctantly from street stalls, where the quality could be dirt-cheap but decidedly not cheerful.

But appearances can be deceiving. The Cantonese mind is not wild about clothes and is mostly preoccupied with food and diets, so many of the new middle class in Guangdong have no qualms about being seen in shorts and flipflops. (Only an observer unversed in the ways of the Cantonese would take them for factory or migrant workers.)

Uncle Ho, a handbag manufacturer and retailer in Guangdong, offers some reasons for the casualness:

> When I was starting my own business, I was very emphatic about what clothes I wanted to wear. I'd often buy brand-named suits, shoes and briefcases. But now I don't wear suits or buy branded clothes unless they're durable. If I dress elegantly, I can feel out of place, and that makes me uncomfortable. I now like casual and sensible clothes, such as shorts, T-shirts and sandals, which make me feel relaxed and comfortable. When buying a watch, mobile phone, wallet, fountain pen, suitcase or shoes, I tend to go for well-known brands. **(Uncle Ho, 49, entrepreneur)**

I see from my research sample that the trend among the older new middle class is to dress casually. Their style is simple, comfortable and wearable – a distinctive 'taste' for them. But they will dress more formally for business functions or important occasions such as weddings, on which occasions they are more likely to buy or use brand-named merchandise.

> I dress very casually, in a T-shirts and jeans. Occasionally, when I meet clients, I'll wear a suit; otherwise, I rarely wear suits. I'll buy brand-named leather shoes, briefcases and fountain pens, no matter how expensive they are. I buy what I want and don't worry about price. **(Uncle Chris, 49, entrepreneur)**

It is quite common for the older new middle class to have friends going or living abroad buy brand-named products for them. These products are mostly for the purpose of gift-giving and tend to be items like mobile phones, timepieces, and jewellery. The usual places are Hong Kong, Japan and South Korea. Uncle Kwok, an entrepreneur, says,

> I buy only durable and expensive items and am not bothered if they are not well-known brands. There are not too many options for men. I go on a shopping spree around once a year, usually around the Chinese New Year. I tend to go to large Western chain stores to buy a T-shirt made by Nike, Adidas, Puma or Li Ning [李宁, a major sports goods brand in China]. I buy my shirts from a large mall which imports them from overseas. These products are durable and last for almost 10 years. (**Uncle Kwok, 40, entrepreneur**)

Uncle Lee agrees with Uncle Kwok. He says,

> I buy suits from Gucci, Emporio Armani and Versace because they are more durable and can last for more than 10 years. It doesn't mean that I am obsessed with brands, but the quality of the local brands is poor and they're easily damaged. (**Uncle Lee, 40, entrepreneur**)

Fashion consumption shows different practices in the old generation between men and women. Take Aunt Jennifer for example. She is a cadre and greatly enjoys shopping. She won't buy any durable products in China, but purchases durable and brand-named products in Hong Kong and Europe. She travels twice a month to Hong Kong for that very purpose:

> I always visit Hong Kong whenever I travel. It's a shopping paradise where I can always buy the most wonderful and beautiful fashions and other products. The most exciting thing I buy is jewellery. On each visit I spend around RMB50,000 [US$7,322 £5,058] on diamonds, jade, gold, silver and pearls. Shopping in Hong Kong really makes me go crazy. All the items I buy are gifts for my business partners. I hardly ever buy for myself. (**Aunt Jennifer, 53, cadre**)

Aunt Lisa tells me the same story of buying durable products in London and Paris.

> I usually go to London or Paris to buy Louis Vuitton, Prada and other brands. I am determined to purchase genuine products since there in China are so many counterfeits which are almost indistinguishable from the real thing. It is shameful for me to use fake LV handbags. **(Aunt Lisa, 40, entrepreneur)**

The fashion consumption patterns of the old generation of women are varied. Some of them prefer to buy brand-named, fashionable, and trendy clothes from Hong Kong, Paris, London or Europe. But some of them have similar fashion consumption patterns of the men in the old generation. They prefer durable brand names instead of some trendy brand-named products. Fashion consumption for the older new middle class tends not to be conspicuous, pleasure-seeking, or luxury chasing. They are willing and able to outfit themselves quite elegantly when occasion calls for it. They prefer serviceable products for personal consumption. But at the same time will use brand products in front of outsiders so as to highlight their identity and strengthen business interests.

With regard to their travel patterns the old generation of the Chinese middle class are very pragmatic and utilitarian. They usually travel with their business partners instead of family members. The most important attitude about travelling with non-family members for the old generation is to 'get on' with friends and business acquaintances for the purpose of doing business. The older new middle class is involved in overseas travel, but values it only if it encourages business. Many of them have over the years built up close links with business acquaintances abroad, especially during the early reform years. In the last ten years or so, however, their attention is turning mostly inwards to the growing domestic Chinese market, mainly because of various changes to the global marketplace and also because of perceptions that the domestic Chinese market is relatively untapped in commercial terms. The attitude of increasingly sticking with China often manifests as full plane bookings during the Chinese New Year (January–February), Ching Ming Festival (清明节, around February–April), Labour Day (1 May) and National Day (1–3 October) holidays. Of course, this does not mean there is any less interest in foreign business opportunities. It just means that there is added keenness for the domestic market.

As a form of consumption, travel is more than a lifestyle for the older new middle class. Its practical function is for business. Travelling with friends and business acquaintances is a form of strategic thinking to safeguard business competitiveness because the sense of bonding between fellow travellers helps enhance cooperation and collaboration. Travelling together has the general effect of imbuing fellow travellers with a sense of togetherness and belonging – what the Chinese would call sentiment (*ganqing* 感情) and a sense of belonging between people (Farrer 2000 in Davis 2000a: 244). Travel therefore becomes part of a commodification process for finding *guanxi* connections to match business collaboration. It becomes a form of social interaction done for the ultimate purpose of furthering business interests. Travelling acts as a form of social capital that comes from doing things on the road together, helping to grow trustworthiness and reliability (Chen & Lu 2005; Gold *et al.* 2002; Baron *et al.* 2000).

In non-business situations, the sense of togetherness and belonging coming from travelling with others translates into a strong emotional affection for the home province. This affection is most visible during holidays such as the Chinese New Year, May Day and National Day, when people 'touch base' with kith and kin and rebuild kinship networks.

## Pragmatic but conspicuous consumption patterns

With the sociocultural production of the Chinese new middle class and the *sui generis* characteristics of this group manifested in lifestyle, and a particular orientation to consumerism, there is no contradiction for the old generation in practising both pragmatic and conspicuous consumption patterns. It expatiates on the claim there is a symbiotic relationship between class and individualisation in Chinese society with reference to the old generation and presents information about the class boundaries and culture of that particular subset of the new middle class in Guangdong. Excerpts from interviews will be used to show that the pragmatic and utilitarian inclination of the old generation towards consumption matters, collective memories, and other aspects are shaped by individual agency rather than by collective norms. The old generation of the Chinese new middle class are individually collectivistic insofar as they seek the ultimate aggrandisement of their individual interests through society. This is best exemplified by the strong collective identities that exist within their personal networks.

The old generation of the Chinese new middle class sometimes do purchase expensive items that seem unnecessary. They invest money on extensive leisure activities and luxury expenditure, which seems contradictory with their practical consumer values. Admittedly, these consumptions are conspicuous by appearance, but, in reality, the old generation utilise the 'conspicuous spending' as a means of gaining social capital in building up their *guanxi* network. The *guanxi* network is well identified in China as the admission ticket to promotion and success. A good relationship with the important people means resources, efficiency, and wealth. The best way for people to enhance their cohesion in businesses is through social activities – karaoke singing, massage and beauty parlours, going to pubs and bars, and having feasts. Consumption and entertainment activities can transform informal socialising into economic or political networking.

> At least four days a week I eat out. The rank of the restaurant I choose depends on how important my guest is. Generally we go to high profile places. This kind of expenditure is simply a basic investment in accessing the top people. **(Uncle Fong, 48, Entrepreneur)**

Indeed, consumption is not about needs or utility, it is purely about the images associated with what is consumed – i.e. consumer items (both goods and services) are pure signs (that is, they act as signifiers). Post-reform China is no longer reliant solely on production, but it is largely reliant on consumption, lifestyles, tastes, and quality of life. The everyday social and cultural practices in today's China exhibit the form of heterogeneity as opposed to homogeneity. Such a heterogeneity (or fragmentation, if you will) challenges the traditional concept of class. Class should now be included in the repertoire of sociocultural terminology because the case of China shows that lifestyles and consumption patterns function to define the class boundary of the Chinese new middle class.

Despite money spent on entertainment, the old generation also invest a lot in the purchase of luxurious goods. On one hand, they buy themselves these products to distinguish their social status. When they attend dinner parties with cadres, these products have the 'sign-values' that indicate to other people that they are members of the same social circle. On the other hand, these luxurious gifts work well in pleasing the cadres and their families. This illustrates how luxury service is a recognition of elite entitlement. The precariousness of life at the bottom of the social hierarchy imprints itself upon consumption patterns and practices. Distinct cultural experiences of consumption separate affluent families from low-income ones. Most of the upper-class women spend lots of time on conspicuous consumption, buying some diamonds, Rolex, birds' nests and durable goods in order to bribe very influential people such as cadres. They plan for the future of their children to go to brand-named universities or enterprises. My study reveals that middle-class women from highly affluent households cultivate distinct shopping skills that focused upon knowledge, quality discernment, and *guanxi* network to help themselves or their children.

The pragmatic and utilitarian nature of consumption is largely anchored in the past histories of the old generation, most notably their collective memories of Maoist-era impoverishment, rising through the ranks in state employment, the winding road to the world of business, and possible involvement in illegal activities. Pragmatic consumption is to a slightly smaller extent also attached to traditional Chinese or Confucian values of life as well as the need to carry out continual self-improvements to offset unknown but potentially threatening variables in a fast-changing economic and social landscape.

Pragmatic consumption habits also establish a certain social class boundary for the older new middle class. Admission or exclusion from that class boundary for our purposes is analysed in terms of lifestyle and consumption patterns. Those who have similar lifestyles and consumption may be more easily regarded by the older new middle class as one of their own, whereas those who do not are less likely to be so regarded until such time as they acquire one. The old generation generally have a collective culture (Hui 1988; Moore 2005: 361) though they are pragmatic and utilitarian in terms of making their consumption patterns and lifestyles. They still share common collective memories with their classmates, villages and former colleagues in the state enterprises. They place considerable emphasis on the importance of *guanxi* networks. For this study, I find that most of the old generation will redefine the social distance with various kin or will attempt to formulate new kinship alliances with different partners, but they tend to seek more *guanxi* network outside their kinship types to strengthen or solidify their *guanxi* network.

## Summary

I have been looking at some features of the consumption of the older new middle class and the factors that account for the pragmatic nature of that consumption. Consumption in food, fashion, entertainment, travel and investments for the old generation is done by default in a matter-of-fact, practical manner. However, it tends to be more extravagant and conspicuous when meeting business-related objectives or extending business connections. Consumption can be used by the old generation to construct and nurture power relationships with friends, colleagues, and business associates because some parts of the state administrative structure are ambiguous or incomplete enough to warrant the building of personal connections with decision-makers and knowledgeable people in the state apparatus. For the old generation, there is no contradiction between pragmatic and conspicuous consumption pattern. This is an increasing form of individualisation for the old generation in post-reform China.

In contrast, as we shall see, the values, attitudes, norms, and practices of the young generation are undergoing dramatic changes when compared with those of their parents. One of the most important changes in attitudes is a kind of individualism that stands in emphatical opposition to the collectivist spirit promoted during the Cultural Revolution (Moore 2005: 357). The young generation glorifies individualism (Cherrington 1997; Furlong & Cartmel 1997), whereas the old generation regards such individualism as not entirely popular and many even regard it problematic (Moore 2005: 375). I'll get back to this point in Chapter 3.

In the next chapter (Chapter 3), I will discuss the consumption patterns and lifestyles of the young generation of Chinese new middle class. This is the group born after 1970 and shows the greatest tendency to practise conspicuous consumption as a means to display their wealth and status. The chapter also addresses the 'spaces' of consumption in Guangdong and looks at some real situations related to the young generation, specifically in Guangdong. In today's China, a consumer revolution is taking place. It also examines the lifestyles and consumption patterns of the young generation of the Chinese new middle class that are symptomatic of inauthentic rather than authentic forms of individualisation that can be best described as 'pragmatic' and 'selective'. They rely on the networks of their parents (old generation) to maintain their intergenerational mobility and the reproduction of their class status in Chinese society.

# 3
# Generational Effects in the Chinese New Middle Class

> A lifestyle can be defined as a more or less integrated set of practices which an individual embraces, not only because such practices fulfil utilitarian need, but because they give material form to a particular narrative of self-identity...
>
> (Pinches 1999: 74–5)

A consumer revolution is happening in today's China. The young generation is acutely aware of the need for educational attainment as a form of cultural capital to boost career and enhance incomes. At the same time, they realise that political and social capital is also crucial to getting well-paid and secure jobs (Coleman 1988, 1990). This cohort is seen as long-term planners of their education. Many tend to map out in advance how to proceed with their first and higher degree studies, and what to do after graduation. Many are ambitious and want to pursue higher degrees at the world's most prestigious universities. They are generally proficient in English and may even speak a third modern language such as French, Spanish or others. For the younger new middle class, conspicuous consumption is directly related to *a way of life* and it demonstrates its superiority over other classes and, therefore, legitimises its position of superordination. The young generation progressively seeks to capture the means of cultural reproduction as a way of securing its own social reproduction (Bourdieu 1984, 1996). On the other hand, they are flexible enough to upgrade their competitiveness in the highly globalising China. The lives of many of the young generation are full of challenges and 'dynamic', but they are quite anxious and uncertain about their future life chances. They cannot follow the same trajectories of success as the old generation.

I argue that in attempting to understand the Chinese new middle class (old and young generation), Western theories of class analysis and individualisation cannot be transposed; they need to be adapted to the nuances of Chinese society. This chapter seeks to elaborate on the dialectical relationship between the Chinese new middle class, generation (old and young generation), and individualisation in China, both empirically and theoretically.

## The emergence of consumerism

Since the mid-1990s, China has been experiencing a consumer revolution. Urbanisation, modernisation, Westernisation and globalisation are all processes and symbols of the rapid pace of economic development and the resultant changes in social life in many Chinese cities (Ma & Wu 2005: 344; Held & McGrew 2002, 2003). This change is dramatic, coming as it did after the Maoist period when consumption was determined by the state. With market reforms, producers have

*Figure 3.1*　Recent growth in consumer spending of selected categories

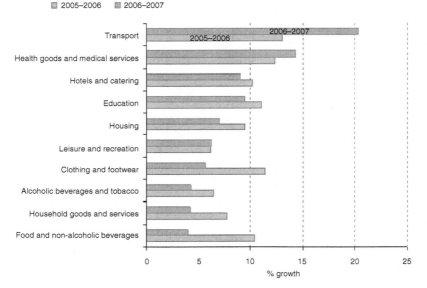

*Source*: Euromonitor International from national sources, 2008.

*Note*: The first row of each item represents the years 2006–2007. The second row of each item represents the years 2005–2006.

become increasingly subject to the demands and tastes of consumers (Jayne 2006; Breslin 2000). The consumption in cigarettes, alcohol, household appliances, leisure, and recreational services in China has risen since 2005 (see Figure 3.1).

Economic liberalisation has contributed to a rapidly expanding Chinese advertising industry (Hung *et al.* 2007: 839), and much of the apparently novelty-seeking materialism of the young generation is cultivated by advertising and marketing. Emulating the lifestyle of Western capitalist societies (usually in a highly romanticised form) is a prominent feature of the current lifestyle ideology of Chinese society. Materialist values and egoistic materialism of making money quickly have become the major preoccupations of many Chinese. That new pivotal function is expressed as a desire for buying homes, modern household appliances, fashionable clothes and services. Fashion magazines, advertising and most facets of commercialism are constantly trying to promote a lifestyle of comfort, elegance, high taste and exquisite behaviour to the Chinese new middle class. Somewhat exaggerated slogans such as 'Giving you a Chinese new middle class home!' or 'Enjoy the life of the bourgeoisie!' stimulate the senses of many people on a daily basis, thereby helping to position the lifestyle of that class as attainable, concrete objects.

In the years ahead consumption will likely be China's locomotive of economic growth. Many of Hong Kong middle class have crossed the border to work in Guangdong since the 1990s. The relocation of Hong Kong factories to Guangdong province since the 1980s, China's accession to the World Trade Organisation in 2001, the enactment of the Closer Economic Partnership Arrangement (CEPA) between mainland China and Hong Kong, and the launch of the Individual Visit Scheme (IVS) bring about close connections between Hong Kong and China. Since 2003, consumption and asset possession have gradually replaced political symbols as the path toward defining one's social status and drawing up class boundaries. It seems to me that consumerism carries more sociopolitical meanings in China than in many free-market societies.

Consumption forms a circle of class distinction by incorporating class privilege into the cultural spaces. This study finds that among most of the Chinese new middle class, using branded goods, wining, dining, and various other entertainment practices have become a distinctly public phenomenon. Consumption of fashionable commodities is the key means whereby the Chinese new middle class creates a new public space for its members. The new public space is a consumer space of commoditised objects, services, and information. Consumption serves as a very important aspect of cultural lifestyle in post-reform China.

The Chinese new middle class is embracing the global marketplaces as eager consumers. Consumer goods have become the new social currency. For the Chinese new middle class, consumer goods play a dual role of both an element of claim and a new communicative medium. In present-day China consumption and trend-chasing are no longer options but necessities. Shared tastes, lifestyles and consumption practices form the new class boundary and the means of admission thereof. Consumption can be defined as 'selection, purchase, use, reuse and disposal of goods and service' (Chambell 1995: 104). It comprises a set of practices that allow people to express their self-identity so as to mark attachment to social groups, to accumulate resources, to exhibit social distinctions, and to ensure participation in social distinction and activities (Warde 1997: 304). Consumption is a way for people to construct, to experience, to interpret and to use spaces and places (Urry 1995; Aldridge 2003; Gay 1996). Consumption is not just about goods that are manufactured and sold. Increasingly ideas, services, knowledge, places, shopping, eating, fashion, leisure and recreation, and sights and sounds are all viewed as consumables. Consumption and lifestyles are the major criteria for drawing class distinction. The Chinese new middle class can afford to buy famous branded products to display their economic ability to consume expensive goods. It is also a way for them to show their sense of taste. Displays of possessions bearing famous brands underscore the personality of the individual and highlight identity differentiation. Featherstone (1991: 21) pinpoints that 'culture is a hybridized synthesiser, which deals with not only what to wear but also how to wear'. The Chinese new middle class uses taste in fashion to differentiate it from all other strata of society, and it can do that because of the advantage of higher economic capital.

The productivist logic of Maoist times has now been replaced by a desire for consumption, one that can only be understood as a yearning for setting the country on the path to global modernity. This is why consumption, rather than production, is extremely important in post-reform China. Consumption then becomes a good means to distinguish the new middle class from the lower classes in society such as manual workers and peasants (Pun 2005).

Michelle Lamont (1989, 1992; Lamont & Lareau 1988) points out that everyday life practices are the key indicators to evaluate distinctions among different groups in society. Life practices are what Lamont (1992) suggests as the moral, socioeconomic and cultural boundaries of the 'upper new middle class' of the USA and France. Borrowing from Lamont (1989, 1992) and Storey (1999), I claim that consumption in the Chinese context has practicality as well as delicacy, which gives rise to 'taste' in living.

Sociologists such as Anthony Giddens (1990) and Featherstone (1991) also point out that people not only consume products as 'utilities' but are also reproducing consumerism as a legitimate way of life. Lifestyle can be defined as a more or less integrated set of practices that individuals adopt because, first, those practices fulfil utilitarian needs and, second, they give material form to a particular narrative of self-identity (Giddens 1990). Consumers in a consumerist culture therefore take on the symbolic value of the items they buy and use. The result is that consumption becomes both a major form of self-expression and a source of identity. An implication in the Chinese context is that both material and non-material items (such as kinship, affection, the arts and intellect) are now becoming increasingly commodified among the young generation.

## Geography and spaces of consumption in post-reform China

On any street in any city or town in Guangdong province, there are certain common images. The imagery everywhere is at once suggestive of the hustle and bustle of Hong Kong. Chain stores and outlets such as G2000, McDonald's, Starbucks, Park n'Shop, Chow Tai Fook Jewellers (some of Hong Kong's brand names) and other well-known names in Hong Kong have sprung up in large numbers along many streets. In fact, Shenzhen, Dongguan, Zhuhai, Guangzhou, Zhongshan and even the ostensible backwaters of Yangjiang now appear more like modern, cosmopolitan cities than Hong Kong.

In addition, many of the main thoroughfares in Guangdong province are plastered with large pictures of brand-named products. Pictures of beautiful models covered in jewellery in freestanding advertising kiosks are publicly admired. In a very short space of time, China has turned into a battleground for international brands, which are increasingly looking to groups such as the Chinese new middle class as the new engine of profits and growth (Friedmann 2005). Many cities in Guangdong province are literally packed with brand-named products, branded chain-stores, and branded fast-food shops. A quick stroll along Dongmen Walk (東門街) in Shenzhen will at once portray the growing cosmopolitan nature that has come to characterise many parts of Guangdong.

Sprawling complexes of street-level restaurants, cafés, and bars are to be found everywhere. Shopping malls and hawker stalls are replete with Hong Kong-style signage. Trendy locals mingle side by side with tourists. People in Guangdong dress every bit as fashionably as those walking the streets of Hong Kong. Pop music and ballroom dancing proliferate. Nightclubs light the night across the province. They are packed with beautiful and glamorous people, crowds throbbing to pulsating music, bars spilling over with patrons consuming fashionable cocktails. There are many shopping malls, restaurants, shopping centres, commercial skyscrapers as well as numerous multinational enterprises in Guangdong.

Guangzhou and Shenzhen, the two major cities in Guangdong province, boast the highest per capita income in the province. When I conducted the first fieldwork, the immediate impression was that there were many newly rich people wherever one looked. There was heavy conspicuous consumption, especially of brand-named products, the latest versions of mobile phones, and big-name cars. These two cities amass vast wealth, which is why prestigious retailers such as Louis Vuitton S.A. and the luxury department store Lane Crawford and others have moved in.

In many parts of Guangdong province, consumption is now no longer solely about buying tangible things. It has now progressed to the buying of services that would improve living standards, for example, the use of babysitters, chauffeurs, family doctors, travel consultants, financial planners, insurance agents, stockbrokers and the like.

These young generation (especially those in management of the bigger companies) of my research samples know well that their 'dress code' of Guccis and Rolexes are crucially important, especially if they wish to project a professional image to others. Because of their jobs, the dress codes of these people are often the readiest identifiers of their social class, even on the very first impressions. They are of the belief – with no small measure of truth – that your dress, your cars, and your accoutrements easily show the social class and this is the strategy to extend business partners. Conspicuous consumption is an important *modus vivendi* for the young generation because they often lack well-developed networks or business associates. Their capacity for conspicuous consumption enables them to impress others that they have the capability to take on major business undertakings.

## Rising consumption of branded goods

The rising consumption of branded goods has swept rapidly through Guangdong since the introduction of the economic reforms. The young generation tend to be more fashionable, stylish, and eager to consume. This explains why the fashion and cosmetics industry in China has opened up lucrative career alternatives for the younger middle class to capitalise on their bodies (Wang Q. 2008). I can therefore see that consumption is not simply consumerism itself but the pleasure of consumption with an emphasis on desirability and status symbols. Consumption of brand-name products gives the younger new middle class a sense of superiority in an increasingly free and open market of life chances. To that extent, Farrer (2000: 244) is right in that a culture of leisure in a marketised economy moves from a culture of production to a culture of consumption.

The young generation appears to have a tendency to consume in ways that suggest the main purpose is to flaunt their wealth and status. The predilection of many of the young generation is to purchase conspicuous 'mansions' and luxury cars to allow them to feel distinctive (Hubacek *et al.* 2007). As I will indicate later, my qualitative data show impressive spending behaviours in the form of expensive merchandise and luxury services that allow them to exemplify their financial power and higher status in society. They patronise luxury restaurants, place high-priced bids on auspicious-sounding mobile phone numbers or car number plates, set up extravagant banquets, and travel.

Generally speaking, the young generation are good consumer targets for a wide range of retailers and service providers in China because of their relatively high purchasing power compared to the rest of the population. They tend to be led by a pleasure-seeking principle, fed by a growing need to be seen as modern and up to date with the world outside China (Wang 2002; Faure 2008: 476).

> I am crazy about brands like LV, Porter, agnès b, Polo, and Vivienne Westwood. I buy them from Hong Kong but not from China. I don't want others to think I'm using counterfeits. I like these brands because they make me feel different from other people. Perhaps they're expensive. Sometimes I accompany my mother and my husband [author clarification: her husband is an assistant professor in Hong Kong] when they go to Europe, Paris and Japan to buy them. **(Lily, 30, professional)**

The rising consumption of brand-named goods in China is not only a quantitative change, but is also an expression of a search for new lifestyles, new identities, and a desire to display their status. Consumption of the big brands gives them a sense of cultural identity and of being distinct from other Chinese people. The young generation consume brand-named products to make them more distinctive, civilised and elegant like the middle class from Western countries. Many ideas and practices from around the world are constantly disseminated and assimilated into Chinese society as a product of economic liberalisation and globalisation (Held & McGrew 2002, 2003; Holmwood 2007).

From my ethnographic data, it appears that the young generation like fine dining and fine drinking, wearing world-famous brands such as Louis Vuittons, Guccis, Rolexes or Omegas almost as a dress code and driving around in sports cars. Those in the upper income brackets parade their social identity through luxury lifestyles in the form of upscale living quarters or villas, shuttling around in limousines, patronising high-class eating establishments and flaunting their golf club memberships. Extravagant consumption is conceived as the best way of displaying capability, wealth, and status. Business networking is essential to display enhanced consumption as an indicator of successful networking.

Ken, an MBA-qualified entrepreneur in an engineering company, says:

> I bought my BMW from Hong Kong because China doesn't usually import them. I wear a Rolex and have the latest models of mobile phones. It isn't because I have to have these luxury items, but I need to show off in front of my friends and business partners. You drive a luxury car and live in a luxury apartment to show that you have money. This is the most important part of impressing someone with whom you'd like to continue to do business. With luxury accessories like BMWs, Rolexes, villas, detached houses and even high-level apartments, I'm in a better position to attract more new business partners. **(Ken, 30, entrepreneur)**

Alex has the same mentality as Ken. Alex is a graduate of a prestigious university and makes about RMB10,000 (US$1,463 or £999) a month. He drives a Chinese-made Honda he bought for RMB350,000 (US$51,210 or £34,916). He usually wears the most fashionable and trendy clothes. He goes to Hong Kong twice a month to buy brand-name products. He says,

> My mantra is 'spend money for tomorrow' or 'realise the dream today.' No need to worry about tomorrow, but seize the moment wholeheartedly while in nightclubs with friends. The word 'saving' doesn't appear in my dictionary. There are many, many temptations in Guangdong. You can find numerous entertainment options here. Money is flowing, there's no need to worry too much. **(Alex, 35, professional)**

It was obvious from my time with Alex that he often travels to Europe to buy famous branded products. Alex cannot afford this kind of luxury lifestyle simply on his monthly salary. This explains why the professionals need to collaborate with entrepreneurs and cadres to do business to maintain their luxury daily expenditure. Alex told me that he usually has part-time jobs like subcontracting trade with some cadres and entrepreneurs. This explains the source of his money and why he can maintain a luxurious lifestyle although his monthly salary is not high by Western standards (Wynne 1998). He is married but he does not want children yet. Alex appears to live life to the full, with no financial worries. His story is commonplace among most of the younger new middle class.

The ownership and display of luxury and precious possessions become part of a larger strategic plan to extend business networks and attract more business associates. The need of or desire for conspicuous consumption is not just a straightforward type of consumption. It has to be the consumption of expensive, brand-name, distinctly foreign and visibly authentic merchandise. They buy for pleasure, status, and to flaunt their wealth in front of their business partners rather than for genuine use. They are ashamed to use counterfeits, although these are very popular in Guangdong. Mary, a French/German-educated accountant, felt that practising conspicuous consumption with her peers is the strategy to strengthen and enhance her relationships with business partners. She explains:

> Dress code reveals status and my peer group can spend a whole month's salary on bags like LV, Gucci or other brands. If we buy counterfeits, there's no difference between us and the blue-collar people. It's a potential source of shame as my friends can identify whether or not they're fakes. To play safe, I'll buy in Hong Kong or in France. An LV bag is a must-have item among my peers. (**Mary, 25, professional**)

Ada, an entrepreneur in a large garment factory, echoes Mary's attitude:

> I don't have any confidence in branded goods in China since there are so many counterfeits. I'll order the latest LV bag from Paris and ask for it to be shipped. Otherwise, when you wear the latest style of LV bags, people can see it's a counterfeit and it'll be awkward. Our business partners assess our wealth and how our businesses are

doing in terms of the branded products, luxury cars, and apartments that we have. They calculate and quantify our wealth through what we wear and where we live. **(Ada, 32, entrepreneur)**

Chiu agrees with Ada. Consumption has its own intangible and intrinsic function in doing business. He says,

I prefer buying a car to buying a villa since we can show off our car to our clients. We cannot show off our house directly to them. In face-to-face meetings, my clients quantify my wealth in terms of my car (whether it is a BMW), watch (whether it is a Rolex), and club membership. **(Chiu, 28, entrepreneur)**

Tong concurs with Chiu. He says,

I prefer an iPhone or Samsung phone, car or suit from a brand such as Prada, since I can show off when I meet my clients. Although I am not a boss, I need to be presentable and dress stylishly when I meet my clients in order to earn bonus and commission. **(Tong, 32, professional)**

The young generation believe that buying brand names and foreign goods indicates their higher status for consumption. With a higher social status, they have more refined personal tastes and a more modern fashion outlook. They need to differentiate themselves from manual workers. They prefer to eat less and save their money to buy genuine rather than counterfeit brand-name products.

I think if entrepreneurs want to attract business investment in China, they need to bring high status branded goods to Guangdong. They need to show us the certificate of each item together with its product code. This can guarantee I won't buy any counterfeit goods. I feel disgusted when I find that I have spent a great deal of money on fakes. **(Ivy, 26, professional)**

Indeed, the young generation mostly has a burning desire for anything with a brand name (Pun 2003: 484). What was once the old-fashioned Chinese way of consumption (for actual needs) and remains prevalent in the old generation is now replaced in quick order by a pattern of consumption revolving around desire (Yau 1994). Consumer goods worldwide are dwindling in their serviceable functionality and giving way to fashion. Today, in contrast to the past, the goal of consumption behaviour is to pursue the satisfaction of desire – a desire that is artificially created and equally artificially excited – rather than to satisfy genuine utility of need (Pun 2003).

The fashion tastes and styles of the young generation are more in tune with those of Hong Kong, Japan, Taiwan, and Europe or any other location that is regarded as 'hip'. Fashion signifies unity with those in the same class while having the power to exclude others. Fashion in the upper stratum of society (such as those of political bureaucrats and the intellectual elite) is never identical with that of the lower groups (such as workers and marginal groups). It is a product of class distinction and yet it also operates as a producer of class distinction for a strategy of inclusion and exclusion. Fashion therefore has the function of reproducing social power and privilege by maintaining social differences and distinctions (Bourdieu 1984, 1996). Storey (1999: 40) considers fashion in the context of power and ideology, and argues that it is 'fashion' *per se* (rather than the content of the fashion) that is the signifier of social difference that helps maintain social status in society. Fashion constitutes and communicates a position in the overall social order while possibly challenging relative positions within it. As such, Barnard (1996: 39) pinpoints that 'fashion and clothing are used as weapons and defence in that they express the ideologies held by social groups which may be opposed to the ideologies of other groups in the social order'. In other words, fashion acts as a resource by which social groups can maintain either a dominant or a subservient position within a social order.

The majority (20 out of 24) of the young generation say that if they have money, they will buy whatever they want. Most of them go to Hong Kong and other countries to buy the latest and trendy fashions. Alex says,

> I like to buy fashion from Japan, such as Ape, Porter, agnès b, Birkenstock and other brand-name products. In fact, we aren't out of step with current fashion, although I know we're always giving foreigners the impression that we're unfashionable. We're now quite trendy and much more fashionable than many middle class people all over the world, including the middle class in Hong Kong. (**Alex, 35, professional**)

Agreeing with Alex, Fai remarks,

> I definitely don't buy any local fashion brands, only international brands like LV, Gucci, Prada, Jack Jones, Calvin Klein, Polo and

Burberry. We are not old fashioned at all. There are many large-scale shopping malls in China. How can I avoid the attractions and temptations? (**Fai, 28, entrepreneur**)

Fashion denotes status and class. It seems as if the Chinese new middle class is trying to steer itself away from the bad sense of dress that it thinks the rest of the Chinese have in the eyes of foreigners – and the undertone of 'village provincialism' (*tuganjue* 土感觉) that comes from it. Thus the fashionable look depends on having that quintessential imported or foreign look.

## The bar and self-commodification

In this section I want to show how bars and similar establishments are 'used' by the young generation to set itself apart from the general population. In Guangdong province there is a bar to which I am frequently invited by members of the young generation. It is about 1,000 square feet in size and exudes happiness. The décor is made by a Japanese designer, consisting of a delicate garden almost fit for meditation and a bar where you can quietly pass an afternoon with a glass of your favourite drink in hand to the sounds of light jazz music. Sweet and shapely waitresses are at your beck and call, all of the services are value-added, and the wide assortment of food and beverages cost at least RMB50 (US$7 or £5) a serving. Meanwhile, the ubiquitous but equally high-priced karaoke bars do a roaring trade. Peter, an entrepreneur, who often brings me to bars and discotheques, says:

Wine and song are our companion for leisure or business if you have the cash to match. Well-dressed foreigners relax on luxurious sofas, and many people have come to use the bar as if it were their second office or a second home. It is a place for me to meet girlfriends, business partners, gossip and exchange tips on fashion, brand-name products and travel. (**Peter, 34, entrepreneur**)

Andy concurs with Peter. He usually brings me to bars and parties.

We drink, dance and hang out with friends in the pub, which is a great place to relax and enjoy life. I can escape from reality. (**Andy, 35, professional**)

Most of the young generation feel up-to-date, trendy, more energetic and young-looking when interacting with other young people. As the hours pass, the night becomes even more beautiful. The bar becomes a gathering spot for a privileged few of the new middle class (men and women alike) (Farrer 2000: 245). Farrer (*ibid*.) observes from dancing activities in Shanghai that discotheques and dance halls are not simply acts of 'consumerism': the discotheque, with its emphasis on desirability, is actually a place for 'self-commodification' – a place for selling oneself to the public. This study finds that this is also the case in Guangdong. Farrer (*ibid*.) believes that the central logic of the market for most young people in China is not the discipline of production or the self-indulgence of consumption. Rather, in post-reform China, he believes it is the pleasure of selling themselves in an increasing open and free market of life chances.

Mary is an accountant who was educated in Germany and France. She spent ten years in those countries obtaining her secondary education and also her first Bachelor and Master's degrees.

> I'm good at dancing. I'm usually the most extrovert dancer and I escape my worries as we dance the night away. In a bar, you treat yourself as though you are your own boss; drinking becomes your quest and the music is what it's all about. **(Mary, 25, professional)**

When the young generation share their own stress and difficulties in pubs or bars, they have their own language to express their distinctiveness:

> We have a certain slang we use when we're in the pub. For example, *In* (*chao* 潮) *hea* (nothing to do, just staying at home), tram guy, *dianchenan* [电车男] (men who stay at home playing on their computers); middle lady [中女 '*zhong nü*' or 剩女 'sheng *nü*] (women aged over 30 who are unmarried or do not have boyfriends). **3S** means Single [单身 '*danshen*'], Seventies [多生于上世纪七十年代 '*duosheng yu shangshiji, qishi niandai*'] (born in the 1970s) and Stuck ['*bei kazhu le*' 被卡住了] (cannot find boyfriends or husbands). *Ku* [酷] means cool. We also talk about cohabitation, sex, gay men and lesbians. This kind of talk energises me and makes me feel young, though I have been working for many years. It is a good way to relax. **(Mark, 35, entrepreneur)**

Most of the young generation feel cool (酷 *ku*) when they use slang in conversations with their peers. Those people who are *ku* (酷) are those who are against dominant culture and support many subcultures in society. They express themselves as being more independent, individualist, strong-willed, friendly and easy-going in everyday life

(Ma 2006; Hui 1988; Hurst 2006). In addition, appearance and following the dress code with trendy fashions and styles are examples of *ku* (酷) (Moore 2005).

## Westernised fast-food shops and Chinese restaurants

Guangdong province is rightly regarded as a food paradise because of the great variety of cuisine there. Indeed, economic prosperity has provided abundant choices of food. The wider choice reaffirms the high importance of food consumption behaviour in Chinese personal relationships. Eating establishments therefore become the hub of socially significant activities and food markets are useful places to investigate changes in consumption patterns.

Veeck (2000) points out that food has long been recognised as a central vehicle for analysing identities, roles, relationships, rituals and ceremonies. An individual communicates the nature of his/her relationship with others through the acquisition, preparation and consumption of food (Bestor 2005).

In fact, the younger new middle class in Guangdong tends to dine out in Western-branded fast-food outlets such as McDonald's, Starbucks, and Burger King. Fashionably dressed youngsters of that class are often seen relaxing in those fast-food outlets during their leisure time and on public holidays. Indeed, dining in Western-style fast-food shops is an integral part of their new lifestyle because that kind of dining apparently makes these people feel as well as be seen as more civilised (Watson *et al.* 2005). They usually utilise this space to chat with their friends or even meet with their business partners. They feel a strong sense of pride and superiority in these Western cafés or fast-food outlets. They feel more civilised, Westernised, and differentiated from other Chinese.

> I usually hang around in Starbucks surfing the Internet and chatting with my friends. I also go to Starbucks when I want to read and have time to myself. This Westernized cafe gives me the feeling that I am a member of the Chinese middle class. It reinforces my sense of who I am. I find myself feeling more civilized and Westernized. **(Lily, 30, professional)**

Consuming 'foreign' foods is an important way for the young generation to set itself apart from the other classes. Many of the young generation interviewed in this study say that while the food and flavours of Western-style fast-food shops are not great, the experience of eating in such establishments made them feel good and appear more modern, civilised and young. Therefore, the appeal of 'foreign' foods is not in the physical sensations of actually eating them, as one frequent patron of Starbucks explains:

> While it's acceptable to go to a Chinese restaurant for my morning cup of tea, I feel that it's a bit outdated. I like to go to McDonald's and Starbucks to enjoy a Western-style breakfast. They provide a private space in which I can 'digest' Western culture. I feel more in step with economic development in China and more civilized, too. **(Chiu, 28, entrepreneur)**

Ben echoes Chiu,

> I personally like eating at Starbucks, cafés, Italian restaurants, and at buffets in hotels. I don't know how to express it, but I like the settings of some Western restaurants or hotels. They give me an individualized, modern, trendy, hygienic, elegant and innovative feeling, which I love. **(Ben, 35, entrepreneur)**

In spite of the fact that overtime work is part and parcel of the daily routine for many of the younger Chinese new middle class, they are trying to look for a better lifestyle within their own limited window for leisure time. Going to some Westernised café like Starbucks, Pacific Coffee or hotels can give them a private space to think about their life chances. They act like some Western middle class since they understand the symbolic meaning of leisure time. Having coffee nowhere else but Starbucks, dining nowhere but Pizza Hut are typical facets of the food lifestyle of the Chinese new middle class. They can give them a taste of 'modernity' (Hsu 2005). Most of the fast food in post-reform China has a kind of symbolic meaning. It is not because of the food *per se*, it is because of the experience. KFC and McDonald's are the two biggest Western fast food chain stores in Guangdong. These fast food shops play a very important role in constructing a non-edible but new and insightful experience for the young generation of the Chinese new middle class. It represents a modern, advanced, high technology, Westernised, and an individualised lifestyle. Fast food is a symbol of equality, freedom, and individualisation. Most of the young generation can spend RMB30 in Starbucks, and they can pass the afternoon by using their notebooks, iPads, iPhones or other advanced electronic devices.

In the fast-food shops, they have to dispose of their own rubbish or leftovers. They feel this kind of practice to be very advanced, considerate, self-restrained, and polite. They believe it is what a civilised citizen should do. But China does not really have this kind of civic education. This kind of reason attracts many of the old generation as well as the young generation to turn their backs on Chinese restaurants and go to Western restaurants instead. This kind of Western restaurant is a kind of borrowed public space to enjoy their private and individualised freedom. It is what Yan (2009: 257) called 'Cultural Symbolism of Americana' (Yan 2009: 257). In Starbucks, Pacific Coffee, or KFC which are smoke free, alcohol free, and full of varieties and choices, men and women are equal in these Western settings in China.

## Mobile phones and portable computers

Like many young people around the world, the Chinese younger new middle class learns about the world around them through the Internet. Because of globalisation, the young generation is somewhat more proficient in English because of a better-quality education. That facilitates the arrival of the culture of the English-speaking world (especially America) to their world. It is also through the Internet that the young generation learns to recognise and cultivate a liking for foreign and brand-named goods.

Communication is a key to the rising knowledge of the Chinese new middle class. They are most likely to buy the latest model of mobile phones and computers with advanced email and browsing functions. However, the mobile phone is also moving away from strictly being a communication tool to becoming a symbol of fashionable lifestyle. It is a symbol of the quality of life. Chiu and Jacky updated me on what mobile phones and computers mean to their lives.

> If you own a fancy mobile, you're effectively transforming yourself from backward to advanced, from traditional to modern. It's a symbol of status, of success. Otherwise, you are asked 'are you still using your old model? You are out of date!' Also, it's now very easy to get high-tech products. I change my mobile phone model frequently, maybe once every two months. I ask my friends in Hong Kong or in other South East Asian countries to buy me an iPhone, a 3G phone or some other high-tech product like a Netbook or MacBook. I'm attracted to the sharp and 'in' appearance of the iPhone and 3G phones. (**Chiu, 28, entrepreneur**)

I cannot live without my iPhone and Netbook. Due to the nature of my job [author clarification: he is a fashion designer], I need to keep up to date in terms of my fashion sense and taste. Therefore, I need to have my iPhone and Netbook to hand all the time to keep in contact with the world and my friends. **(Jacky, 30, professional)**

There is a preoccupation with mobile phones and other electronic devices with a multiplicity of advanced functions. The consumption of these goods gives the younger new middle class a sense of greater connectedness with the rest of the world and helps them to overcome the limitations of their physical locations (Xu 2007: 373). That sense of connection with the more faraway and more advanced outside world also helps the Chinese new middle class to adopt newer status symbols.

## Residential preferences and brands of car

There is a yearning among the Chinese new middle class for spacious, comfortable living quarters. Indeed, these people often live in large homes, normally of around 150 square metres (1,500 square feet), with beautiful gardens and multiple parking spaces. Their homes are comfortable and elegant in décor and typically located on a hillside or by the seashore. Western-style houses built on green grassy knolls or near a stream are meant to display harmony. The home is usually constructed in a way that is evocative of a natural, healthy, and sunny environment for a life of comfort and leisure in a strongly cultured atmosphere.

In fact, the Chinese new middle class can go to some lengths to ensure their homes show exquisite levels of naturalness as much as discriminating taste and status. The new middle class are sometimes known to spend in excess of RMB1 million (US$146,316 or £99,796) on interior decoration alone to achieve good taste and stylishness. I was once invited to a picture-perfect home: a three-storey building with a sloping roof, a huge front garden, a modern kitchen and elegant rooms done up in tasteful pastels in a blend of modern and traditional design.

A dream home is no dream home unless, of course, it is matched by a good network of transportation and amenities. It should be within easy reach of Western-style shopping and entertainment facilities. Geographically, it should be near lakes, hills, forests or parks and also have panoramic views – qualities that help the new middle class to display outstanding social status. Tsang owns just such a dream home:

My home, where I live with my wife and two daughters, occupies 150 square metres. I spent about 1 million yuan [US$146,316 or £99,796] furnishing it. The house isn't just for living, but provides a tasteful environment where my family and I can have a high quality of life. I didn't have it designed for luxury but, rather, with a taste for the modern. I bought materials from France, Italy, and other European countries. I simply pursued my tastes. I don't like to follow popular Chinese furnishing styles, which I regard as tasteless and without character. We wanted to have our own swimming pool and now only the residents have the privilege of gaining access to it. **(Tsang, 37, entrepreneur)**

Raymond and Peter seem to confirm Tsang's views.

Quality of life is very important. I want more than a simple shelter. I'm looking to experience the art of living. A clubhouse is a must-have item for me. **(Raymond, 30, professional)**

When I invite my business partners to my home, they see where I live and which brand of car I drive. It's all related to the pursuit of business opportunities. **(Peter, 34, entrepreneur)**

Many high-class recreational establishments in China are prohibited from the otherwise well-heeled because they are restricted to members only or to government officials. I can see that one of the ultimate goals of the younger new middle class is to consume for showing status so that they can extend social circles to include cadres with a view to extending their social circles even further.

## Gender relations and the attitudes of the young generation

The young generation of the Chinese new middle class generally tend to marry later. In my in-depth interviews and participant observation with the young generation, most of the discussion is organised in terms of generational changes within the three major 'own class' categories of entrepreneurs, cadres, and professionals. From my samples of the young generation, men generally get married around the age of 30 while women generally get married around 28. There is an increasing trend for some of the young generation, women in particular, to decide not to marry. Most of the women making such a choice are highly educated and they are most likely professionals.

Ivy is a professional from a middle-class family in Guangdong. She has a boyfriend and says,

> I personally think that guys from the outset focus on my physical appearance, figure, body, and personality. It doesn't relate to my talents or abilities. It took me several years to look around and then I finally selected this guy as my boyfriend. However, most Chinese guys are stressed now since they need to pay the bill when they dine out with their girlfriends. They need to buy apartments if they want to get married. They also need to feed their parents and grandparents. Luckily I am not a PhD student. I won't pursue a PhD since this will become a burden for me in finding a husband. My parents told me that a Master's is sufficient for me right now. **(Ivy, 26, professional)**

Some members of the young generation state that it is quite difficult for young and well-educated women to find boyfriends or husbands. This is the case in particular for those women who pursued their studies abroad. Betty earned her Bachelor's degree in Guangdong and earned her Master's degree abroad. She says,

> If you can speak fluent English, this makes many Chinese guys run away. In Guangdong, not too many can speak and write good English, but if they can, they are potentially dream boyfriends or husbands. But I can say that in our company, actually, I cannot find any good-quality guys. I prefer a foreigner to a Chinese guy since most of the foreigners are more interesting, and have a sense of humour. **(Betty, 30, professional)**

Sung is a young professional with a Bachelor's degree. He is now single, but he would not consider choosing a PhD holder or even a master holder to be his girlfriend or wife.

> It's very difficult for me to talk to a woman with a PhD. I don't mind having one as my girlfriend, but I am afraid I will not be academic enough to communicate with her. I want to find someone who can share my work, happiness and pain, instead of someone who is so knowledgeable that it will make me feel stressed. **(Sung, 30, professional)**

Dan, a professional, also shares the same view with Sung. He says,

> I need a wife who can share my life and with whom I can have fun, without the need for books or dictionaries... **(Dan, 29, professional)**

However, Sunny is a very trendy, young and optimistic entrepreneur with a different perspective. He is still single and says,

> I'm not worried about the educational level of my girlfriend. I only have a Bachelor's degree. If my girlfriend or wife has a PhD, it'll show how attractive and cool I am... My wife will know how to educate my son or daughter in the future. **(Sunny, 34, entrepreneur)**

It is a common phenomenon in today's China for some of those women who are PhD holders to hide their PhD identity in order to find their future husbands. In China, there is a very famous motto to describe the highly educated women. If you have a Bachelor's degree, you are *Huang-rong* (beautiful, intelligent and easy to communicate with. *Benkesheng shi huangrong* 本科生是黄蓉). If you have a Master's degree, you are *Li Mo-chou* (intelligent and good at *gongfu* but quite difficult to get along with other people. *Shuoshisheng shi limochou* 硕士生是李莫愁). If you are a PhD holder, you are *Miejue shi tai* (very good at *gongfu* 功夫, but is very eccentric and superbly terrible to talk to and communicate with. *Boshisheng shi miejue shi tai*, 博士生是灭绝师太).[1]

In contrast, Dan finds that highly educated men, such as PhD candidates, are the dream men for many Chinese women. Dan says,

> Once most girls learn that I am a PhD candidate (*boshisheng* 博士生 ), they pay more attention. If they are over 30 and still unmarried, they will be regarded as a 'middle lady', whereas I will be easily able to find a high-quality girlfriend. I want my wife to have a good career. I don't want to find one who relies on me financially. **(Dan, 29, professional)**

Jiang, a professional, is a son of the old generation who got his PhD from Hong Kong and he absolutely agrees with Dan. He got married and now has a daughter. He told me that he had tremendous choices for a wife since he represents the 'dream man' for many women in China. He is intelligent and young, comes from a middle-class family and can speak good English. The most important thing for

Jiang and Dan is that they earned their PhD from abroad (*jinguo xianshui* 浸过咸水) and are now working in China. Jiang says,

> I'm not looking for a woman with a PhD to be my wife. It doesn't necessarily mean that I will marry one who has acquired only a primary or secondary education. My wife should have a Master's degree, be beautiful, intelligent and gentle, able to cook well, and be docile. (**Jiang, 31, professional**)

The men in the young generation in general prefer their girlfriends/ wives to be more economically and financially independent. Ben says,

> I can say that women in China are normally dependent on their future husband. However, I would like my wife to be financially independent. I would hate it if my future wife wanted to be highly dependent on me. (**Ben, 35, entrepreneur**)

Melody is a professional who is now working in China after finishing her MA in Hong Kong. She believes that most women are relatively richer than men[2] of the same age. But she needs to be independent and needs a job even after getting married. She says,

> I foresee the need to have a full-time job after I get married. I don't have any fantasies. I cannot fully rely on my husband. I cannot act like my mother who never worked after she got married. She has been a housewife since she was 20. I expect that if I get married and have children, I will need to work. My future husband will not be able to meet all our expenditures if I don't. I want to be financially independent as well. (**Melody, 28, professional**)

Lily, married, concurs with the views of Betty and Melody. She has a full-time job, although she also has children. She says,

> I don't want to rely on my husband since I can work. I want to have my own salary. I like buying branded goods and jewellery. Otherwise, I need to ask my husband to buy them for me and I feel embarrassed if he refuses. (**Lily, 30, professional**)

Well-educated men use different criteria when choosing their girlfriends or wives in China today. There are no common patterns for this phenomenon. But one thing that can be guaranteed is that men with

PhDs, particularly those who study abroad, are the 'dream men' for many Chinese women. Well-educated men also want their wives to have good jobs and be more economically independent. They want to find someone who is intelligent and economically independent instead of being good at doing domestic chores. The marriage patterns of both men and women of the young generation show relatively different patterns from those of their parents (Zhang 2006).

## Parent–child relationship between generations

In terms of consumption patterns and lifestyles, the young generation do not act like their parents. Why do the younger middle class not have a more frugal or workmanlike lifestyle, like their parents? There are two main areas in which the young generation do not act like their parents. These are consumption patterns and marriage practices.

My respondents are well aware of the hard and impoverished lives of their parents, and many would have been instructed by them on the benefits of frugality. Yet the childhood memory of the young generation is mostly of fun, good food, good clothes and nice toys, with parents doing their best to afford the best-possible surroundings for them.

In Chapter 1, I explored some conceptual frameworks describing the Chinese parent–child relationship and why it is different from that in Western societies. In analysing the parent–child relationship between the old and young generation, I can view that relationship on two fronts.

First, middle-class Chinese parents tend to indulge their children. The unique and perhaps most astounding aspect about the parent–child relationship in post-reform Chinese society is that a very high proportion of young urban people are in fact the only offspring of their families. The one-child family policy is more strenuously enforced on urban families than on rural families, which are normally, if not formally, allowed to have more than one child.

As the only child, most are highly dependent on their parents. Broadly speaking, the only child is the king or queen of the household in the eyes of many Chinese parents. Parents are often involved in planning career paths for their children, preparing them for overseas studies, using their *guanxi* networks to find jobs, and even helping them to find boyfriends or girlfriends. Many parents in fact look on their progeny as the torchbearer of the family.

My sample of the old generation illustrates different views about their relationship with their children. Uncle Fang's son is currently studying abroad. He does his best to provide whatever his son wants, and says,

> I don't think I spoil my son. I just want him to enjoy his studies without worrying about money. I am proud of him since I know that whatever he achieves will be good for us as a family. I pay for his tuition fees, around RMB110,000 (US$14,641 or £11,134) per year. I provide him with RMB5,000 (US$732 or £506) for his monthly expenditure and I pay for his accommodation [around US$800/£400 per month]. I don't want him to get distracted from his studies. **(Uncle Fang, 49, cadre)**

Indeed, Chinese parents are unable to release their offspring and are apt to do and plan everything for them since they have relatively more cultural capital than the lower-class or peasant families (Wang *et al.* 2006). The result is that many sons and daughters of the Chinese new middle class never learn to be independent. One interviewee explains:

> Some of my friends are very protective of their sons and daughters. They want to send them abroad when they're only eleven or twelve years old. Most of them send their sons to the UK, Australia, the USA or Canada in order to learn more English. But most of my friends just send them away without parental supervision. The result is that most of the kids learn nothing and end up badly behaved. Not only are they weak in English, but they're also bad morally. They're not mature enough to learn how to be independent or have critical thinking. So they've wasted their parents' money and become a paobuji [跑步机 i.e. making no progress]. **(Uncle Vicky, 45, professional)**

The country's one-child policy provides a driving force for these attitudes as many urban parents see their only offspring as the object of hope and expectation to carry on the family line. Meanwhile, the one-child policy also produces a negative aspect especially for nuclear families in that it tends to encourage an egocentric personality in the young generation. Broadly speaking, the only child in an average Chinese family is cared for and indulged by roughly six adults who all want to push that child to become a high achiever (Faure 2008: 479–80). Uncle Tom, the father of Mary, told me that he hadn't spoiled Mary when she studied in France. Instead, he taught Mary how to be independent and earn for her own daily expenditures.

> I paid her tuition fees in France for the first year. For the remaining years she received a scholarship from the university since her academic results were quite good at that time. She also tutored privately, teaching Mandarin. She took care of all her living expenses in France. I would say that whether or not you spoil your children, it really depends on how you teach them. (**Uncle Tom, 45, professional**)

Uncle Tom's attitude about how to teach children, however, is not common in my sample. Indeed, my findings indicate that the Chinese new middle class do not seem to know much, if anything, about Western-style parenting, especially more so among the old generation. While the Chinese new middle-class parents put a great deal of resources into their only child, it does not necessarily mean they have any close affection with their child. The parent–child relation-ship between the old and young generation does not seem to have the kind of friendly quality that is often seen in Western middle-class families.

In general, the Chinese parents, whatever the class, have authority. So they command respect and expect obedience. In some, there is a high level of intimacy and affection, with parents in the habit of coddling their kids and generally treating them like cherubs, even if the children deep down do not necessarily respect their 'god'. By and large, the parents among the Chinese new middle class tend to fit the profile of domineering parents, although there are pockets of liberal-minded attitudes depending on the historical conditioning and education level of the parents concerned.

From the dialogues recorded for this study, I could see that many of the young generation receive a great deal of care from their families. Sometimes this can be transformed into a kind of pressure because they need to preserve their family reputation. Indeed, for the post-80 generation (*bashihou* 八十后, those born after 1980) or post-90 generation (*jiushihou* 九十后 those born after 1990), their childhood is mostly one of cramming and swotting (Huang 2008).

Ivy is a 26-year-old accountant in a top accounting firm. She is the only daughter of an old-generation family and obtained her first degree in Hong Kong.

> How to describe the relationship with my parents? It's full of bitter-sweet emotion, including respect, love, conflict and obligation. They want me to be an accountant, a prestigious job that can guarantee work until I retire. This job has no age barriers. Usually, I tell my parents good news and conceal bad news. My parents want me to be Number One in front of my relatives. I don't want my parents to lose face. I need to take care of their upkeep since they'll be retiring very soon. I don't have any siblings and the pressure is quite huge. **(Ivy, 26, professional)**

Jiang concurs with Ivy. Coming from a reputable family in Guangdong he took more than a year to find a teaching post outside China after receiving his PhD. Now he is only able to find a teaching post in a city in Guangdong. The low salary is very disappointing to him. But it is better than remaining jobless. In fact, he wants to work in Hong Kong or Macau to secure a better future and a well-paid job. He cannot do something that will ruin the reputation of his family.

> If I end up with a low-paid job, I will ruin my family's reputation. I am under pressure to please my parents. Now you can imagine how frustrated I am. I will keep trying to find a prestigious and well-paid job either in Hong Kong or Macau. My family has invested a lot in me and I cannot let them lose face in front of my relatives. **(Jiang, 31, professional)**

So it appears that middle-class parents tend to have greater ambitions for their children because of the one-child policy. They therefore show a need to maintain or improve family and social status through their only child. Education in today's China is still ascriptive, dependent on family inheritance, social connections, and *guanxi* networks, rather than on the students' own effort and achievement. Under the dual influence of economic reform in the country and globalisation, intergenerational upward mobility for the middle class is full of anxieties and uncertainties, and needs to be maintained over generations mainly through cultural capital (education), social capital (tastes and distinction), and political capital (cadres).

## Anxiety, uncertainty, and individualisation over generation

From my study of the Chinese new middle class, I discovered that both the young and old generation of the Chinese new middle class have a kind of anxiety and uncertainty about how to reproduce their social status and privileges over generations. The young generation can no longer fully utilise the favourable factors in the 1980s and all the businesses have been saturated in today's China. It is more difficult for them to do business since everything seems to be more institutionalised in post-reform China. Cultural capital (education level) will become the entry ticket but this means little if they don't also have social capital (social networks). The young generation has a strong degree of status inheritance from their parents and are members of the Chinese new middle class in terms of academic achievements, occupation, and career paths (Bian 2002a: 104–5). Education serves to reproduce differentiated cultural patterns. A dominant economic class is able to have better or higher education and so have improved access to higher culture (good taste). Both generation think education is the best way to keep their middle-class status (Gladney 2000).

For many in the old generation, it can be a lifelong plan of making investments to help their children study abroad so as to maintain the social worth ('face') of the family. Uncle Fong considers sending his elder son to the USA in the future. He says,

> I don't worry about myself but worry terribly about my two children because it's pretty difficult to secure a good position or to start doing business in China today. The business sector is currently running at maximum and has little room for growth. What I can do is provide a good education and buy two apartments for my elder son [author's clarification: one to occupy and one to rent; at the time of the interview this boy is only seven]. **(Uncle Fong, 48, entrepreneur)**

In fact, the life of an average mainlander is laden with escalating costs of family needs such as food, hospitalities, and education. Furthermore, while China has something like 'nine years of free education' (as most Westernised countries do) children get schooled only if they have or can secure an urban residence.[3]

In Guangdong, for instance, tuition fees in state schools are half subsidised by the local government. Private and international schools are not subsidised and all fees are privately funded by the students' families. Uncle Yang and Uncle Lee share the same views about their children's tuition fees.

> I need to earn more and more money. This is to cover the cost of the children's education and expensive sponsorship fees. It costs me around RMB5,000 a month [US$732 or £505] to look after my five-year-old son. He studies in an international kindergarten. I want him to speak English fluently and I am going to send him abroad if I can. If my child fails to get the offer of a place at university, it might possibly cost me more than I will be in a position to afford. **(Uncle Yang, 40, professional)**

> The investment in children's schooling – like having them attend different courses and training programmes – can cost you as much as RMB55,000 a year (US$8,052 or £5,565). **(Uncle Lee, 40, entrepreneur)**

That most of the old generation of the new middle class in my sample (20 out of 35) need to keep financial reserves for their children's education explains why the old generation are apt to buy real estate rather than investing in equity or other relatively riskier securities. Most of the young generation tend to have far-sighted, broad horizons for their future. They also tend to have working plans in place to pursue higher degrees in Hong Kong or overseas at some point in the foreseeable future. The other reason why the young generation are stressed is their obligations to their parents. They will have to feed at least four elderly members (their parents, their grandparents or father or mother-in-law if they get married). King says,

> It is stressful for me to feed four elderly people in my family. I know I need to maintain a competitive status in society since it is quite difficult to get and keep a job in China today. I need to give my parents a comfortable life. This is my promise. **(King, 30, entrepreneur)**

Kong, 30, a professional, feels the stress, although his parents had helped him to buy an apartment for his marriage. He says,

> My parents have their pensions because both of them are cadres. They also have their own savings which are sufficient for their retirement. They have helped me to buy an apartment. But I am still under stress as I want to get married to my girlfriend next year.

I need to take care of my own family. Can I rely on my parents to feed my wife and children? **(Kong, 30, professional)**

The parents of the old generation (the first cohort) were most likely employed by the state enterprises which provide their pensions until they die. They had secured their pensions and medical services with the existence of *danwei* system. The second cohort of the old generation is most unlikely to have pension and medical services with their job. Therefore, they need to rely either on their only son or daughter to provide their living expenses after they retire, or on their own accumulated resources (some of which they would have invested in that son or daughter).

I argue that the old generation are pragmatic and business-oriented, rather than being personally-oriented in their consumption. They also show strong collective identities, but these are rooted in personal networks rather than in a sense of a common class location that they share with others outside their personal networks. In contrast, the young generation tend to be more flexible, individualistic, and materialistic in their career planning and lifestyles. Therefore, I argue that the Chinese new middle class (old and young generation) are undergoing the process of individualisation in post-reform China. Chinese people are generally described as *collectivist* in contrast to their individualist counterparts in the West. Thus, in Asian societies, it is the traditional and communal bonds of the extended family, neighbourhood, and wider communities that are the primary forces assumed to shape the individual's identity, choices and biography. The plenitude of Western theories of class analysis and individualisation cannot be transplanted and need to be adapted to the nuances of China.

## Individualisation of the Chinese new middle class

In the sociological literature, Ulrich Beck's *World Risk Society: Towards a New Modernity* (1992) is the *locus classicus*. It claims that individualisation is the 'new contradictory mode of socialisation' which has altered the reproductive modes of industrial society in the form of social class, gender, marriage, parenthood and occupation. In a much later text entitled *Individualization: Institutionalized Individualism and its Social and Political Consequences*, Beck and Beck-Gernsheim (2002) opine that individualisation must be understood as a complex process that depends on:

> ...economic prosperity, the construction of a welfare state, the institutionalization of interests represented by trade unions, the legal

underpinning of labour contrasts, the expansion of education, the growth of the service sector and associated opportunities for mobility and the shortening of the working week.

In my ethnographic study in Guangdong carried out since 2002, I have observed that the decline in rural living standards is the result of China's socialist conditioning that disadvantages the working-class peasants who were too 'ill-prepared to cope with the sudden rigours of competitive capitalism' (Lingle 1997: 109) at the expense of augmenting the wealth and living standards of the middle-class urban dwellers. As the economic revolution gained momentum during the 1980s and 1990s, material possessions and consumption replaced political symbols as the measures of one's social status (Yan 2009: 208). A mandate was therefore provided for a flourishing advertising industry (Hung *et al.* 2007: 839) to cultivate the desires of the new middle class. The defining characteristics of the different groups that comprise China's emerging new class may remain somewhat inchoate. Nevertheless, consumption and a fine taste for designer accoutrements are the prerequisites that one must exemplify to be admitted to this echelon (Smart & Smart 2003; Smart & Li 2006). The predilections of the young generation to 'consume' a Western education (Gladney 2000) and to conspicuously flaunt their status by purchasing luxury 'mansions' and expensive cars (Hubacek *et al.* 2007) are emblematic of a self-conscious mentality and anxiety to secure the reproduction of their class status. As consumption is not simply the act of consumerism itself, but the hedonistic desire to experience leisure or pleasure through consumerism, Farrer (2000: 244) is right in deducing that the ubiquity of a culture of leisure in a marketised economy represents a shift from a culture of production to a culture of consumption. Their pleasure-seeking habits and self-consciousness suggest they remain enamoured with Western modernity's individualised lifestyles of consumerism and consumption that will be at odds with the hegemony of their ascribed identities and collectivist values.

The effect that money has in changing one's cultural values, according to Simmel (2004: 344), is the 'atomisation of the individual person, as an individualisation that occurs within the person'. Money, then, in conjunction with the consumption of material culture, individualises a person. In our current climate of late modernity defined by the ubiquitous consumption of fashion and style, Roberta Sassatelli (2000) insightfully illuminates the way in which the consumption of fashionable commodities is central to individualisation. Sassatelli (2000: 214) said:

> Fashion allows the individual to be up to date. Yet, although it is ephemeral and doomed to disappear, fashion also appears as a semblance which alludes to other, deeper and firmer features of the individual [...] In other words, fashion offers a space of difference, which nevertheless is expressed in terms of a relative indifference because of both its transiency and its public availability. For a moment it yields to a strong sense of self; and, as indifference, it brings the subject to continuously re-establish a distance and a space of difference for him or herself in the pursuit of such heightened individuality.

Sassatelli's arguments on fashion also resonate with Giddens' findings that the human body plays a pivotal role in enabling the individual to attain self-actualisation. Fashion, dress, and modes of facial adornment 'are to some degrees a means of individualisation' that remains 'signalling devices of gender, class position and occupational status' (Giddens 1991: 99). In equating material success with materialistic consumption patterns, China's emerging new middle class have cemented consumption and financial wealth as the hegemonic matrix for class stratification in contemporary post-reform China. It is therefore this power to ascribe value to the objects of material culture that is *par excellence* definitive of one's personal identity and attainment of 'enlightenment' that distinguishes a member of the new middle echelon from the rural working milieu. In calling for a shift from class to culture in our globalised and neo-liberal era, Beverley Skeggs (2004: 66) maintains that the reconstitution, progression and progressiveness of the world's new middle classes are 'predicated on holding in place – fixing – that which must signify stagnation and immobility'.

The individualisation of the new middle class is, however, characterised by the government's supreme right to pre-emptorily censure and enforce that individualisation when doing so would be instrumental to the *summum bonum* of the organised collective community (see Yan 2009, 2010). The distinguishing hallmark of China's state management of individualisation is the party-state's use of economic or political rewards to encourage individuals who will choose pathways preferred by the government, and exert their self-autonomy only within clear and distinct boundaries (Yan 2009: 289). However, there is little the government can do to eliminate the 'dissident' forms of individualisation that are not expedient to economic growth. The communist party-state has been ineffectual at suppressing the desires of China's middle-class youth to express themselves in the cultural arena (Fung 2009). Thus, through the commercialisation of youth culture and the proliferation of consumption as a value, 'liberalising values have developed amongst young people which might impinge upon society and politics' (Fung 2009: 295). The CCP is powerless.

The young generation is flexible enough to improve their competitiveness in the highly globalising China. They are quite anxious and uncertain about their life chances in the future. They tend to be more individualistic, materialistic, and oriented to personal gain like those in Western countries. However, on the other hand, they are unlikely to practice the form of individualisation that happened in some Western countries. The young generation never experience the Cultural Revolution and the impoverished childhood. They tend to practise conspicuous consumption patterns. But they rely a lot on the *guanxi* network, and cultural capital to maintain their middle-class privileges over generation. The development of individualisation for the young generation can be regarded as 'pragmatic and selective'. They rely on the networks derived from their parents (old generation) to maintain their intergenerational mobility and stratification and the middle-class status over generation.

The promotion of social trust and universal values have become an urgent moral and social issue in China as the discussion of it is becoming increasingly popular in post-reform China. The untying of the individual is one of the distinguishable features in post-reform China. This partly explains why state-owned enterprises collapsed. China does give the individual more mobility, choice and freedom. But given the fact that the social level in all aspects are increasingly individualised, social relations are being further instrumentalised and fragmented, and collective norms and values collapse. In the light of the lack of a viable welfare system, retirement scheme, and public educational fund, the process of individualisation is astonishingly obvious to the young generation of the Chinese new middle class. There is a low level of trust in institutions because of the corruption of the power holders at the local level.

For the young generation, if they want to be re-embedded in a new safety net, they have to rely on their family or parents' personal networks or *guanxi*, to be part of the social trust. As a result of individualisation promoted by the central government, individuals should face the indivisible and isolated self if they feel a great sense of anxiety in today's China. The level of identity construction should rely on their cultural capital (education) as well as cadres and their own social network. The second generation of the Chinese new middle class is situated in the process of 'railroading with self-interest' (Yan 2002). This means the Chinese Communist Party tries to indoctrinate the attractive economic or political rewards to allow individuals to freely choose the way favoured by the party-state and to exert self-control or self-management while staying within the boundaries that have been drawn by the party-state (Yan 2009: 290). The multilayered and multitemporal individualisation project exists in post-reform China. It is an ongoing project which individualisation, party-state and social groups put efforts to well establish it to get it into shape.

The old generation (those born between 1940 and 1969) is characterised by their pragmatic frame of mind in their way of life and utilitarian consumption habits. They stand in marked contrast to the conspicuous consumerism of the young generation that has followed them. Starting from the establishment of the People's Republic of China (1949), the Great Leap Forward (1958–1960), the Cultural Revolution (1966–1976), economic reform (since 1978), and globalisation era, their pragmatic and utilitarian nature of consumption is largely anchored in the past histories of the old generation. They are most notably collective memories of Maoist-era impoverishment, rising through the ranks in state employment, the winding road to the world of business, and the possible involvement in illegal activities. Pragmatic consumption is, to a slightly smaller extent, also attached to traditional Chinese or Confucian values of life as well as the need to carry out continual self-improvements to offset unknown but potentially threatening variables in a fast-changing economic and social landscape.

With regard to the issue of individualisation, the old generation of the Chinese new middle class are still in the form of collectivisation but this type of collectivisation is somewhat different from the traditional Chinese form of collectivisation. The empirical data reveal that they are *collectivist* not for the sake of the society/citizenship/state, but for self-gain of their families. They also show strong collective identities, but these are based in personal networks rather than in a sense of a common class location that they share with others outside their personal networks. The old generation, use their *collectivist means* to achieve their *individualised ends* to well secure their middle-class status over generation.

Finally, it is worth highlighting that the cultural identities of the new middle class in China are currently inchoate owing to the fact that many would, by their own admission, disavow the fact that they are members of a new echelon (or any other kind of middle class). Traditional class theories and individualisation would therefore be ineffectual for the purposes of analysing contemporary Chinese society. The emerging 'Chinese new middle class' departs from the standard developmental pathways portrayed in Western-oriented middle-class theories. It is likely that the currently amorphous Chinese new middle class will evolve into a much more diversified group than imagined.

The Orthodox Chinese political leaders formed the extreme fetishism and commoditisation process which could lead to the degrading and perversion of social norms and values in society. The individualistic attitudes of conspicuous and pragmatic consumption patterns that have developed can be regarded as an apolitical response to the changing politico-economic context in China. This kind of conspicuous and pragmatic pattern is more compatible with the PRC's policy. This serves to divert the middle class from critical discourse of civil engagement that could undermine state legitimacy. From my ethnographic account, I can obviously see that a kind of individualistic and utilitarian pragmatism has emerged as a dominant logic for the Chinese new middle class which displaces political ideals, social morality and self-criticism and reflections. Such cultural values in the imported popular culture create a context for the formation of the local structure of pleasure for the audience (Fung 2005: 290).

This explains why the old generation has both pragmatic and utilitarian consumption patterns. The exorbitant speed of the expansion of consumption for the middle class accounts clearly for the rise of the consumer revolution, and of the individualistic pursuit of desires. The Chinese new middle class works harder for job security as well as maintaining a form of middle-class intergenerational mobility by extending *guanxi* networks and cultural capital (education).

## Summary

While the young generation of the Chinese new middle class construct for themselves a system of signs that codify social differences and human relationships (Baudrillard 1998), there is simultaneously a desire to be shorn of an air of provincialism and to adopt overt signs of modern culture or civility. The overt signs of embracing the modern culture or civility are largely provided by merchandise and services associated with foreign (or at least non-Chinese) cultures and lifestyles. The ability to consume at high quality and in increasing quantities creates and reinforces the appearance of conspicuous consumption because that is the most notable way to showcase that they are more economically and culturally successful than other people and that they are more capable of success.

Foreign merchandise and services are ready-made icons of modern life in China because (*a*) their availability is increasing in all parts of China because of globalisation and the marketisation of the entire Chinese economy, and (*b*) the merchandise or services are so distinctively un-Chinese and therefore unconnected to possible Chinese provincialism. The ever-increasing need to keep up a distinct social status for themselves as a means to emphasise economic ability and cultural aptitude in consumption leads to increasing levels of consumption, in both quantity and quality.

In a globalising world, people in post-reform China are more market-oriented than before, and the young generation is more so than the rest. Many Chinese living or who have lived abroad bring to China a more heightened sense of a globalised world. In this new world, the Chinese new middle class has a market-oriented identification, one that blends and emphasises instrumentalism and pragmatism in consumer choices (Yu 2005; Hung *et al.* 2007). In short, the globalising nature of China offers ample opportunities for the acquisition of cultural capital, social networks and economic capital for the young generation to build their own careers and their hometowns. This provides a new challenge for the young generation (Brown 2003; Cao 2001; Chen 2006). They need to maintain their competitive power in order to provide a comfortable life for their parents.

In relation to the issue of individualisation, the old generation of the Chinese new middle class is more collective in nature but this type of collectivisation is somewhat different from the traditional Chinese form of collectivisation. My ethnographic data revealed they are *collectivist* not for the sake of China as a whole, but for extending their own business network and securing a good position in post-reform China. They also show strong collective identities, but these are based in personal networks rather than in a sense of a common class location that they share with others outside their personal networks. The old generation, using their *collectivist means* to achieve their *individualised ends* to secure their middle-class status over generations, want to maintain the status quo since they are the beneficiaries of the economic reform.

In the next chapter, I will explicate the details about the Chinese new middle class and *guanxi* networks. The *guanxi* network is a common survival kit for both the young and old generation in today's China.

# 4
# *Guanxi* Networks and the Chinese New Middle Class

Max Weber [1951] considered the lack of trust in Chinese society to be a major factor in explaining why historically the development of China's credit and commercial activities were considerably hindered. When trust remains only based on kin community and when personal links, reciprocity, moral obligation, and duty towards the community as a social capital remain essential, then the transaction costs for finding a reliable counterpart, negotiating a contract and enforcing it become extremely high. A moral attitude prevails only within kinship or circle of friends and acquaintances.

(Faure 2008: 485)

As argued in previous chapters, the way that institutional structures in China have evolved since 1978 has important consequences for the formation of the Chinese new middle class (Gilley 2008). The role of cadres remains important, influencing the collaboration with professionals and entrepreneurs. Institutional mechanisms of regulation are unbalanced and weak, and riddled with loopholes. The new middle class and others often exploit loopholes in the system for pecuniary or other gains, thereby reinforcing any grey areas that exist in the system. The rush to economic performance causes due diligence in governance to fall by the wayside. It leads to the growth of *guanxi* networks and affects how the old generation fully utilises their *guanxi* networks to achieve their *collectivist* form of individualisation. It also influences how the young generation utilises their *guanxi* networks derived from their parents to form a pragmatic and selective form of individualisation. It highlights the ambiguities and incompleteness of national and local policies, and the networks that arise from them as a counterbalance.

This chapter aims to investigate the importance of *guanxi* networks to the Chinese new middle class. The development of a reliable personal connections with powerholders (cadres) becomes a key business strategy for the entrepreneurs and professionals of the new middle class. Collaborations involve bargaining, negotiations and mutual accommodation through informal situations (social gatherings) but within an institutionalised setting (institutional polices). These help to maintain a balance between individual and group interest and advantages.

## *Guanxi* as an internalised process in China

Bian (1994, 2002a, 2002b) provides the most relevant definition of *guanxi* with respect to the Chinese new middle class. *Guanxi* is the dyadic, particular and sentimental ties that have the potential to facilitate exchanges of favours between parties that are connected by the ties. The close relations (called affective or emotive *guanxi*) contain strong expectations of cooperation. The thickest of those relationships merge into family ties, making the parties 'one of the family' or 'one of us'. Building and maintaining *guanxi* networks is a dynamic and lifelong process for every Chinese person (Lin 2001; Zhou & Pei 1997).

*Guanxi* network building and rebuilding may well have become an internalised habitus for the Chinese (Bourdieu 1984). Since the 1980s collaboration to do business and make profits has provided a practical impetus and lubrication for cadres to meet professionals and entrepreneurs from other parts of China as well as the Hong Kong middle class in the same groups. Since post-reform Chinese society is more business-oriented, *guanxi* networks now appear everywhere. As Wank (1995) has stated, 'As markets develop, the resources requirements linked to bureaucratic discretion are also greater, obliging entrepreneurs to cultivate official patrons.' Therefore, Wank (1995) also places an emphasis on the importance of institutional policies to do business since the economic reforms reinforce the development of informal ties.

In building and the use of *guanxi* networks, the Chinese new middle class seems to rely on using different kinds of social capital to create what is called a 'cultural nexus of power' (Duara 1988; Li 2001: 189). This phenomenon is viewed throughout our samples in Guangdong. What has been observed during the course of the fieldwork in this study is that the most powerful *guanxi* networks involve personal connections with the police, local cadres, and district officials who have direct control over land use, resources, and the enforcement of statutory regulations. For example, if an entrepreneur operates without a business licence (and a 'special business' licence in particular), the institutional process will often regard that entrepreneur as a criminal and he or she will be subject to all sorts of harassment by the police and other authorities (Li 2001: 190).

This study finds that local bureaucrats still exercise great authority in many areas of the economy in urban China, particularly in matters in relation to contracts, investment, land and property, financing and taxation. The building of relationships with cadres is often most easily undertaken through the exchange of gifts. Material and non-material gift exchange helps launch reciprocal assistance and continuing indebtedness between parties. In that sense, gift exchange can be understood as a process of building interpersonal relationships to facilitate economic activities. Businessman Uncle Fong elaborates that pleasing cadres' family members is crucial. He says,

> If you want cadres to give assistance to your career, then you have to be prepared to provide more gifts and money. You're not only setting out to please the cadres themselves, but also their family members – their wives, sons or daughters. I and my wife usually go to Hong Kong to buy jewellery, birds' nests, Rolexes, gold and brand-name handbags [like LV, Gucci and Prada] in order to please cadres' wives, sons and daughters and even other relatives. **(Uncle Fong, 48, entrepreneur)**

Businessmen Uncle Beck and Uncle Moss echo the words of Uncle Fong. The more expensive the wines and cigarettes, the more sincere you will appear in the eyes of the cadres. Uncle Beck says,

> The price paid for a dinner shows the value you place on the connection. And it also says a lot to the cadres about the sincerity of your commitment. It is also quite common to spend a few thousand RMB on famous branded wines or cigarettes for the cadres. **(Uncle Beck, 56, entrepreneur)**

Uncle Moss tells me that he will have a greater chance of succeeding and maintaining a good relationship with that cadre if he pays 'gigantic' *laisee*.[1]

> Most of our friends compare how much *laisee* or red packet money we give to cadres for their birthday, for their family's birthdays, for their children's marriage or even for their funeral. The more money you give, the more sincerity you show. **(Uncle Moss, 48, entrepreneur)**

Social connections are most evident in social events, which provide a venue for 'extra legal functions'. In China, it is commonplace, and indeed almost expected, to pay respect to and maintain or improve connections with local cadres through gift-giving (Yang 1989, 1994), especially during the Chinese New Year or the Mid Autumn Festival. Gifts are not just mooncakes, or the like, but also contain cash.

> One of the more influential cadres in Guangdong province always receives a lot of gifts from different kinds of people. But these people [cadres] are always too busy to take care of those gifts, which are processed by their domestic helpers, who put the gifts away for a while and then throw them out when the freshness of the moon-cakes is expired. The cleaning ladies who scrounge mooncakes for a living may well be blessed with an unforeseen income, as there is nothing but money inside those gifts. Wine and cigarettes are among the popular items for this and red packets also. (**Uncle Tony, 50, entrepreneur**)

In such cases, *guanxi* goes beyond mere emotional bonding and becomes a quasi-formal structural element of the Chinese new middle class. Even as a special form of *guanxi*, interpersonal exchanges are still normally, in terms of reciprocal obligations, where a cycle of gift exchange takes place to assure the value of wages, contracts or donations (Migone 2007: 182). Like the regular *guanxi*, the exchange of favours is trans-acted through emotional expressions of sentiment (*ganqing* 感情), human feelings or compassion (*renqing* 人情) and face (*mianzi* 面子) (Yang 1989, 1994). Interviewees never tire of pointing out that inter-personal relationships have been of supreme importance in China since time immemorial (see also Anderson & Lee 2008). In fact, many of the interviewees go on regular shopping sprees in Hong Kong, buying expensive merchandise as a favour to cadres and entrepreneurs back home. The maxim is, 'The more gifts you provide, the more business opportunities you will get. The more you pay, the more you gain'. So the prevailing theory is you have to spend money to make money.

My interviewees reveal that *guanxi* networks and gift-giving are rather intricate in practice. Gift exchange in the Chinese context is hardly as straightforward as buying privileges with cash. It takes a certain degree of cultural understanding to sense where the balancing point is and how the value of the gift is assessed in non-monetary terms. In many cases, non-material gifts are more valuable than material ones because somehow they express a higher degree of friendship or loyalty. What matters more is not the gift itself but the message conveyed by the gift-giving (Ong 1999: 153; Yang 1989, 1994).

From my own participant observation, some of the Hong Kong middle class claim that they have trouble in maintaining a long-term business relationship with their Chinese counterparts, although they enjoy the same types of lifestyles and consumerism. The old generation are deemed the most inscrutable and inassimilable to the Hong Kong middle class because they have their own 'insideness' (Wank 1999). 'Insider categories', through a sense of solidarity and mutual sentiments, set up reciprocal relationships within the class boundary. The sense of solidarity and mutual sentiments comes from having the same forms of lifestyle practices, which in this context mean having matching accents, matching dialects, similar kinship, or blood relationships or even the same surname. In the context of the Chinese new middle class, one develops a connecting train of thought with a common acquaintance by infusing a common identity into two people which draws them into a single circle of 'insideness' (Wank 1999: 164). In a broader sense, whether or not the new middle class actually gathers together on their matching forms of lifestyle practices is an unclear matter of circumstances. Nevertheless these are all elements of culture and refer to cultural practices in everyday life.

Since the *guanxi* network builds on the common attributes of its members, it can be regarded as the lifeblood of the development of private entrepreneurs everywhere in China (Tsai 2007). These *guanxi*-network relationships could either be seen as a form of corruption or be rationalised more innocuously as a practical means of reducing transaction costs in a transitional economy. What is clear is that strong ties often exist between cadres and entrepreneurs. This is because *guanxi* embodies the idea of social closeness. A society that still operates on relationship networks almost in the way of an institutional process will have the kind of atmosphere that carries on with a rule-*by*-law spirit of governance.

The problem is that institutional governance in China today is now largely skewed towards dependence on social bonding rather than on institutional rules. Social bonding is now fully immersed in much of Chinese daily life and is manifested in a wide range of corruption and bribery that are otherwise regarded in liberal countries as a straightforward matter of procedure. For instance, applications for passports, residential permits, business registration, or property registrations are now all carried out with little regard to actual regulations. In this sense it is accurate to state that China has a weak 'rule of law'.

Weber (1951) considers the lack of trust in institutions in Chinese society to be the crucial factor in explaining why the development of credit and commercial activities in China was considerably hindered for much of the time in Chinese history (Faure 2008: 485). The Weberian argument (1951) is that the transaction costs of finding a reliable counterpart and negotiating a contract is extremely high in China where social capital (based on personal links, reciprocity, moral obligation and duty towards the community) remains important. If a 'proper' system of governance like those in liberal democracies were ever to appear in China, an absolute majority of Chinese people would have to follow rules and the influence of *guanxi* networks would be diminished substantially. Most of the Chinese new middle class, due to the lack of trust in institutions, are therefore reliant on *guanxi*.

## What do the cadres understand by the term *guanxi*?

In post-reform China, the cadres still play an influential and leading role. The bureaucratic hierarchy of the Chinese political system in many senses determines the personal interests of party or government officials in matters of power, promotion and, ultimately, corruption. Local protectionism is strong in many parts of China. The link between the fiscal revenue of the state and the personal interests of officials lies in the omnipresent and unchecked power of the Chinese state apparatus. But most of the cadres think that even if they have received gifts from citizens or from their friends, they have integrity and are honest in upholding the doctrines of justice, equality, and transparency as local cadres. All cadres (11 out of 11) say their work units give them clear operating instructions and even run courses on how to avoid corruption.

> My work unit often keeps us informed about the integrity of the PRC and CCP. We cannot receive any gifts, presents, money and cash from citizens. (**Aunt Monica, 60, cadre**)

> Our work unit is very transparent. If someone wants to obtain a business registration certificate, it's very easy to do so in Guangdong without bribery. The residents come to our office to ask for our help, but we ask them not to bribe us. (**Uncle Leung, 48, cadre**)

One cadre thinks China is actually moving towards democracy and the village election is the breakthrough for democracy in China.

Now, villagers in many parts of China can exercise their right to elect their representatives. The pace of political development in China can be neither slow nor too fast. Political democracy should be achieved only step by step, otherwise it may go out of control. China has already done a good job in improving democratic development. **(Uncle Leung, 48, cadre)**

The aforementioned cadres see that political development in China today is much better than in pre-reform times. *Guanxi* is not directly related to corruption since even the Western democratic political system has instances of corruption. They see that one-party rule is suitable for China, which has improved a great deal in political terms.

The official account of the cadres is that they think government departments are increasingly transparent and more workmanlike, so that the average person is able to deal with officials directly without recourse to social connections or giving gifts. Most of the cadres gave an official account about their integrity and honesty to the PRC or the CCP. Uncle Fang, an influential cadre, usually receives gifts from professionals and entrepreneurs. Uncle Fang says,

My work unit often invites professors from Tsinghua University (which ranked No. 1 in China in 2010) to give lectures on socialism, politics and economics so that I can be up to date and keep up with what's going on in society as well as in the current political and economic systems. They always instruct us on how to avoid corruption and say 'no' to gifts and money. The Communist Party gives us clear instructions. We vowed not to receive gifts from our friends, partners, colleagues and relatives when we agreed to become Communist Party members. I remind myself repeatedly to follow these guiding principles. **(Uncle Fang, 49, cadre)**

But when I asked Uncle Fang whether or not he would receive red packets or gifts, he said that cadres are not allowed to receive gifts from 'citizens', by which he means the ordinary members of the public. Professionals and entrepreneurs are not classified as ordinary citizens; they can afford the expenditure and it also represents payments for the role of cadres in facilitating the businesses from which their incomes derive. With regard to the 'ordinary citizens', he is required to maintain the high morale of the integrity and honesty of the cadres. The cadres in Guangdong are sufficiently well organised and enthusiastically good enough to service 'ordinary' Chinese citizens without any bribery and red packets. He continually receives admonition, education and indoctrination from the CCP and his working bureau that corruption and bribery are serious offences.

## The influential role of the cadre-entrepreneurship

As set out in Chapter 1 and Chapter 2, it is the majority of the old generation who are the main beneficiaries of the economic reforms introduced in recent decades. To what extent do the age-old Maoist social institutions (*danwei* and *hukou*) still play a role in the formation of the new middle class under China's reforms? The linkage between *danwei*, *hukou*, and *guanxi* are closely intertwined. Since the 1990s, most of the cadres 'jumped into the sea' (*xiahai*) and became entrepreneurs. But they still have close connections with their previous affiliations (work unit – *danwei*). *Danwei* is officially dismantled in rural China but it continues to operate in urban areas. Ultimately, *danwei* is a collection of welfare benefits because it is associated with the 'market situation' of some forms of employment. Given that *danwei* affects work situation and influences welfare, it also impacts on class relations. *Danwei* is significant in class distinction because of its role in forming *guanxi* networks inside the boundary of the Chinese new middle class. Therefore, *danwei* is a major institutional factor that directly contributes to the emergence of the Chinese new middle class. Most of the old generation have an urban *hukou* (household registration) once they get a job in state-owned enterprises. The *hukou* has been influential in post-reform China, forming an integral part of their households with a *specified legal residence*, which is registrable and registered with the public security apparatus. The *hukou* classification cannot be changed easily. Registrants receive unalike essential services and welfare benefits. Most of the Chinese new middle class prefer urban *hukou* since it is important for their children to study in the so-called key primary schools (*zhongdian xiaoxue*) as well as key secondary schools (*zhongdian zhongxue*).

By building up *guanxi* (关系) networks with political, social and cultural capital, many members of the Chinese new middle class convert these advantages into material wealth within their class boundary. The creation of a mixed-market socialist economy has not in fact eroded the institutional foundations of a cadres-dominated social hierarchy. That domination is attributable in large measure to the household registration system in operation since the late 1950s. The linkages between *danwei*, *hukou*, and *guanxi* are closely intertwined. The old generation of the new middle class have significant common experiences that they draw upon in their interactions. However, what binds them together is not just that they have experiences in common but that most entrepreneurs and professionals in the old generation were previously cadres. So for this generation, the roles are not clearly distinguished. The rise of a hybrid elite of 'cadre-entrepreneurs' (Nee 1989, 1991, 1996) is particularly significant in post-reform China. Thus, cadres are frequently also entrepreneurs, at least part-time, and professionals also engage in entrepreneurial activity. Equally, given continued state ownership, some positions – for example, in health – that in Western contexts would be identified as professional also overlap with cadre roles and provide opportunities for various kinds of private activities. In this way, it is not simply an issue that entrepreneurs need to make contact with cadres, for example, but that in some contexts, the entrepreneur in question is also a cadre. In this way, the different groups have no difficulty in understanding the world of the other and its expectations, because they occupy that world not just in terms of common background, but also in their everyday activities. When entrepreneurs talk about the qualities expected in a cadre they know what they are talking about not just in terms of their own entrepreneurial interests, but also because they have experiences themselves of occupying the role and facilitating similar entrepreneurial activities.

This explains the continued significance of cadres in a system that might otherwise be seen to be moving in the direction of a market system in which their role would be diminished. Cadres are the ones who have benefited the most from the economic reforms. They have job stability as well as *officio* and *ex officio* capabilities to mobilise resources that the state and the market both want. Aunt Jennifer, a veteran cadre, explains about doing business in post-reform China. She says,

> We cannot earn as much money as entrepreneurs and professionals, but we have certain powers. We are not influential cadres like central government officials, but they need our referrals and information when they do some part- time job or some consultancy work for each other. Most of them need our help. (**Aunt Jennifer, 53, cadre**)

Uncle Robert, previously a cadre, echoes Aunt Jennifer:

> On the criteria list of being a cadre, interpersonal networks come first and then your personal achievements. The basic entry-level salary is RMB5,000 [US$732 or £505] a month. Pay rises are possible.

Cadres have power. I also seek help from cadres. As a famous saying goes, 'It is beneficial for your business if you have connections at Court.' Corruption can also be found among officials of the Anti-Corruption Bureau. The reason is that their income is very low. **(Uncle Robert, 50, entrepreneur)**

Another entrepreneur, a former cadre and vice-director of a factory in a collectively-owned company, gained his networks in state-owned enterprises, which meant that it was easy for him to develop his 'special business' with *guanxi* networks before setting up his business in Guangdong:

Luckily for my established networks and connections with my existing colleagues [cadres], I chose here [Guangdong] as my base. I had worked in the government bureau for fifteen years and established networks with many cadres in Guangdong. I rented land and set up my cement factory in 1995. If your network connections are poor, officialdom will make trouble for you even if you've done nothing wrong. **(Uncle Henry, 50, entrepreneur)**

There are two types of cadre. Administrative cadres (*xingzheng ganbu* 行政干部) are those in major government establishments at the municipal, town or village levels. For want of a better term, they are civil servants or government officials. 'Business cadres' or operational/line cadres (*shiye ganbu* 事业干部) (this is not the official differentiation, but I learnt from the interviewees of Chinese new middle class of the differences) are effectively state or government employees who operate in state-affiliated organisations such as hospitals, schools, public utilities, and so on in a kind of semi-professionalised capacity.

In theory at least, administrative cadres (much like any other civil servants across the world) are barred on penalty of dismissal from running private businesses or making personal gains from their activities. In reality, many administrative and business cadres have outside jobs and investments through unreported collaborations with entrepreneurs and professionals. This is no secret and they did not mind sharing it with the researcher.

I'm also engaged in capital construction with my secondary-school classmates – and there's no need for us to report profits to our superiors. In addition, my wife and I also run a real-estate business. Actually, most cadres in China are engaged in their own businesses. **(Uncle Leung, 48, cadre)**

I'm an engineer in a government department. I run my own business in pile drivers and escalators, and I often take up different projects. This is my way to survive. (**Uncle Chan, 60, professional and cadre**)

We always do some consultancy to private corporations, including land developers and national enterprises. It is normal to have a part-time job, but you cannot be greedy and obviously corrupt. (**Uncle Man, 40, professional and cadre**)

My workplace doesn't prevent me from working part-time jobs or having other investments. No one has the time to check up and investigate whether or not you have additional involvements outside of the workplace if you are not too greedy. (**Aunt Jane, 40, professional and cadre**)

Most of the cadres have part-time jobs. The average basic salary of most cadres is only around RMB5,000 (US$732 or £505) a month. If a cadre refuses grey income or *laisee* money, the question in the minds of most professionals and entrepreneurs is: how is it possible for the cadre to support his fairly prosperous life? Indeed, the constant receiving of gifts and favours is the *modus vivendi* in the professional life of a cadre. It has been said that one of the traits of a successful cadre is to be acquisitive without being avaricious. Uncle Chung updates me on how the quality of the cadre has a direct relationship with the *laisee* money.

The quality of the cadres is very questionable. They cannot speak clearly and coherently in public. They definitely get promoted not because of their talent but because of their *guanxi* with their supervisors. They give gifts like birds' nests, diamonds and branded goods to bribe their supervisors or other influential cadres in Guangdong. (**Uncle Chung, 56, entrepreneur**)

Most of our entrepreneurs and professionals echo the following saying with the researcher:

Don't you see that many regional cadres go to Hong Kong for shopping with cash only? They don't like to use credit cards because they don't want to have any record in black and white. They are afraid to reply to their emails. We meet face to face to settle every deal. All cadres are corrupt, but it all depends on the degree of corruption.

> It's normal to receive money and gifts from professionals and entre-
> preneurs. I can't believe cadres are not corrupt. (**Informal interview
> with Uncle Victor, 11 June 2008**)

Deep and close relationships developed in this way also extend into
business activities, as one entrepreneur illustrates in relation to the
sharing of work and costs:

> I know many regional cadres who have spent RMB600,000
> [US$87,796 or £60,605] purchasing a lychee garden, while others
> have spent more than RMB 6 million [US$877,960 or £606,050] dec-
> orating two three-storey houses that are being built nearby. Also, a
> dozen gardeners were hired to work on the lychee garden. Some
> regional cadres have spent RMB100,000 [around US$14,631 or
> £10,004] on providing an access road to the lychee garden, while
> and one cadre spent more than RMB100,000 on road renovations
> and repairs like paving the road with cobblestones. Most of the
> money has come not directly from their salaries, but from the red
> packets they received in their work. (**Uncle Fong, 48, entrepreneur**)

Raymond, a doctor, echoes Uncle Fong,

> The norm for both administrative and executive cadres is to moon-
> light and receive gifts from fellow doctors. The senior doctors spend
> the gift money on investments in Hong Kong or other places, other-
> wise they don't know how to make all this money look right if the
> authorities start inspecting. That's why so many mainlanders spend
> at least a hundred thousand dollars on buying flats and on con-
> sumption in Hong Kong. It is very common for doctors, lawyers and
> engineers to bribe cadres to buy houses. Usually they can buy a
> house at a cheap price. Normally, for example, I'll pay RMB600,000
> [US$87,777 or £60,313] when buying a house. Of the total cost,
> forty percent goes to the estate agent, forty percent to government
> officials and only twenty percent goes to buying the actual house
> itself. (**Raymond, 30, professional and cadre**)

The norm for both administrative and executive cadres is to moonlight
without reporting the fact to their establishments. It is observed that if
the cadres are not greedy, brash, obvious, and overmaterialistic, neither
their close colleagues nor friends will report to their supervisors.

Professionals have appeared abruptly on the scene in post-reform China. The Communist Party had long regarded them with political suspicion mainly because of Mao Zedong's love–hate attitude towards intellectuals (Laliberte & Lanteigne 2008; Ryan & Musiol 2008). That stance turned around after Deng Xiaoping rose to power and the economic reforms started in the 1980s. Deng and other pragmatists took the view that it was possible and necessary for the party to make use of capitalism to strengthen its political legitimacy and also to fend off any negative political consequences (Zheng 2004). The definition of the 'professional' in the post-reform era is somewhat different from that of Mao's regime. The professional in the reform era possesses a marketable skill based in knowledge that is organised and sanctioned by a corporate body. Those professionals in post-reform China should usually define themselves in meritocratic terms (expert, *'zhuan'* 专) and by political allegiance (red, *'hong'* 红), but not only based on the latter.

In the switch from a socialist economy to a capitalist one, professionals are mostly of the view that breaking free from the risks of poverty is only achieved through industriousness and education. But many professionals know full well that cultural capital alone is not the magic wand to success. Of course, there is no denying that cultural capital (in the form of education) helps get people better jobs and work partners. In addition to meritocratic requirements, it is also true that doctors, lawyers, and academics normally get a job or work opportunities through the social networking of old school friends. Therefore, social capital is a necessary ingredient for stabilising or safeguarding the job (Goodman 2008: 167; Li 2010; Hasan 2005). With this social capital, professionals, cadres, and entrepreneurs form their class boundaries, based on *laisee* and *guanxi* networks.

A doctor who works in the public/state sector is in fact a professional and a cadre rolled into one, and this is particularly true in the case of senior-level medical practitioners. There is keen competition for professional appointments and doctors compete with one another for special treatment from their superiors.

Without any social connection, it's very difficult for me to find work in hospitals – and public hospitals especially. Thanks to a relative, I got a job as a doctor in this hospital. I do hope he will always help me. If you know a senior doctor and he wants to employ you, then he'll put out a recruitment notice according to your personal particulars. The recruitment target, male or female, the required qualifications or working experience – these things will all be confirmed beforehand. There's no such thing as 'transparency' – even the superiors emphasise that – it's all ridiculous, and a lot of information is kept well in the dark. **(Raymond, 30, professional and cadre)**

That is a common experience for doctors in China today. A careful use of social connections could help even an inexperienced or under-qualified doctor to get a hospital job without too much trouble. By contrast, good doctors with few or no social connections could end up working in places like Hunan, Hebei, or Sichuan where incomes are low even for doctors and lawyers. In Guangdong, however, the incomes of public-sector doctors are relatively high. Moreover, many public-sector doctors supplement their official incomes with 'grey' income from work undertaken outside their official hospital duties. It is quite common for them to work as private family doctors (i.e. general practitioners), run private clinics or other businesses, invest in the stock or property markets, or just teach at a college or university. Many doctors take every opportunity to secure a second income. Indeed, for many, the sideline often proves to be the gateway to personal fortune. As both a professional and a cadre, the doctor is particularly able by position and training to earn extra incomes and mobilise resources for it. That ultimately becomes a motivator for many doctors to stay on in the government sector rather than break out into the private sector.

In addition to the official and grey salary, public-sector doctors normally receive gifts and emoluments from fellow doctors as well as from patients. They circumvent official auditing by spending or investing gift money outside the country, usually in Hong Kong. Evading traceability by supervising authorities may explain why so many of the Chinese new middle class are able to spend upwards of RMB1 million (US$146,316 or £99,796) on buying a flat without needing a mortgage.

Some Guangdong public hospitals already allow doctors to take up officially arranged or permitted secondary jobs because of the low level of official salaries. The health authorities let doctors give and receive red packets, so long as it only involves their own patients. However, *songhongbao* (literally means giving red envelopes or packets) is very necessary if you want to maintain good relations with your superiors. Most Chinese usually give gifts to cadres or other influential people to help them to get things done during the Lunar Chinese New Year, Mid Autumn Festival, Labour Day (1 May) and National Day (1–3 October). Holiday corruption is the *hongbao*: red envelopes that traditionally contain gifts of money.

You can get other good benefits in the workplace. A doctor comments,

> If you can maintain a good working relationship with your supervisor, you'll be assigned to a better job with bonuses and commissions. You'll be asked to buy medicinal products, medicines or equipment. Not only will you get repaid for what you've paid out, but also be repaid ten to fifteen percent extra as a bonus for your hard work. But not every doctor gets such a privilege. This goes to those who are on good terms with their superiors. (**Aunt Jane, 40, professional and cadre**)

Chinese citizens enjoy by right many forms of free medical treatment in public hospitals. The cultural norm among the Chinese is to try and get a higher quality of treatment by using incentives like the red packets. If you are rich, you could expect to have a doctor specially assigned to you, in which case you are compelled to do *songhongbao*.

Conversely, your inability to *songhongbao* suggests that you might be in some sort of financial difficulty. No *hongbao* and you get rude and apathetic attitudes from a lot of medical personnel. Put out *hongbao* and their attitudes will be patient, serious and honest. The *hongbao* money becomes an additional allowance or commission for the doctor and, in fact, the extra cash can figure as a major portion of the monthly income. Aunt Jane is a senior doctor in Guangdong and the health authority she works for permits her to work part-time outside of the official workplace and also to make personal investments. She runs private clinics with her husband (also a doctor) who manages other clinics, a transport company, and a dockyard. Her father was a former director-in-charge of one hospital in Guangdong:

> With allowances and commissions from *songhongbao* my basic monthly income is actually RMB10,000 [£999]. My husband and I have two clinics. Also, we're medical consultants in government sectors and to private corporations. Only rich people call us for treatment. My patients are grateful to me because I've treated their illnesses well. I have investments in transport companies, property and land speculation, and own some shares. These extra investments have become a major part of my monthly income. (**Aunt Jane, 40, professional and cadre**)

Lawyers face a situation similar to that encountered by doctors. They need to have their own *guanxi* networks so that they can do their job efficiently. This is evident in the way in which land transactions are dealt with. When an entrepreneur seeks to buy land rights, he or she hires a high-level lawyer or senior lawyer to deal with land transaction procedures (Michelson 2007: 400). The latter will use their social capital from the government sector like the Bureau of Justice. Some of them were former bureau chiefs and deputy bureau chiefs from the Bureau of Justice who have left the government sector and established their own law firms in Guangdong. Therefore, they have close relationships with the police, prosecutors, and law courts at the local level. Most of the professionals make full use of their own social networks to enjoy preferential access to the land transaction procedures in Guangdong.

Uncle Man, a lawyer in one government sector, updated me about the situation of a lawyer in China today.

> I need to maintain good relationships with my colleagues in various sectors in order to be able to visit my clients (suspects or defendants) with convenience [*fangbian* 方便]. Without a network, I'd be unable to help my clients. It wouldn't be possible to accomplish things. **(Uncle Man, 40, professional and cadre)**

Most of the professionals and entrepreneurs will pander to and ingratiate themselves with the cadres. Lawyers are no exception. Private developers may outsource private law firms to host the contract procedures. The legal institutions do not always consist of properly trained lawyers. Even with the so-called lawyers present to sign the contract, it is hard to guarantee that they received formal training. There are terms used to describe this situation: 'black lawyers' (*hei lushi* 黑律师), 'fake lawyers' (*jia lushi* 假律师) and 'underground lawyers' (*di xia lusi* 地下律师) (Michelson 2007). The post-reform context is that the local policies are unsystematic and no authorised organisation exercises the formal power for the implementation of the existing land and property policies (Michelson 2007: 401).

Second, the land market, structured by ambiguous property rights, has helped produce rapid growth in urbanisation in coastal regions since 1988. That in itself has helped to encourage the emergence and evolution of the Chinese new middle class in those regions. China had no property developers before the 1980s. By 2001, there were 29,552 registered developers (State Bureau of Statistics 2002 in Zhu 2005: 1378).

> The ambiguity of the land reform makes me so confused. But I don't bother to know what the revisions are. I receive updated news from my friends who are ex-colleagues at state-owned enterprises. They

keep me updated and informed on where is the best place to invest. They reserve the 'gift' (land or apartment) for me while still observing the formalities of the process of so-called 'formal tendering'. **(Uncle Billy, 56, entrepreneur)**

Uncle Cheng, an entrepreneur, who is not an ex-cadre but who aligns his consumption patterns and lifestyles with those of his business partners like entrepreneurs, cadres and professionals, can buy an apartment before the formal procedures of land transaction.

There are no actual formal procedures of public tender or public auction. The most important aspect is whether you know the cadre or not. The so-called formal procedures of land transaction are only 'on show' by the regional officers [in Guangdong] to demonstrate that they are just, equal, professional and transparent. This is the 'show' and 'face' party only. I live here and I know what happens....
**(Uncle Cheng, 40, entrepreneur)**

Land-use rights (LURs) are a somewhat murky area following changes to the Chinese socialist land law. Prior to 1980, there was no investment or speculation in land in China. Article 10 of the 1982 State Law provides that all urban land belongs to 'the State' (i.e. the central government) and that suburban and rural land is under collective ownership unless the law specifies state ownership. The state and the collective own the lease of the land usually for a period of 20 years. Therefore, collectives own residential land and family land plots, so no individual and family is legally permitted to transfer land on their own to third parties unless proper conveyance permissions are obtained first. But the state and the collectives (*danwei*) still own the lease of the land though some of the cadres can manoeuvre via loopholes in the land law.

This situation changed in 1988. In that year, the National People's Congress passed a constitutional amendment that 'the right of land use can be transferred in accordance with the law' (Zhu 1999, 2002, 2005). Two years prior to the amendment, the Ministry of Land Management was set up to coordinate the use of state-owned urban land nationwide. The ministry operates in each local government through a Bureau of Land Management. Each bureau coordinates national policy on land use in the local jurisdiction and its work includes preparing yearly land-use plans, allocating quotas of farmland converted for non-farming use, issuing land-conversion permits, monitoring the sale of land-use rights, and collecting tax on land transactions (Ma & Wu 2005: 173).

The 1988 constitutional amendment legalised the leasing of public land such that urban land now becomes rentable to developers or users for a fixed term on payment of a lump sum to the central state (Zhang 1988). That means land-use rights are derivable from property rights. The state does not formally recognise these derived rights but it does not actively deny them. Therefore, land-use rights never automatically replace the long-standing system of administrative allocation of land. In fact, both systems coexist with each other (Ma & Wu 2005: 169; Zhu 2005).

The PRC seems to have systematic institutions to monitor the land reforms but these do not work in practice. There are still many collaborations among cadres, professionals and entrepreneurs that have been recorded, involving 1.2 billion square metres (1,200 square kilometres or 436 square miles) of urban land (Sun 2004: 36). The loss of state land assets through illicit land-use transfers has been estimated at around US$1.4 billion per annum since the late 1980s (Sun 2004). It is really the revenue from the asset that is lost, rather than the asset itself, since the leases remain state-owned or collectively-owned.

The Chinese government has put land-use rights into practice since the 1990s chiefly to counteract the problems faced by the public housing sector in an emerging market economy. Housing shortages began to surface in the 1980s soon after the economic reforms started. For a long time previously, the *danwei* was the primary housing provider in Chinese cities. *Danwei* built or provided affordable housing to employees usually at one-fifth the cost of commercial housing because *danwei* was able to acquire cheap land through administrative allocations. Bigger problems started appearing by the early 1990s. Many state enterprises went into financial trouble because of various episodes of global economic downturn. Many state enterprises in Guangdong started to sell their premium city-centre landholdings in a bid to rejuvenate their business or to stave off bankruptcy. Other state entities such as universities or even military or government establishments followed suit. Some state enterprises were given land through administrative means on the basis of capital investment plans (Ma & Wu 2005: 168). Some sold their landholdings by forming joint ventures with established property developers or directly to multinational companies (Ma & Wu 2005: 171).

I and my wife have been workers at state-owned enterprises since 1988. We have two apartments. I bought the two apartments (one 60m$^2$, the other 80m$^2$) which cost me around RMB80,000 (US$11,705 or £8,003) and RMB100, 000 (US$14,631 or £10,004) respectively from our *danwei* in 1993. I sold one apartment at a relatively high price in 2005. The other we have been leasing out since 1999. **(Uncle Ho, 49, entrepreneur)**

Uncle Yuen seems to concur with Uncle Ho.

I think this was the privilege of being a former cadre. I bought the apartments more cheaply (£15,003 for 100m$^2$) from our *danwei* in 1992. I sold it profitably in 2005 (at least 300% on the buying price since the market at that time was soaring). **(Uncle Yuen, 56, entrepreneur)**

Most of the housing was priced at *chengben* (cost 成本) price but not *biaozhun* (standard 标准) price before 1998. Most of the cadres benefited from the *chengben* price. The cadres or ex-cadres were heavily protected by the *chengben* price to buy their apartments. They gained extra discounts to buy public flats (10–20% of market prices) from their *danweis* (Lee & Zhu 2009; Li, C. L. 2009). In addition, before 1998, there was the so-called Existing Housing Stock Subsidy (EHSS) for the cadres. EHSS refers to the lump-sum housing subsidy provided to the cadres before 1998. The subsidy was based on the rank and number of working years to multiply cadres' wage level in 1998 (Li, C. L. 2009: 48–9). Therefore, most of the Chinese new middle class who worked in state-owned enterprises for more than ten years gained substantial subsidies from their *danweis* according to this calculation. This largely explains why they are the winners in post-reform China.

To alleviate the disparities between the poor and the rich in urban China, the housing monetisation policy (HMP) was announced in 1998 by the State Council (Lee & Zhu 2009; Li, C. L. 2009). All *danweis* were not allowed to build or buy housing from the market for any rental or development purpose. Instead cash subsidies would be given to the cadres to encourage high-income groups to buy private housing, while medium- and low-income groups are encouraged to buy low-cost housing (Lee & Zhu 2009: 39).

However, only SOE employees are eligible for the so-called 'recommodification of urban housing' (meaning that the *danwei*'s requirement to provide housing function to its staff was replaced by the market, for details see Davis 2003) of the HMP. Staff from private sectors and collective enterprises are totally excluded from the HMP. The HMP is being regarded as the marginalisation of city residents outside of the state system (Li, C. L. 2009: 54). Therefore, the so-called cadre-entrepreneurs

I considered in Chapter 1, are the winners under the system of land reforms.

*Danwei* to a certain extent regulates the land price. Some of them lease out housing units to parties unaffiliated with any *danwei* at higher-than-state-stipulated or even market prices, violating the applicable rules. The *danwei* and other state entities are able to do all this mainly because of a definitional uncertainty over ownership. Urban land con-stitutionally belongs to the public – but who is the public? And who represents the public? In the absence of any clear-cut answer, many *danweis* just set up land development companies to take advantage of their tax-exempt status with respect to their landholdings. These *danwei*-based companies often earn substantial profits when they trans-fer the land-use rights to commercial developers in the secondary land market (Ma & Wu 2005: 172). In the process, the *danwei* passes *de facto* rather than *de jure* property rights in state land to third parties (Macuse 1996) – a situation of *ultra vires* that any lawyer could recognise. Uncle Chan is familiar with this transition because his job closely relates to land transaction.

> I bought my house from my *danwei* in 1989 with RMB100,000 [£10,004] for 100m². This price, I think, is a least 50% lower than the market price in 1989 for a house of similar quality and size. When I bought it in 1989 we still thought it was a little bit expen-sive. Now, I sold this house in 2004 and at the same time, I used this money to buy other private houses. Of course, I was able to contact some of my ex-colleagues to buy the apartment at a rela-tively lower market price. Regulations are not taken seriously here [Guangdong]. It seems my *danwei* used its identity as a state-owned enterprise to earn profits by transferring land use rights to private commercial developers. I don't know any further details...this is all I can tell. (**Uncle Chan, 60, professional and cadre**)

The ability to behave *ultra vires* ultimately comes down to the power of the cadre operating in conjunction with entrepreneurs and legal pro-fessionals. If the cadre has the proper jurisdiction, he or she is the val-idator of the conveying of land-use rights. If not, he or she can fairly easily find the proper cadre to arrange for the desired result. The desired result comes in a number of ways, depending on which way best fits the interests of the transacting parties. In China today, leaseholds are acquirable by public tender [*zhaobiao* 招标] or by public auction [*paimai* 拍卖]. Both are formal and transparent methods. Of course, transactions are also done through private negotiation [*xieyi cuoshang* 协议磋商], which are not formal or transparent (Ma & Wu 2005). Predictably, most land in China is leased or transacted through negotiation. Table 4.1 presents the full picture of land allocation, mainly by private negotiation, but not by public tender or auction.

Table 4.1  Land allocation by different land-leasing methods

|  | Guangzhou | Shantou | Shenzhen |
| --- | --- | --- | --- |
| Lessor and period | 1992–2002 | 1992–99 | 1998–99 |
| Area leased | 251 sq. km | 17 sq. km | 36.4 sq. km |
| By private negotiation | 57% | 98.8% | 97.7% |
| By public tender | 42% (combined) | 1.2% (combined) | 2% |
| By public auction | | | 0.3% |

*Sources*: Shenzhen Bureau of Statistics (in Zhu 2005: 1372), Shantou Bureau of Statistics (2000), Li, C. (2009).

Guangdong provincial authorities do in fact have strict prohibitions on the sale and purchase of unfinished buildings in order to maintain social and market stability. The problem is that the government at the national and regional levels has at best weak control over the private sector. The government has little control over many quasi-state enterprises because they operate more like privately held enterprises in a market economy.

> My friends also do it the same way. They spend RMB1 million [US$146,316 or £99,796] buying quarries, petrol stations and other real estate. With the help of a friend of a cadre, I placed a reservation on some desirable building land. Dealers placed bids of RMB10 million [US$1.6 million or £1 million] for it, although RMB300,000 [£30,367]...had to go to local officials. This was a big deal but it guaranteed I could buy the land. Also, the bidding activities in Guangdong are not open to others. If the local authority chooses to publicise, what you're bidding for is unwanted building land. (**Uncle Fong, 48, entrepreneur**)

In fact, a substantial number of our entrepreneur interviewees managed to obtain low-priced apartments from ex-cadres. Many cadres obtained apartments from SOEs and sold them off to commercial developers in the early 1990s. However, if you don't have any connection and rich information from your cadre friends, you are the loser. Sunny is an entrepreneur and he shares his experience below.

> I needed a house urgently in 2006. I followed the formal procedures and approached the property agency near my office. I spent RMB1 million [US$146,316 or £99,796] on 100m². Since buying that house, I have learnt from my friends that 40% (of my total budget) goes on land and to the property developer, 40% goes to government officials and 20% goes to the contractor. If I network with the cadre beforehand, I can save up my 40% of my budget. It's a huge difference. That's unfair, isn't it? **(Sunny, 34, entrepreneur)**

This is a recurring storyline from our entrepreneur interviewees. Some who owned suburban farmlands in the province became obviously rich, mainly from converting farmland into residential buildings that they let out. Uncle Pan was previously a cadre. He comes from a peasant family and his family has owned some lands in the peripheral area around Guangdong. He says:

> Developers contacted me about my farmland. I'm native to the area, owned some farmland in my village that belonged to the suburban area in 2000 but was converted to cosmopolitan shopping malls or residential areas in Guangdong. I was lucky. I couldn't believe my dreams of becoming a millionaire were coming true, and all thanks to the help from my friends, ex-cadres. After I sold all of my farmland, I quit my job in state-owned enterprises and teamed up with my partners to set up my own property investment company here [in Guangdong]. **(Uncle Pan, 40, entrepreneur)**

The peasants living in the cities in China also benefit from the burgeoning economy in post-reform China (Zhou 1996; Ho 2001). They sell some farmland to the government. Uncle Pan's recollection concurs with depictions in the literature by many sociologists, such as Ma & Wu (2005), Zhu (1999, 2002, 2005), Ho (2001) and Li, C. L. (2009). Cadres have taken on a leading role in stimulating the market for private property in Guangdong. Most land and private properties sold in the situations described by Uncle Pan are almost never sold by public tender or auction but by behind-the-scenes negotiation facilitated by meals and gift-giving. Officials and ex-managers of land-owning *danwei* are, in fact, among some of the more successful landbrokers. Those officials and ex-managers, like Uncle Pan himself, have connections to government agencies with responsibility for approving development projects or hold details about the availability of land lots. It is through such landbrokers that premium land parcels owned by *danwei* go to commercial developers (Ma & Wu 2005: 172).

With regard to housing units, some are leased out at higher-than-market prices (market prices tend to be the highest price, but some cadres can lease out at rates even higher than the market price) to people or establishments unaffiliated with any *danwei*, violating the applicable rules.

This explains why some cadres and ex-cadres such as Uncle Pan have become powerful personalities in land and housing acquisition in post-reform China (Ma & Wu 2005: 171). With political capital, cadres and ex-cadres are able to acquire land through behind-the-scenes channels at lower-than-market prices and then sell them to private developers at a substantial profit. However, not all the peasants have been benefiting from the transformation of urbanisation in Guangdong. If they don't have any friendship ties with regional cadres, they cannot benefit. Uncle Pan is lucky because he has close friendship ties with some cadres. But there are still many peasants who cannot receive profits although they want to sell their lands to private developers just like Uncle Pan. The close ties to regional cadres become the crucial factor for the peasants (if they have their lands) to get profits. I believe that to avoid the ambiguities of land polices, it is the responsibility of the central or local government to closely monitor the implementation of land policy and administration so that it can guarantee its social credibility (Ho 2001: 421). There is still considerable room for improvement in land and property restructuring in Guangdong.

## 'Special businesses'

'Special businesses' (*tezhong hangye* 特种行业) include hotels, tour agencies, fitness centres or salons, karaoke bars, massage parlours, sauna baths, and various entertainment establishments. These are quota-restricted businesses, so licences are difficult to obtain from the Licence Registration Bureau. In Guangdong province, it is not difficult to run a 'normal' businesses, but running a 'special business' is exceptionally difficult. Local authorities specify quotas on the number of entertainment clubs, hotels, travel agencies, bars, discotheques, restaurants, coffee shops and massage salons. The only way to launch these lines of business is through social connections with important people, i.e. regional party cadres.

A cadre explains the formal process of how a major government department such as the Industry and Commerce Bureau in Guangdong issues business licences:

> The Industry and Commerce Bureau will carefully investigate the nature of the business. If it involves prostitution or other 'exotic' elements, the Bureau will absolutely ban these illegal practices and crack down on prostitution in karaoke lounges, bars and nightclubs. Simultaneously, the Police Bureau will check to see if any karaoke sessions involve prostitution and 'exotic' business. Moreover, they will also check the sanitary situation, fire alarms, and safety facilities, to ascertain whether they fulfil specified Industry and Commerce Bureau regulations. The final decision of issuing special business licenses isn't decided by one person but is approved and decided by all of the committee members in the Bureau. (**Uncle Fang, 49, cadre**)

Guangdong provincial regulations prohibit the establishment and operation of an entertainment venue of a commercial performance nature until it has been issued with no fewer than four different licences: a 'business operation licence' by the Administrative Bureau for Industry and Commerce, a 'licence for entertainment business operation' by the Ministry of Culture, an 'inspection certificate of fire-fighting facilities' by the Fire Department, and a 'special business operation licence' by the Ministry of Public Security. The process of getting just one permit could take months or even a year or two.

However, ownership of a licensed 'special business' is a clear indicator that the business owner enjoys strong *guanxi* with the local authorities. A connection with a strategically placed cadre is the most effective and efficient way to circumvent compliance. Cadres still play an influential role in today's China. Most of the party-state is still in control over the scarce resources required in doing business, particularly bank loans and special business licences. Our entrepreneur interviewees confirm that such activities are quite usual in business licensing matters.

> Although getting business licences isn't difficult, the procedures are pretty complicated and bureaucratic. I tried for ten years before successfully getting one with the help of one of a good friend. He introduced me to a cadre. Everything can be settled through referrals and meetings in restaurants. The trade-off is to give red packets and gifts to

the cadres. This cadre helped me by arranging all matters relating to the setting up of the factories in a smooth, efficient way. Otherwise, if you want to get licenses for special industries in Guangdong, it is extremely difficult. **(Uncle Cheng, 40, entrepreneur)**

Part of the collaborative strategies involved is by reference to common tastes in everyday life practices in matters of food, fashion, entertainment, travel, cultural activities, smoking and drinking, and developing *guanxi*. A cadre confirms as much:

> I receive gifts and invitations to restaurants from friends and partners. I have the power to access certain documents related to setting up business in Guangdong. Everything about setting up a business should be directed to the Industry and Commerce Bureau. Some clients will buy air tickets and provide hotel accommodation for me because they want everything to be handled in a smooth, efficient manner and do away with formal bureaucratic procedures. I am selective about the gifts I receive as I get so many requests. **(Uncle Yip, 48, cadre)**

Most entertainment venues are located in upstairs premises, thereby creating a complication in terms of property rights for the premises, and quite a number of them do not hold occupation permits. That is why many of these venues are unlicensed in their operation. The authorities generally tend not to investigate licensing status, contrary to specified regulations. By virtue of the existence of unlicensed establishments and the concurrent failure of the authorities in enforcing health and safety requirements, that state of affairs points to a potentially significant level of collusion between local officials and interest groups. Owners of such venues are too impatient and business-wise to go through the massive amount of red tape. They instead dodge the system by dealing directly with cadres in the government establishment who have the authority to shelve or delay regulatory oversight.

A 'special business' is often put into operation while licensing registration is still pending. Official inspection teams would be told that the venue is 'on the pending list of registrations' or, even more expediently, temporarily shut down while inspections are imminent. It is also highly likely that inspection team members (who are cadres themselves) are recipients of bribes and so turn a very blind eye to such matters. The problem is quite insidious within the 'special business' sector, and it is an open secret that many such venues are partly owned by government officials (*Ming Pao Daily* 2008).

On one occasion I was invited by a member of the new middle class to a karaoke session. It soon transpired that prostitution and other 'exotic' business was also going on in the venue. Women in heavy makeup and low-cut dresses half exposing their cleavage were sent in to 'work the floor'[2] there (Zheng 2005 in Lee 2005). The venue, licensed as a 'special business', was subject to regular inspections by the police and the licensing authorities (usually once or twice a month). One can infer that the venue owner is well connected.

Anecdotal evidence suggests that the authorities have long known about prostitution and other unlawful activities in many entertainment centres. They have taken no action and instead act as if the activities are not going on. As one regional cadre says:

> If my friends need my help, I help them wholeheartedly. I really don't like to have to turn them down or cancel their special business licences if and when their entertainment places involve prostitution or erotic business. I may have to depend on their help when I want to set up a business of my own in the future. (**Uncle Yip, 48, cadre**)

Uncle Yip's conversation (above) confirmed that the Chinese new middle class have a common social circle in their everyday lives. It's a reciprocal relation and trust for their friends and business partners. The Guangdong Police Bureau is the most powerful of all in the province and is the one that is particularly prone to bribery. Uncle Fong says:

> When you report cases of prostitution and erotic business in places of entertainment, the police come quickly, often within five minutes. The reason is that they will be receiving bribes from the owner of the business, who will cope with the situation immediately. Usually, the owner will bribe the police with money to prevent them from disclosing the scandal to the public. Otherwise, their reputation will be affected. However, when you report cases like robberies and theft, the police are late in coming because they need time to handle and solve them, which usually involves red tape. These cases don't affect an individual's reputation and prestige, so the police require more time and effort to solve them. Normally they come late. (**Uncle Fong, 48, entrepreneur**)

I can infer from my interviews and dialogues with cadres that they are nearly always the first port of call when one attempts to solve problems. Cadres would be bribed to keep scandals from erupting into the open. Cadres in leading government departments would not intervene even if prostitution or serious criminal activities were established in entertainment centres. The standard operating procedure among cadres is to maintain the status quo, unless the central government orders otherwise. The authorities know full well what is happening, where it is happening, by whom and with whom. They will do nothing, certainly nothing on their own initiative. No licence will be revoked and no police will come. If cadres' hands have been greased, action is even less forthcoming. Bribing regional cadres is the best ticket out of trouble.

## The privileges of cadre-entrepreneurship

As economically important as entrepreneurs are, they need to maintain close relationships with cadres and professionals to upkeep their businesses. Currying favour is a two-way street: cadres also want to develop good relations with entrepreneurs, especially those connected with multinational corporations. The only awkward part is that relationship building with cadres is less straightforward than with entrepreneurs or professionals. The reason is that the cadre is the human interface of the state and that makes the nature of the work carried out by the cadre a sensitive one. Therefore, building relationships with a cadre relies more on having a prior trusted introduction. The status, integrity, and credibility of the introduction could be crucial. As one interviewee explains:

> I'm used to maintaining good relations with regional cadres like the police bureau, tax bureau, industry and commerce bureau and licence registration bureau. Relationships between professionals and regional cadres are interdependent and intertwined. If a reliable and trustful person isn't introducing you, the regional cadre won't dare to take your red packet and gifts. Regional cadres are now very cautious simply because they don't know your background. They don't know whether you're a spy from the central government or from western countries to test the water or probe the honesty of regional cadres in China. It's useless for you to have in-depth interviews with regional cadres. They won't tell you the truth. (**Uncle Fong, 48, entrepreneur**)

Uncle Bryan, who was previously a cadre (as vice director of a factory), says he built his networks over the years when he worked in various state enterprises. He updates me on the differences between *guanxi* in China and in Western countries.

> Cadres and professionals need to maintain good relationships with each other. You don't know when you will need someone's help. I think everywhere is the same. Even Western countries still practice *guanxi,* but within a different context. **(Uncle Bryan, 40, entrepreneur)**

It seems universally true that human relationships (*guanxi*) are of significant importance in everyone's career development, particularly (if not only) in China. Most of the Chinese new middle class (40 out of 59) tell me that you may not need close business partners or friends, but the primary caveat is that you don't have any enemies within your class boundaries of the Chinese new middle class. Guangdong is such a small place and any foe will hinder their business expansions. But the major difference between Western countries and China is that *guanxi* is a formal and institutionalised habitus in China. The Chinese new middle class relies on *guanxi* as a 'code of law' or 'rule by law'. The advantage of cadre-entrepreneurship is a crucial factor for them to form business partners within their same class boundaries as I argued in Chapter 1.

Most of the entrepreneurs are former cadres. They have close connections with the remaining cadres in Guangdong province. The collaboration among the Chinese new middle class is the result of shared lifestyles, tastes, collective memories, and shared profit-making. The most important aspect, however, is that most of the Chinese new middle class are members of the Chinese Communist Party (*dangyuan* 党员) and membership is the entry point for collaborations. Entrepreneurs and professionals have typically made fortunes by colluding with influential cadres, or have taken advantage of market chaos to get away with the ambiguity and incompleteness of institutional polices (Li, C. L. 2009).

In 1998 only 46 out of the more than 2,000 representatives of the Ninth Chinese People's Political Consultative Conference were private businesspeople (Zheng 2004: 74, Li *et al.* 2006). The state is effectively the single largest employer in the country. There were all together 30,000,000 cadres in China in 2008 (*China National Bureau of Statistics* 2009). The state (and therefore the party) is still prominent in managing the country's flow of funds, from loans for foreign investment to subsidies via local banks. The state is a major source of capital and the chief controller of the use of capital throughout the country at all levels. The corporatist and exclusionary relationship between politics (the state) and economics (the business world) is forged by the economic reforms and restricts the autonomy of capital. Therefore, private entrepreneurs are compelled to cooperate with the state as part of their risk management strategy to protect investments (Li 2003: 78).

The Chinese middle class is in a good position to borrow money from the Chinese government to take on big projects such as collaborating with different parties to build entertainment establishments and shopping streets in Guangdong. Broadly speaking, private companies in China have a hard time getting bank loans. Having the right kind of public sponsors and the proper cooperation with bank officers significantly eases the difficulty.

In China, local banks are considered to be administrative agencies because they are delegated the work of dispensing state subsidies to state enterprises and collectively-owned corporations under the guise of loans. If you have the right connections with administrative cadres, one (as an entrepreneur or professional) could probably collaborate on difficult kinds of investments or business areas at the provincial level. Some cadres interviewed for this study say that they have had business ventures with professionals and other cadres since the 1980s using bank loans that were secured through their well-established network of fellow cadres in the local government and local banks. An example below from Uncle Tang will show the general situation with reference to entertainment establishments and shopping streets.

Uncle Tang is a cadre who went into business with other entrepreneurs in 1993. They were partners in a joint project with a Japanese company to set up a resort and entertainment centre somewhere in southern China. The all-inclusive facility has hotels, parks and gardens, farms and stables, a golf course, bars, restaurants, nightclubs, massage saloons, karaoke lounges, pools and sports and recreational centres, all set in a beautiful landscape. The resort resembles the famous Country Garden (Biguiyuan 碧桂园)[3] and other famous property development in Guangdong (not undertaken by Uncle Tang). Uncle Tang's group of principals borrowed RMB5 million (US$731,689 or £504,212) from local banks and another RMB5 million from the local government, investing a total of around RMB9 million (US$1,317,041 or £907,582) in the project. The *bu* (部 the regional administrative level of the government) in Guangdong approved their development plan.

Although the principals on the Chinese side have to repay the loans before even making a return on investment, Uncle Tang says it was very easy for a regional cadre in Guangdong like him to obtain resources such as loans, investment rights, and the priority processing of licensing documentation. Apart from that project, Uncle Tang also borrowed RMB5 million (£504,212) from the local government to invest in a complex of commercial and residential buildings elsewhere in Guangdong province. Uncle Tang's case is a fine example of the high degree of autonomy cadres and ex-cadres enjoy when they engage in business or other activities that are otherwise restricted or banned by their workplace regulations. Uncle Tang is a cadre of a land-owning *danwei*. His close relationship with the local government and banks stems from his position as a party secretary in the 1980s and son of a former cadre. In our example above, he sets up an outside company and simply transfers the land-use rights of the *danwei*-owned land to developers in the secondary property market for a large profit (Ma & Wu 2005: 172). Uncle Tang says that if he were not a cadre, he would be unable to make outside investments or engage in outside business or qualify to borrow from the local government or the local banks. He reaffirms the opinions of many that cadres today have more advantages than ever before, especially in Guangdong province where already ambiguous local policies or regulations are enforced more laxly to regulate relationships between cadres and entrepreneurs.

Many entrepreneurs have set up local chambers of commerce as an institutionalised way to assure and enhance self-sufficiency and to seek to formalise relations with the state (Cheng 2000: 70). This then accounts for the heavy schedule of formal annual meetings, publication sponsorships, and exchange of information that goes on in most chambers of commerce in Guangdong. Many private entrepreneurs and professionals are eager to set up or join work-related institutions because good relations with the state stimulate improvements in their money-making potential. There is a feeling of vulnerability to political shocks among the new middle class after the vicissitudes of the 1989 Tiananmen Crisis. The numbers of private enterprises in China fell sharply following that event (and after the Asian and global economic crises of 2003 and 2008). The Chinese new middle class is more concerned about the consistency of official policies for the private sector and seeks whatever few political means are at hand to protect and advance commercial or social interests. This explains the eagerness of many entrepreneurs and professionals to join business associations and meet cadres, since officials exercise substantive power over commercial destinies. Professionals and entrepreneurs therefore prefer to wear the 'red hat' of a party member. They build or strengthen channels of communication for expressing concerns.

What is absent is a well-functioning system of courts to regulate relations. Most of my respondents stated that they have never used the national or provincial court systems to enforce contracts or solve problems. The Chinese court system is in fact quite rudimentary. Officers of the court are amenable to corruption and influence-peddling because their job positions are relatively low down the government hierarchy and their educational backgrounds are quite basic. Courts are also seriously compromised from an operational point of view in having to enforce sometimes contradictory statutes that are haphazardly enacted by different legislating bodies. Because courts are generally seen as ineffectual and their officers corruptible, the solution employed by the new middle class to use gifts is perhaps a more efficient and effectual problem-solving technique. Close personal ties with officials in government departments that supervise their areas of business activities can prevent administrative harassment. Gifts and favours to cadres in the police force can forestall investigations.

## Limits of *guanxi* networks for the young generation

*Guanxi* networks have become the main mechanism to do businesses. The young generation thinks that jobs are hard to come by and harder to hold down. They try to secure their footing in society by acquiring very high levels of cultural capital (education) and political capital. However, they also seem to find that the value of social capital for securing jobs is slowly diminishing over time.

Uncle Leung has a deep understanding of the importance of cultural capital. He earned his MA studying part-time.

> Now, education is an important threshold for your admission to any government institution. Lack of educational qualifications means that you have no guarantee of promising career prospects. Pursuing further studies is the critical factor for successful career prospects in today's China. We use written tests when recruiting regional cadres. That means more consideration will be given to your ability and skills, but less importance is attached to your interpersonal network. **(Uncle Leung, 48, cadre)**

The young generation needs to be more independent than the old generation in their careers, in that it has unprecedented autonomy in employment matters. The 'iron rice bowl' system that operated in the old days of state planning came to an end when the labour market became more market-led since the 1990s (Sheng & Settles 2006). Occupational mobility has become more common and the level of job security is reduced. The country no longer operates on the socialist package of lifelong employment, automatic job assignments, fixed salaries, housing, healthcare, retirement benefits, ration coupons, and so on (Hoffman 2006).

*Guanxi* plays an important role in job hunting but it is not a magic wand for the young generation (Guthrie 1998). There are two debates about the importance of *guanxi*. One version is that *guanxi* is becoming less significant in the hiring process in the sense that employers in China today are putting more weight on merit-based hiring policies. Recruiters are increasingly using more formal, standardised and transparent recruitment procedures. Recruiters are increasingly able to design procedures that safeguard the integrity of the hiring process.

One entrepreneur from a multinational enterprise says roughly the same thing:

> We have positions for accountants and administrative officers in our company. I have been invited to dinner by a number of people who hoped to entice me to offer these posts to their sons or daughters. There are many candidates applying for them. In the end, I offered the posts to the brightest candidates who were proficient in both English and Chinese and had good analytical and logical skills. I rejected candidates who tried to bribe me since they didn't perform well in the written test and interview. I think performance in the written test and in the group and individual interviews is very important. A bachelor's degree is essential. The *guanxi* network is important but it's not a magic wand. **(Uncle Jimmy, 49, entrepreneur)**

Today, job interviews often involve a variety of writing and aptitude tests plus one-on-one and group interviews. Many of the third and fourth generation of the Chinese new middle class have had similar experiences. Kong, a programmer in one multinational enterprise, says:

> Though my parents know some cadres, they couldn't help me find a good position in a foreign-owned business. I am not competitive enough to speak fluent English and don't have a good grounding in

it. I had to take courses to improve my spoken English. I sent out more than a thousand application letters for trainee posts with multinational companies. Initially, I didn't receive any responses. It took more than half a year before I was given my first written test. A standardised and strict recruitment process was in place. Finally I got a job after being short-listed for both individual and group interviews. **(Kong, 30, professional)**

The other version of the importance of *guanxi* is that it still plays an influential role in job hunting. Jiang, a professional, shares this perspective on the new development of *guanxi* networks in China. He says,

Education is only an entry ticket. The most important factor is the *guanxi* network. It seems that everyone has a bachelor's degree now. Someone may get a well-paid job in a state or national enterprise without any interview. Or they have already been selected, but you are still asked to attend an interview. **(Jiang, 31, professional)**

*Guanxi* sometimes is important only when the legal system related to the labour market is either weak or non-existent. Many of the Chinese new middle class accept *guanxi* ethics and apply them either consciously or unconsciously in interactions with others. This is because *guanxi* ethics arise from internalisation processes, such as from socialisation in the family unit and throughout the life course of the individual. Therefore, *guanxi* building and rebuilding becomes a habitus for most Chinese people (Huang 2008). It is clear that education is of paramount importance or at least that it is an entry ticket in today's China. But the middle-class children have comparative advantages over lower-class children in terms of securing a job or career. The young generation are generally more able to gain access to higher education if their parents also had higher education. Most of the young generation tend to have farsighted, broad horizons for their future. They also tend to have working plans in place to pursue prestigious job positions or high-end salaries due to the substantial seeking of *guanxi* network from their parents.

## Summary

In 'socialism with Chinese characteristics', national as well as local official policies in various areas are unclear or even non-existent. The lack of clarity gives rise to a degree of decentralisation and regionalism in urban China. Incompleteness and the fuzziness of institutional policies results in unique development and features of the new middle class, and this facilitates its collaborations within and outside its class boundary.

The ambiguity of reforms or restructuring in the land, property and *danwei* segments is still important to the Chinese new middle class because it provides it with manoeuvring room in the market. Some state-owned enterprises had closed down or were even transferred to private or multinational enterprises, and many cadres have used their insider positions to become wealthy (Chen 2003: 54; Roberts *et al.* 1999; Anderson & Lee 2008). Agents of state-owned enterprises make decisions for loans and land sales more by negotiations than by tender. A reciprocal relationship becomes established among cadres, professionals and entrepreneurs. The ambiguous property rights are to the advantage of local coalitions and at the expense of the land revenue to the central government. Cadres are clear beneficiaries (Zhu 2005: 1377) and become the leading targets for collaborations with professionals and entrepreneurs.

There are still some professionals and entrepreneurs who do not want to rely on *guanxi* networks. They prefer to rely on their credentials to find jobs by themselves or through head hunters. However, they also need connections to form special business, entertainment establishment and shopping centres. These are obtained through the channels of the chambers of commerce and social gatherings. While the importance of business principles and credentials also helps to accomplish things and reliance on *guanxi* is no longer sufficient by itself, the latter remains important. The unsystematic nature of most institutional structures in China today, and in the foreseeable future, simply encourages *guanxi* networks to fill the gap.

In Chapter 5 we'll explore more details about the identity of the Chinese new middle class and China's political development. The Chinese new middle class are in the vanguard of consumption, but they are not in the vanguard in terms of democratic advocacy.

# 5
# Class Formation and Political Development

There is no hope for Chinese politics. What is the meaning of *minzhu* [民主 democracy]? The citizenry is *min* (民 people) and the state is *zhu* [主 master]. We need to obey the state. I took part in the June Fourth movement when I was a university student. We couldn't say the June Fourth incident was a massacre – otherwise we'd expect to spend the rest of our lives in gaol. It is extremely useless to advocate democracy. If there is promise from the Chinese government to promote democracy, they are telling lies and the reality will never come true.

**(Uncle Yang, 40, professional)**

What roles or effects do economic reforms and globalisation have on the process of deconstructing political hierarchies in Chinese society today? My study finds that there are distinctive differences between the young and the old generation in terms of class culture. The young generation are individualistic, materialistic, and money-making in attitude. They seem to have moved away from traditional cultural values like frugality, modesty, self-restraint, and upholding the family reputation (Hui 1988; Faure 2008: 475). The old generation tends to be more collective in terms of personalised networks. But their distinctive solidarity is far from being a form of class consciousness, as it is normally understood. There are some similarities shared by both the young generation and the old generation. The fact that my interviewees, by and large, do not recognise themselves as members of the Chinese new middle class (or any other kind of middle class) speaks volumes that self-image and cultural identity is still in flux.

The Tocquevillean and modernisation theories argue that a burgeoning capitalist economy brings about democracy and civil society. Corporatist theory also asserts that state-created corporatist groups control or even suppress autonomous associational activities. However, those theories are not applicable to the relationships between the middle class and the state. With regards to political development and democratic development, the roles of the Chinese new middle class are dependent on the state. The Chinese new middle class and the Chinese government can be regarded as symbiotic, pragmatic and utilitarian. The cultivation of ties and *guanxi* (connections) is aimed to share the profits and interests derived from their mutual interaction and cooperation. This chapter finds that the Chinese new middle class tends to make good use of the business opportunities arising from the land and property reform mentioned in Chapter 4, that is, members of the new class are in no sense activists or agitators working against the government. Rather, the *guanxi* networks go beyond mere emotional bonding and become part of social capital, contributing to an extension of business webs of the growing middle class.

## Reconceptualising the Chinese new middle-class culture

It can be said that in the near future the Chinese new middle class is unlikely to act in a way resembling the middle classes of the West. It is not a pillar of society that advocates social and political change in China. The regime discourages and suppresses challenges to its rule from any quarter and any free expressions of political opinion. The Chinese new middle class is not, and does not see itself, as being in the vanguard of democratic advocacy. Whatever the Chinese new middle class might or might not be, it is a strong supporter of 'socialism with Chinese characteristics' and therefore allies itself with the government.

The Tocquevillean[1] and modernisation theories on democracy,[2] and corporatist theories are often applied or believed to be of relevance to China. Modernisation theory maintains that a country develops by moving from an agricultural economy to an urban, industrial, and service-oriented society. As a consequence of these structural changes, more people move to cities with concomitant expansions of education and job opportunities, rising incomes and living standards, a transformation of family structures from extended families to nuclear families, changes in social norms and ideologies, and the rise of consumerism. The rising interdependence and collaborations among various societal sectors promote economic prosperity, and bring about peace, democracy and civil society. The key agent for change in the process is the bourgeoisie (the new middle class), which transforms the regime into a democratic one. It is, however, not the case in the developing parts of East Asia. Focusing on the Indonesian civil society from the 1950s to the 1960s, Aspinall (2004: 62) says that 'most large civil society organizations were affiliated to political parties that aimed to hold or seize political power and civil society became a mechanism, not for generating civility and "social capital" but rather for magnifying socio-political conflict and transmitting it to the very bases of society'.[3] Alagappa (2004) also points out that in Singapore, the most Westernised society in East Asia, an active and strong civil society does not lead to a strong democracy.[4] It is even less likely in the yet still authoritarian China.[5]

Corporatism theory has two variant forms. One identifies how capitalism and nation-state consolidation challenge corporate organisations in society.[6] The second discusses how the state creates or incorporates different kinds of corporate organisations in society, like those formed by some of the Chinese new middle class.[7] Corporatism is supposed to thrive in strong authoritarian states (like China) that restrict political pluralism and freedom of association. Naturally, the Chinese new middle class, particularly entrepreneurs and professionals, works closely with the cadres. Therefore, they do not pose a challenge to the cardinal principles of the Communist regime. Unger (2008) concludes that 'China's major associations were in fact founded by the state and today remain firmly under the control of a state or Party agency'.[8] In short, they are state corporatist. I tend to use the concept of the contingent symbiosis (Spires 2011) to capture the relationship between the Chinese new middle class and the government (both central and provincial). Their relationships can be regarded as pragmatic, practical, and reciprocal. The exchange of mutual benefits and cooperation all depend on the profits and interests from their cooperation. They are in a contingent symbiosis relationship, rather than a hostile relationship. The word 'contingent' in general refers to a relationship that is 'dependent on or resulting from a future and as yet unknown event or circumstance' (*Encarta World English Dictionary* 1999: 411). In China, there is an argument that authoritarian rule is required to prevent massive chaos and dislocation during periods of rapid economic growth (Li 2006). Cadres still play an influential role in present-day China. A democracy in China is more likely to lead to the emergence of independent trade unions. It will in turn harm the vested interests of the new class. The party officials as well as the middle class have managed to come up with novel and creative ways of maintaining that rule. The non-confrontational policy of these bodies with respect to the party-state indicates that as yet any radical change towards the rise of civil society in China has not progressed beyond even a minimal level (Ma 2006: 208). The middle class is loath to confront the power elite in the party-state who are still in control over the scarce resources required to carry out business, particularly bank loans and special business licences. The business sector and political elite also have a shared interest in suppressing labour costs. In cases of social conflicts, members of the middle class remain docile and are supportive of the policies handed down by the Chinese government. Their pro-status quo stance seldom converts to political opposition or triggers any demands for political change. It is therefore less likely that the Chinese new middle class will become an agent for political change in China.

Chen and Dickens (2008) find that most of the entrepreneurs (the Chinese new middle class) prefer to maintain the status quo in China. They tend to support the conservative and authoritarian regimes in today's China and to act in accordance with the CCP's political policies in order to maintain a harmonious, peaceful, watchful, and conservative relationship with the state. They wish to fully utilise the advantages gained from their close ties with the CCP, like tax exemptions and a favourable investment environment. In cases of social conflicts, they remain silent and try to support the policies proposed by the Chinese government. They are never the political vanguards. Rather, both the Chinese government and the Chinese new middle class take good advantage of the extended *guanxi* networks to do business by collaborating with multinational enterprises.

All this explains why the Chinese new middle class is unable to form a uniquely 'new middle class' political culture. As China still lacks a progressive middle-class element in its social stratification, the question here is how the political stance of that new middle class will evolve and whether it will produce a middle-class political culture of the kind associated with the middle class in Western societies. Ever-widening income disparities, the waning capacity of the state to redistribute income fairly among its population, and the inability of social institutions to deliver timely and equitable public services all raise serious issues. But on the basis of the attitudes of those interviewed in this study, the new middle class is hardly the agency likely to address them. The weak degree of class awareness and class-based socialisation means that the Chinese new middle class are less prominent in Chinese social transformation than is the middle class in Western societies.

## The middle-class culture of the old generation

The old generation exhibit strong collective sentiments, but their collective identity is in terms of personalised networks rather than what might properly be thought of as a *class* consciousness. They are strongly collective oriented in terms of their collective experiences, but they are generally flexible (at least not static) in their methods, as social, business, and other conditions around keep changing in the post-reform era. Some have acquired additional marketable skills in order to maximise their personal and organisational competitiveness.

The old generation are quite cautious about the future, expressing a sense of uncertainty and anxiety about their status. Without higher cultural capital, they think that if processes are institutionalised they will have little room to manoeuvre.

> I cannot imagine what will happen if my factory collapses or the business goes bankrupt. I don't have a high level of education and marketable skills. What else can I do? Most jobs require a master's degree. I only finished senior high school and infrastructure is all I know about. Can I become an employee? I don't think so... **(Uncle Henry, 50, entrepreneur)**

The comparatively wealthy old generation in fact express the greatest extent of anxiety. They claim their businesses are potentially an anachronism. They do not have the business acumen to try another new business in a globalising China if their factories are forced to shut down. They don't know how to invest in the newly-developed industries such as IT, shares, funds and investment business. They don't have any marketable skills and foresight in accordance to social change. They are winners and reap profits simply by taking advantage of a cheap workforce and the favourable tax concessions introduced since the early 1990s. Self-interest dictates a cautious attitude towards the future and a reliance on the government to maintain the conditions for their continued success. Greater economic liberalisation, and further changes in the wake of globalisation, are among their fears. Insofar as political liberalisation and economic liberalisation are perceived to go hand-in-hand, the old generation is no advocate of the former. They are averse to the risks which may affect their future. Today, many Chinese invest in a diverse range of financial products at home and abroad. Real estate is a major investment area for the older new middle class, despite its having endured a long history of market downturns. It is very common to find the old generation investing in as many as eight shop premises for the sole purpose of earning profits from rising property values.

> I only know how to manufacture garments. I buy property because I am scared. I don't want to be poor again. It wasn't any fun being poor. I will need to rely on my former colleagues [cadres] and class-mates to seek out new opportunities if my factory closes someday. **(Uncle Chris, 49, entrepreneur)**

The central government started to implement macroeconomic regulatory measures around 1993 in an attempt to control the continual overheat-ing of the property market. Before then, many of the Chinese new middle class bought property at high prices, and when the property bubble burst, many suffered huge losses or had their investments wiped out.

> Most people like us were poor. We're now rich, but no one can guar-antee you won't become poor in future. I lost money in the stock market in the 1990s and now I'm much more cautious in managing my wealth and finances. A financial tsunami won't affect only me, but will impact on the whole family. I'm not young anymore. Luck won't always be with me. I have to be conservative and prudent in managing my finances. **(Uncle Victor, 50, entrepreneur)**

Some of them have never recovered from the property or share market fiasco in 2005–06. Those who did survive the mess became extremely cau-tious about matters in general – a fear that ranks only second to the primal fear of returning to the poverty from where they came. Therefore, the older new middle-class cadres and entrepreneurs in particular, are marked by a very cautious mentality in relation to investment in general, and towards securities, bonds, insurance, mortgages and other financial instruments in particular. The objective is to multiply the resources for their retirement years and preserve money and asset value for future gen-erations. Their orientation to the future is concerned with personal secu-rity and the most important experiences governing their attitudes lie in the past.

## The middle-class culture of the young generation

The young generation shows class identity in more individualised and mobile than collective ways (Mendez 2008). For want of a better description in today's China, the young generation exhibit the characteristics of a 'post-communist personality' (Wang 2002; Faure 2008: 476). That personality is apt to be individualistic, materialistic, and money-making in attitude (Ting & Chiu 2000; Ting *et al.* 1998; Sun 2004), while moving away from traditional cultural values such as frugality, modesty, self-restraint, and maintaining the family reputation (Faure 2008: 475). Although family reputation and personal social status may be important enough, they are inadequate on their own within the materialistic orientation of the personality. So a money-oriented attitude takes increased prominence. To prevent any possible demotion along the social strata, the Chinese new middle class resorts to 'extensive investment' in its social status and way of life.

Generally speaking, the young generation are good consumer targets of a wide range of retailers and service providers in China because of their high purchasing power relative to the rest of the population. Their consumption patterns tend to be based on a pleasure-seeking principle, fed by a growing need to be seen as modern and developing in line with the world outside China (Wang 2002; Faure 2008: 476). High purchasing power and pleasure-seeking consumption needs mean that there is a rising trend for the younger Chinese new middle class to buy real estate, invest in various financial instruments and gambling. They usually have mortgages and enjoy their lifestyles, rather than seeking to play an active role in politics. Indeed, the shift from production-oriented state-centred socialism to market-centred reforms is developing China as a consumer economy. In this way, the young generation is in the vanguard of a consumer society, with that consumerism replacing political ambitions. They do not seek to be cadres (except where it might be for personal advantage). They have not developed a different kind of political sensibility oriented to extending economic reforms into the political area.

The young generation, as I have explained in Chapter 3, need to work hard to maintain their competitive power. There is a kind of circularity to their life: they work hard for their needs, display their superiority to others, and then work hard again to sustain that superiority. In time, they seem to develop a sense of superiority by consuming conspicuously amid an anxiety about the origins and destination of their lives. Ironically, they also develop an almost outright adherence to sensual pleasures, a need for excitement, and sensationalism from nights out on the town. Night after night, they congregate around town after a hard day's work.

Personally, I think I was indeed 'poisoned' unconsciously. I was born into a competitive society in China and learned that the ends are more important than the means. For the majority of society, money comes with a nice job. A diploma from a famous university, certifications and academic awards tend to be the concern of the boss [in China], who will consider it important whether you graduated from a famous university or got a high GPA (grade point average) or not. I studied very hard for my undergraduate and master's degrees with a high GPA. Now I have a job, but it is not very stable. I usually go shopping twice per week. No one will see the effort you made and the pressure you endured. I am sick of this way of living and don't think we can do anything to improve this vicious circle. (**Melody, 28, professional**)

The other interviewees pinpoint the contract-based nature of employment as the other reason to explain why the young generation indulge in lavish consumption. The so-called prestigious university and brand-named company are ingrained in the young generation. This phenomenon makes people today more utilitarian and pragmatic. They think that grades represent everything and that employers only focus on their results and grades.

The contract-based nature of my job makes me insecure. I'm always uncertain about the future. I was forced to work hard to enter a more exclusive primary school, secondary school, and university. Now I need to work in a reasonably good company so that I can maintain a good quality of life and feed my parents or even my grandparents. Society doesn't pay too much attention to the process and the effort involved is somehow overlooked. Even if I don't like my job, it will at least allow my parents to show off in front of our relatives. This explains why I so often go shopping for brand-named goods. (**Ivy, 26, professional**)

Society changes rapidly and most of the young generation feel powerless and desperate to determine and shape their future. The contract-based job gives them a sense of insecurity (Liu 2008). Most of the young generation have well-organised plans, but have an unconscious concern that they cannot control their future. The market in China is growing. It is impossible for them to have a frugal life and they spend lavishly as a means to reduce their stress and lay aside uncertainties.

As argued in Chapter 3, the young generation know that today's China is potentially becoming increasingly institutionalised and formalised. Initially, laws and political policies allowed for a relatively more permissive or depoliticised enforcement of the *hukou* and *danwei* systems. The reforms have made it possible for the country to operate in a more deregulated mode and the young generation perceive this to be changing. Dan, a PhD holder, informed me that it is very difficult to get a full-time teaching post even though he wants to work in China. Currently, he can only find a part-time job in one university in China. He says,

> Four or five years ago, if you graduated abroad, whether from Hong Kong or further afield [the UK or the USA], your salary would be three times that of people educated in China. Now academia has been saturated. After many failed attempts, I cannot get a full time teaching post in China. There are many people with PhDs who studied in the USA and the UK; so many that my PhD seems valueless. I can get only a part time job. I feel lost and very uncertain about my future. **(Dan, 29, professional)**

Stiff competition for jobs and the ever-growing competitive nature of modern Chinese life means that social connections and the ability to use social networks for non-political purposes are both less effective and also perceived to be of great significance. Fai informed me that he belongs to the so-called post-80 generation group (in that he was born after the 1980s). In China this group is well-planned, flexible to change, individualistic, ambitious, and aspiring in their career planning. He reasonably cares about his future. Therefore, he is reasonably stressed. The post-80 generation groups need to be well-equipped themselves to face the challenges, both from their careers and with regard to political development in the future. He says,

> I need to be tough and independent. I got used to this sort of livelihood when I was a customer liaison officer two years ago. The job market is daunting in today's China. This explains why I want to be a boss [author's clarification: he resigned after working two years at a service company and has been an entrepreneur since 2006]. Most university students can only afford to live in a 'container' house (a tiny house like a container [*woju* 蜗居, *huoguiwu* 货柜屋[1]]) in Guangdong. Although they have a job, their low salaries cannot maintain their living standards here [in Guangdong]. It is extremely hard to get a position in today's China. I need to pay the mortgage

every month. I don't dare to have children yet. All this makes me stressed and insecure. **(Fai, 28, entrepreneur)**

Fai's conversation reasonably explains why the young generation place a great emphasis on the self and one's 'interior' life (Faure 2008: 476): on the individual level there is an effort to enhance personal development and achievement. In other words, members of the young generation think only on a personal interest level rather than on a higher level of making contributions to the improvement of general society.

## A Chinese middle-class culture in the making?

The transition to a market economy has allowed the emergence of a Chinese new middle class but it has yet to develop its own identity as a politically significant group. For the young generation, their consumption orientation seems to be an obstacle to any such identity formation. At least part of the problem is that many respondents make unreasonable comparisons of their lifestyles and circumstances with those of their counterparts in Western societies. Mary is a 25-year-old Guangdong native who works for an advertising agency. She was educated overseas at a renowned tertiary institution and holds a Master's degree from the United Kingdom. She makes around RMB100,000 (US$14,631 or £10,004) a year, owns an 80-square-metre flat and an imported car, and is artistically accomplished.

> All my salary goes on mortgage and car repayments. The mortgage will take more than 10 years to pay off. A holiday is a luxury to me. Somehow I relax whenever I can. The term 'middle class' sounds impressive but means nothing to me [*zhongchan, duo haoting de mingzi* 中产，多好听的名字]. If I don't have a lifestyle as good as that in the West, I can't honestly say that I am middle class. **(Mary, 25, professional)**

By the standards of most mainland Chinese, Mary is handsomely paid for her work and her parents enjoy high social prestige. However, high income does not necessarily equate with the kind of life that she believes is similar to the highly paid individuals in the West. Like most people of the Chinese new middle class, the pace of life for Mary is hectic and intense, with very large daily costs. To upkeep her high quality of lifestyle, she perceives herself as having to work harder and harder all the time.

Some members of the old generation make similar statements. Uncle Man is a professional and cadre, and the Chinese new middle-class identity seems too abstract to him. He says,

> Do I belong to the Chinese new middle class? I doubt it. I can't afford to buy a residential unit or a flat with the amount I have saved so far. I bought a house of about 80m$^2$ that cost me about RMB800,000 [US$117,154 or £80,938]. My mortgage is for thirty years. Now I have my own flat and car, but I find myself heavily indebted. **(Uncle Man, 40, professional and cadre)**

Of course, a mortgage is a key indicator of the emerging culture of the Chinese new middle class that it shares with the Western middle class. Equally, many members of the Western middle class also regard themselves as being money-rich, 'time poor'. Many of the Chinese new middle class grumble about their stressful life and about being constantly under great pressure. That China today is deficient in not having a comprehensive social-welfare policy helps to explain the lack of leisure time or leisure activities for most people. Many individuals are deeply concerned about raising sufficient resources to secure their future in old age and possible ill health.

Lamont (1992) finds that the American middle class is far less willing than are the French to establish class boundaries on the basis of cultural factors such as taste. The Americans prefer to establish moral boundaries instead. By contrast, the cultural and moral boundaries of the Chinese new middle class are different from either the Americans or the French because it has yet to develop anything concrete in this respect (Mendez 2008). In Guangdong, most of its citizens are in the early stages of adopting global forms of cultural appreciation and sophistication (Tsui *et al.* 2006: 666). Cultural activities for the Chinese new middle class are still in flux and still indistinct. When I conducted my fieldwork in Guangdong, I noted that the Chinese new middle class (with the exception of some intellectuals) as a whole rarely visit bookshops, libraries, museums, or art galleries. I can suggest that the transition of China to a market economy shows a weakening of both traditional Chinese and socialist culture without a replacement by anything distinctive (Jim & Chen 2009).

It appears from my interviews that the Chinese new middle class is still developing its moral boundaries. Ethics are weakly developed in China at present and that is largely caused by the weak development of civic education in the country. The rigid educational curriculum and syllabus cause the Chinese new middle class themselves to state that there is room for improvement in moral development. They do not share any common imagery of the middle classes in advanced capitalist societies such as a stable lifestyle, mainstream values and active political participation (Bian 2002b: 297–8; Wright 1997: 23–6). Also absent are a developed middle-class value system (So 2001, 2003) as well as an internal political motivation to encourage the rise of a civil society (Pearson 1997).

The Chinese new middle class is still very unsure of its identity within the middle-income bracket. Strongly individualised endeavours as opposed to collectivist efforts typify the social behaviours of the middle-income bracket (Wang X. 2008). However, some of the professionals believe that the role of the Chinese new middle class, like those in Western countries, should have the initiative and motivation to pursue democracy and freedom, human rights, and civil society (Fewsmith 2007).

> I don't have the sense that the Chinese new middle class enjoys any feelings of cultural superiority. I question that it must necessarily have its own political advocacy and enjoy a distinct and unique social status and prestige. We've not achieved this, but we still want to keep the status quo. We don't want to provoke any riots, protests or demonstrations that will show China in a bad light. (**Uncle Yang, 40, professional**)

Ken concurs with Uncle Yang, believing that the Chinese new middle class is an integral part of a highly stable society, which might otherwise lapse into a state of chaos if there is no such social class.

> I don't feel a sense of accomplishment in having become a member of the middle class in China. I don't think that we are so powerful that we can keep the balance between the poor and the rich. Also, the middle class are not capable of maintaining a stable political system. But at least I can show off in front of my clients... (**Ken, 30, entrepreneur**)

Paradoxically, the Chinese new middle class is somehow quite self-conscious of its class identity even though that class identity is still quite fragmented in nature. Even so, the individuals who make up that class do indeed make a special point of distinguishing themselves from the rest of society – especially in terms of higher living standards and education (Brown 2003; Cao 2001; Chen 2006).

## Debate on Chinese political development

Up to now I have suggested that the Chinese new middle class is generally unable to contribute anything constructive to the political development of the country. It has almost no room to promote political democratisation under the current political arrangements in the country.

However, since the time China joined the WTO, the Party has gradually been repositioning itself as responsive to social demands instead of just shaping the social arena. This trend to reposition basically started around 1989 in the aftermath of the Tiananmen emergency. Broadly speaking, the voices for and against political progress are manifold and conflicting. Cadres generally think China is heading in new political directions. Professionals and entrepreneurs are conservative and realistic about political progress. It seems that all groups accept the determining role of the party and the cadre. Professionals and entrepreneurs alike adapt to it, while cadres are required to be more positive in their endorsement.

Cadres follow rules set for them by the party and state. They cannot express anything that diverges from the party line and that is to be expected of party bureaucrats anywhere in the world. Yet cadres are the most optimistic group about political developments in China. The majority of my cadre interviewees (9 out of 11) indicate that they are passionate public servants.

Why do cadres, regardless of age, admire the party and the glories of the People's Republic so much in their daily life? Like most other people in the country, cadres receive a fair dose of political indoctrination through their schooling in their formative years. Most mainland Chinese history schoolbooks are replete with tales of the Eighth Route Army, which was an army of, and for, the common masses in the Sino-Japanese War and the Chinese Civil War, and the glorious achievements of Chairman Mao and other revolutionary heroes. It is quite easy to appreciate that the more politically disciplined individuals like cadres would toe the party line. Indoctrination becomes internalised and reinforced by key socialising agents in everyday life.

> The Communist Party I work for is the most democratic party in the world. China is improving in political development. I personally think that is pretty much enough for Chinese political development. (**Uncle Hui, 60, cadre**)

The reality is that China has a long way to go in terms of its democratic development before it will be able to fast-track political developments in the ways that occurred in Western countries. Jacques (2009) pinpointed that whether China is a developed or a developing country 'is a matter of fine print, depending on which side of the definition you want to define yourself with'. In fact, the physical standards of much of the infrastructure in China surpass that found in many developed countries. The quality of the financial stimulus package that Beijing carried out in 2009 to save the national economy was better designed and better implemented than that put out by Washington for the American economy. In politics and human rights, China has some way to go.

Most of our entrepreneur and professional interviewees believe that the current political developments in China will see no major change anytime soon. The confused state of regulations means that it becomes quite normal for a cadre to accept *laisee* money and gifts from citizens as a part of their official duties (Liu 1983). Indeed, our entrepreneurs (25 out of 31) and professionals (8 out of 11) are of the opinion that the Chinese bureaucracy is rife with nepotism, favouritism, and corruption. They see that the Chinese leadership has never claimed that the country is actually carrying out different forms of capitalist activities. So, in effect it is unwilling to legitimise capitalism in the country (Zheng 2004: 65). The party at an abstract level retains a prestige that is denied in terms of the local implementation of its policies, but the new middle class is able to negotiate those local difficulties and secure advantages for itself in the process.

Many of our entrepreneurs and professionals see that the party-state still tends to be heavy-handed in its dealings with dissenting citizenry. Probably the best example is the violent ending of the 1989 student movement (Tiananmen Incident). Since then, there have been open elections in some select provinces but only at the village level. The government still subdues separatist movements among ethnic minorities of the country. It performs censorship of the mass media and restricts Internet access. It is also active in the management and monitoring of the educational sector. In all fairness, though, the Chinese government has also relaxed its control over the economy for the sake of general wealth-building of the nation, and this has allowed many people at all levels to have a chance at prosperity. China is still taking nascent steps on the road to democratisation driven by the nascent and precarious development on democracy. This is what Zheng called the change-induced legitimacy crisis (Zheng 2003). However, the legitimacy crisis is primarily internal to the party in terms of its need to recruit and reproduce senior cadres, rather than between the party and the emergent new middle class outside it. The dependence of entrepreneurs and professionals upon facilitation by local cadres keeps them tied to a system that secures their economic advantages. As long as the latter is secured, the new middle class appears happy to be de-politicised.

Cadres and their work are largely unregulated and unsupervised. Corruption and unlawful activities among officials are fairly widespread, but the central government has carried out countermeasures. Scandals and corruption of cadres often compromise the administrative and legal systems. There is no institutional organisation to monitor the integrity and alliances of cadres. No direct elections are held for the heads of towns and townships. Indeed, there is no such thing as an 'accountability system of principal officers' in China. This is the overwhelming consensus of opinion of the interviewees found by this study. They see there is much room for improvement on an everyday level but they do not necessarily challenge the government in the mildest way.

For most members of the Chinese new middle class, the topic of human rights is a taboo. Most of them are more content to talk about current economic trends and how they can make money. The more widely read and intellectual members of the new middle class (like college professors) are guarded in speaking their minds on political reforms (Zweig & Chen 2007). In China, sometimes you pay with your life if you speak your mind, as exemplified by the case of PRC *vs*. Ching Cheong (程翔) (2005).[10] However, those at risk do not belong to the particular categories of the new middle class that were the object of my study.

Indeed, they want nothing like the Hong Kong model of governance because that is so well organised that there are practically no exploitable loopholes. Zheng (2004) found that, following the strict measures of discipline after the 1989 student protests, the leadership deliberately constructed an interest-based social order for the country. This order has brought much stability and rapid development. People from all walks of life turned their main attention to the private economic arena when political passions were transformed into economic ones (Zheng 2004: 82). The result was political indifference. They prefer the status quo.

I can safely say that the road to democracy in China is hopeless after I was heavily involved in the June 4th incident when at university twenty years ago. I don't think I can improve the current tense situation and differences that limit the participation of everyone in China. I only want to maintain status quo after the serious attempt to fight for democracy twenty years ago. To me, change now represents challenge rather than opportunity. **(Uncle Yang, 40, professional)**

I wrote something to express my opinions about the June 4th incident. I expressed my concern that the central government should
stop censoring some websites in China. If people knew more about
the facts of June 4th, then they would more accurately judge the true
nature of the event. This article appeared on my university home-
page, while I was studying for my undergraduate degree in Hong
Kong in 1999. I received an 'invitation' from the China Liaison
Office [*Zhonglianban* 中联办] (author clarification: the organ of the
PRC based in Hong Kong, responsible for PLA's Hong Kong Garrison
and the Office of the Commission of the Foreign Ministry in Hong
Kong. It is also responsible for liaison with Chinese companies in
Hong Kong). I almost freaked out because I was now probably seen
as an anti-communist. I couldn't help picturing the very serious
consequences for my future. I blamed myself, too, for probably
involving my family. At the time, I was nervous and upset. I told
myself I shouldn't do that kind of stupid thing again. **(Ken, 30,
entrepreneur)**

Even if we wanted to improve political freedom and democracy in
China, the current system and polices would not allow us to do. We
see clearly that all the activists who have advocated democracy and
justice in China have failed. They were either put in jail or lost their
freedom. Who can go against the CCP? We can only work for the
CCP. **(Uncle Lam, 40, entrepreneur)**

These excerpts help to explain why the Chinese new middle class in
my study is less sensitive to politics than are middle-class people in
other countries. The overall level of surveillance has become tighter
since the Tiananmen events of 1989, and now extends from traditional
media to the Internet. Under the current political set-up, the professionals cannot see themselves as having any influences over the policy
directions of the country, although many of them are in fact active
party members. My interviews reveal that many of my respondents
have foreign passports. While they live and work in China, their children live abroad. Many hold overseas bank accounts in their own
names as well as in those of their children and relatives. They are well-
prepared in case something drastically wrong occurs in China.

In China capitalism has certain distinct characteristics. Tsai (2007)
points out that 'socialism with Chinese characteristics' has become a
structural constraint for democracy to develop – capitalism without
democracy. Gallagher (2005) describes the situation in China as 'contagious capitalism'. If there is no legitimacy crisis, there is no democrat-

isation in China (Welzel 2006). Many people (including the Chinese new middle class) will not advocate anything radically different from the status quo for fear of arrest by the authorities.

Indeed, a number of political or ideological reforms that took place in China even with the blessings of the government never actually took hold. Public attention simply turned to economic matters, especially after 1989.

> There is no hope for Chinese politics. What is the meaning of *min zhu* [民主 democracy]? The citizen is *min* [民 people] and the state is *zhu* [主 master] – we follow in the footsteps of the state. I took part in the June 4th movement when I was a university student. We couldn't say the incident was a massacre, otherwise we'd have spent the rest of our lives in jail. It is worse than useless to advocate democracy. If there is the promise from the Chinese government that it will promote democracy, it is a lie. In reality it will never come to pass. **(Uncle Yang, 40, professional)**

> I appreciated Zhu Rongji. He was very effective in getting rid of some corrupt officials and syndicates in China. But regrettably, we don't have too many like Zhu Rongji in China. Right? There are many corrupt officers in our country. How do we get rid of them completely? Only one Zhu Rongji is not enough. **(Peter, 34, entrepreneur)**

For more than 20 years, the Tiananmen shootings have been a 'no-talk' zone for discussions about democracy in China (Zheng 2003). There is a noticeable pattern of 'don't tell, don't ask' about the event at all echelons of state organs as well as in Chinese society in general. The authorities divulge no details, admit no wrongdoing, and expunge any references to the event. In the public eye, the government exercises a wilful loss of memory. Behind closed doors, participants and survivors from the event are just now starting to be released from incarceration. Two interviewees offer their views:

> I think there is no hope for democracy taking root in China before I die. I have never administered cases relating to human rights and political issues in Guangdong. It's a difficult thing to say, but politics is a very dark area in China. China won't let things become transparent and totally unveil them. **(Uncle Man, 40, professional and cadre)**

> Some foreigners think that we have lost our freedom. I know what the government has done and what they are trying to hide from us.

But we won't disturb this peaceful atmosphere. We won't go against the government unless it gives us no space in which to live. With one ruling party it is hard to make any actual change. We can do nothing but take advantage of the opportunities for our own advancement [in this globalising China]...However, I think China could achieve more in the area of political development now. **(Sung, 30, professional)**

By all Western standards, the Chinese new middle class has not come of age yet insofar as politics is concerned. The fact of the matter is, the new middle class is largely apolitical and unconcerned with regard to appeals for the government to improve human rights and freedom of speech since, to them, the cold reality of life in China is to maintain the status quo. The new middle class poses no challenge, political or otherwise, to any level of government.

Uncle Yuen's conversation (below) examines the four leaders of the PRC. Most of the Chinese new middle class share the belief that Mao Zedong was an uncorrupt leader. He could maintain justice and integrity since he aimed at achieving an egalitarian society or even a communist society. But in fact it proved to be a utopia. Deng Xiaoping had loose policies to deal with outrageous corruption in China though he led China to the road of prosperity. Jiang Zemin has no particular political and economic contributions; he only followed in the footsteps of his predecessors. Jiang's major contribution was to close down many state-owned enterprises since the 1990s. Hu's regime focuses principally on economic development but has made little progress in politics. Hence, the Chinese new middle class reiterated that they need to maintain the status quo in politics.

I don't know how to describe Chinese politics at this moment, but I am not optimistic. I think it's rather like this: 'Mao Zedong is like the sun who shines for a brighter future in China' [*Mao Zedong xiang taiyang zhaodao nali nali liang* 毛泽东像太阳，照到那里那里亮]. 'Deng Xiaoping is like the moon, who makes society more extravagant and corrupt, with people going to karaoke lounges' [*Deng Xiaoping xiang yue liang, ka la OK dao tianliang* 邓小平像月亮，卡拉ok到天亮]. 'Jiang Zemin [3rd President of the PRC] is like the star who laid off or made redundant workers since the 1990s' [*Jiang Zemin xiang xingxing xiagang gong ren shu buqing* 江泽民像星星，下岗工人数不清]. How about *Hujiantao*? I have no more fantasies and hope in politics... **(Uncle Yuen 56, entrepreneur)**

Uncle Moss concurs with Uncle Yuen,

> Mao Zedong advocated that everyone needs to be self-reliant. He also advocated integrity in society. I remember one famous proverb: *'woyou yishuangshou; buzai cheng li chi xianfan'* [我有一双手，不在城里吃闲饭] (I have my own hands. I can work and don't want to wait for government subsidies. Everyone needs to work and find a job to make their own living). We had a strong sense of integrity during the Mao period. No-one bothered to bribe their supervisor. Society at that time was very poor but egalitarian and just. Corruption got worse when Deng Xiaoping, Jiang Zemin and Hu Jiantao become President in the PRC. **(Uncle Moss, 48, entrepreneur)**

Stockman (1992) says 'the power of the Communist party-state is weakening' in terms of its control over Chinese society during the reform era, while Nee (1989) suggests that the power of cadres is declining. Stockman's (1992) contention rests mainly on economic reasons: the devolution of power to managers; the encouragement of foreign investments over which the party has minimal control; the declining capacity of the state to restrain corruption; the reduced capability of the state to extract financial resources in a market-led economy; the commercialisation of the state coercive apparatus; and the general rise in crime across the country. This does not quite seem to be the case in China today. In fact, the vast majority remark that there is no challenge to the authorities. Indeed, theirs is a desire for a stable, safe and secure life within the status quo in a booming economy and prosperity. A few intellectuals and professionals might go so far as to espouse ideas about freedom of expression and association, but, all in all, they are still comparatively more enthusiastic about enhancing their economic and occupational potential than about democratic pursuits (Li 2006). There is no loss of power of the Communist Party in modern Chinese society.

Bruce Dickson (2003: 134) seems to be closer to the mark: 'the priority given to political stability is one of the strongest and most enduring features of the Chinese political culture, and seems to be shared by both state leaders and members of society'. The leadership and the average person are unwilling (at least at present) to be advocates of radical political changes; instead they prefer incremental democratisation.

In the Chinese context, there is at least some logic to the argument that some kind of authoritarian rule is required to prevent massive chaos and disintegration during periods of rapid economic growth (Li 2006). Bluntly speaking, prudent progress is difficult enough with the support and encouragement of the government, never mind dramatic progress. Democracy is a frightening prospect for China. For the local party authorities, alignment with the rich has long been a reality: for instance, local governments typically take the side of capital in labour disputes. It is a hardly veiled symbiosis in which the business world provides much of government revenue through tax and employment and contributing to the local economic development that is one of the key criteria for cadre promotion. In return, cadres offer tax breaks and government contracts or loans, often deriving from them not only career boosts but actual shares of private profit (Chen 2003: 58).

The Chinese new middle class wants to get rich and not meddle in politics. It tries to profit from the economic reforms of the country by cooperating with, rather than challenging, the government (Li 2003: 77). As that class is widely regarded as the biggest gainers from the economic reforms of the past 30 years, it desires the status quo and is very unlikely to speak or do anything that might jeopardise its position in society and its interests. Therefore the Chinese new middle class will be unlikely to be the communication bridge between powerless groups in society and the government. It is therefore quite difficult for China to achieve the so-called 'second democracy' (Beck and Beck-Gernsheim 2002), which refers to a new era of post-democracy and a post-welfare state. But at present, most of the Chinese individuals still follow the first modernity which is derived from Western Europe. The first modernity means that the majority of the people pursue primarily materialistic lives, focused on secure employment, quality of life, welfare benefits, and the freedom to travel, speak, and engage in social movement or forums. This explains why in post-reform China, the young generation, as well as the old generation, work industriously to pursue materialistic lives, and capitalise on their *guanxi* networks to secure a well-paid job. These kinds of individuality and self-reliance have been created by the market economy and global capitalism in the context of the political authoritarianism of the party-state in post-reform China (Yan 2009). This explains why the Chinese new middle class is still located in the 'first modernity'. It is difficult for them to pursue the 'second modernity'. The strategy to create the 'second modernity' has to take political, ideological, and institutional contexts into consideration. But the individual-state relationship in post-reform China is bestowed with both red ideologies and the authority of the CCP. This is what Beck (Beck and Beck-Gernsheim 2002) called 'cultural democratization' meaning that democracy has been widely accepted in the society. The emergence of civil society and the close individual and state relationship is clearly appearing. But this is not the case in post-reform China. Chinese individuals never rely on the systems of education, social security, medical care, employment, and employment benefits granted by the Chinese government. Rather, they rely heavily on rule by law rather than rule of law.

## Summary

The Chinese new middle class constitutes only a small fraction of Chinese society. It forms only 12% of the Guangdong province and less than 7% of the national population of China (CASS 2007; Zhou 2005). The class is far smaller than the middle class in Western countries. As such a very tiny community, the Chinese new middle class does not have a well-formed recognition of its own self-image and cultural identity (Tomlinson 1990, 1999). The Chinese new middle class is a new concept and it takes time to establish the Chinese new middle-class culture. Despite three decades' worth of economic reforms and economic growth of the country, the Chinese new middle class is still heavily geared to gaining the maximum possible economic benefit from society. This causes a shift in focus away from politics and general social responsibility and towards educational qualifications to secure better careers (Fladrich 2006; Flew 2006; Hannum 2005). The result is that the Chinese new middle class as a whole has a low sense of obligation to making contributions to the social development of the country.

The fact that most of the Chinese new middle class do not recognise themselves as being members of the Chinese new middle class (or any other kind of middle class) clearly illustrates that self-image and cultural identity are still in flux. One major reason right now is that the Chinese new middle class has no channel to express political sentiments and has no desire to pursue political democracy in China at this time. Their advantages seem strongly tied to that of cadres and they have always been the actual beneficiaries of the economic reforms. The non-confrontational policy of these bodies *vis-à-vis* the party-state indicates that any radical change in civil society in China has not even progressed beyond a minimal level yet. There is no obvious sign to show that the Chinese government is anywhere near moving in the direction of greater political liberalisation or the emergence of a civil society even with the appearance of the Chinese new middle class and the liberation of economic reform (Dickson 2004, 2006). The young generation of the Chinese new middle class even prefer to retain the status quo and they do not want to challenge the Chinese government, given their hyper-consuming lifestyles and their ultimate reliance on traditional networks as detailed in this book.

# Conclusion: A China in the Making with a New Middle Class?

The purpose of this study has been to apply a sociocultural perspective to the study of the rise of the new middle class in post-reform China. The Chinese new middle class can be identified and studied by using the sociocultural perspective that considers their lifestyles and consumerism. Ideally, they can act as an agency to promote social changes and historical transformation to protect (or expand) its class interests and lifestyles. The overall argument that the Chinese new middle class is best defined through cultural markers, and that it is economically progressive but politically conservative, is original, important, and interesting. The 'thick description' of consumption practices and attitudes, and their role in producing a shared sentiment, is similarly novel, and potentially of interest to a more general type of readership curious to learn about contemporary China.

## Summary of the book

In Chapter 1, I argued that the established class theories or class analyses from the West address class as an economic formation and are not directly helpful in understanding the transition from communism to capitalism evident in China. In many ways, China provides a new twist to the meaning of class. The transition seen in Chinese society diverges from Marx's trajectory of societal development. However, Weberian and neo-Weberian (John Goldthorpe's) approaches can be applied to China more readily.

The Chinese new middle class brings together the concepts of class, status, party, and political determinism in ways that allow us to think about the special nature of the market situation that applies to 'socialism with Chinese characteristics'. At the same time, I suggested that

Bourdieu's sociocultural approach is also applicable to China (Jacksons 2008; Robbins 2000; Webb *et al.* 2002), although the situation with the Chinese new middle class goes beyond the taste, habitus and field in Bourdieu's French-centred work. In China, class positions are tied to economic, cultural, political, and social capitals. All of these capitals follow the mode of consumption that acts as a normative mechanism and also demarcates the tastes shared by the same group inside a relatively similar class boundary. In this chapter, I also developed this sociocultural approach further, applying it specifically to the nature of the transition undergone within China and the role of residues from the state-centred period of Chinese economic development. This sociocultural approach contributes to the originality of this study (Ryan & Musiol 2008). There are a few studies in the literature about Chinese class dynamics, and almost none of these take a sociocultural line. Post-reform China is no longer solely reliant on production and work. Producing for consumption has become one of the more lucrative means of profit-making (Fraser 2000), particularly in the light of growing inflows of international capital into China. These developments are working to start a new chapter in the cultural globalisation of China. The everyday social and cultural practices seen in China today exhibit a form of heterogeneity as opposed to homogeneity. Such a heterogeneity (or fragmentation, if you will) challenges the traditional concept of class. Class should now be understood in the repertoire of sociocultural terminology because the case of China shows that lifestyles and consumption patterns function to define the class boundary of the Chinese new middle class.

In Chapter 2, I presented the old generation of the middle class as largely pragmatic, politically apathetic, and conservative in personality and desiring of the maintenance of the status quo (as vested in the ambiguities and incompleteness of institutional changes and political reform in urban China). The old generation have often been seen as the biggest winner in post-reform China. Part of its 'winnability' is in being able to collaborate with others inside class boundaries. The fact that the old generation is able to exploit the system is in itself indicative of the resourcefulness to operate in transitional conditions. The sharing of past memories help the old generation to build up a sentiment (*ganqing* 感情) of being in the same group (*zijiren* 自己人 'our own people'). Gatherings and leisure activities act as important socialising agents for them to form class boundary and class admission within the same circle of 'insideness' and identity.

In discussing the ongoing consumer revolution in China and the emergence of the young generation in post-socialist China, Chapter 3 demonstrated that the young generation are more inclined to practise conspicuous consumption patterns owing to the rapid pace of impacts brought about by globalisation forces and the 'spaces' of consumption in Guangdong. They are gradually moving towards late marriage, independence, a lack of leisure time, and being individualised, egocentric, and Westernised in their everyday life practice.

In Chapter 4, I presented different types of collaborations and utilisations of *guanxi* network within the middle-class groupings of entrepreneurs, professionals and cadres. Since the current economic reforms that began three decades or so ago in China, everything has been done through *guanxi* networks. Social scientists such as Weber (1951) and Faure (2008) argued that the transaction costs of finding a reliable party and negotiating a contract are extremely high in China where social capital (based on personal links, reciprocity, moral obligation and duty towards the community) remains highly significant. In economic activities, a shared insider identity can enhance the level of trust between people. This results in a reduction in the costs of negotiating and enforcing contracts (Shirk 1984, 1993). The 'insider categories' (same group) within the new class boundary develop reciprocal relationships through the same tastes in lifestyles and consumerism (Sulkunen & Holmwood 1997).

A defective and deficient monitoring system of governance in China encourages many professionals and entrepreneurs to put more weight on social connections with cadres and vice versa. Institutional structures conducive to the existence of *guanxi* networks are flourishing in China. Gifts and mutual reciprocities are culturally deep-rooted in Chinese society and are employed as pragmatic survival tactics to build interpersonal connections for defending or advancing economic interests. However, altogether, they impede the progression of a civil society in China.

In Chapter 5, I argued that as yet there is no real and definite middle-class culture in China. The young generation are increasingly becoming more individualised, Westernised, and independent. The old generation are more collective in nature. But they both show no strong class awareness and culture as the members of the Chinese new middle class. Instead, they both show a high degree of anxiety and uncertainty about the future. The political landscape is unlikely to change, even minimally, for a number of reasons. First, the current regime provides for the best-possible climate to maximise profit-making and maintain social stability. Second, there is a substantive need to associate with government officials in fostering economic benefits. Third, there is a need to cultivate *guanxi* network because mutual relationships are important in a society that is often described empirically as a 'low-trust society'. Finally, the new middle class mostly prefers to maintain the status quo because it works to its own advantage.

The theoretical framework incorporates a spatial-temporal dimension to current Western-oriented approaches to debates on class analysis, consumption patterns and institutional changes in post-socialist China. Up to now, most research on class structure and formation has been based on Western European concepts originating within a classically conceived Western experience of modernity. This is because Europeans were the first to write about the development of modernity and, therefore, took their own experiences as 'normal' from which others provided 'deviant' cases.

For this reason, as I have set out at the start of this study, the classical Marxist point of view is conventionally the starting point for the analysis of class formation. However, notwithstanding the role of Marxism in the ideological self-understanding of Chinese (socialist) modernity, Marxism provides a less than satisfactory guide to understanding a society in transition from state-centred socialist modernity to market-based modernity. The Chinese transition complicates the Marxist analysis by including a trajectory not recognised by Marx. Moreover, if market capitalism tends to be a class society, it is not a class society in the Marxist sense. I argued that Weberian and neo-Weberian approaches will provide a better fit, albeit by drawing on different aspects of the Weberian legacy than those normally utilised in Western sociology. It is not only that the Chinese Communist Party remains important in determining class relations, perhaps especially those within the new middle class given the continued significance of cadres and professional employment within the state sector, but also that significant political and cultural 'formations' from the state socialist era remain.

Thus, I have referred to how residency status or *hukou* continues to structure not only the labour market for unskilled labour, but also the new middle class. In addition the *danwei* remains a significant institution providing opportunities (for example, in terms of access to development land) for the new middle class. There were few members of my sample who were entrepreneurs outside those structures. Moreover, all entrepreneurs required access to what those structures provided and, therefore, were embedded within them in terms of how their business affairs were conducted. In post-reform China, the same occupation (in class terms) is rewarded differently in different regions because of how *hukou* and *danwei* operate. *Hukou* creates spatially distributed inequality. *Danwei* continues to be significant on class and class distinction in urban China. Both *hukou* and *danwei* create differences in work situations by forming *guanxi* networks inside the boundary of the new class.

The perceived wisdom of traditional class theories, then, requires adaptation when we try to analyse contemporary Chinese society. The emerging 'Chinese new middle class' departs from the standard developmental pathways displayed by Western-oriented middle-class theories. The new class emerging in China is more diversified and heterogeneous than its equivalent in most Western societies would be. The cultural and social identification of the Chinese new middle class operates mainly through cultural practices and consumption patterns.

The work of Bourdieu also has an important bearing on how the new middle class is formed as a cultural entity alongside its economic formation. He went beyond the traditional studies by including first cultural capital and then social capital into the accounts of economic inequality and social stratification. In the West, education is a key institution by which the established order is maintained and reproduced. There is evidence that a similar pattern is emerging in China. However, in the meantime class formation is under much influence of such cultural factors as lifestyles and consumption patterns. With a rise in standards of living, it is argued, Chinese people's consumption and lifestyles rather than their occupation and ownership play an increasingly important role in shaping one's social attitudes and behaviour.

In the consumer revolution that is happening in China today, using branded products, wining and dining, and various other entertainment practices are a distinctly public phenomenon. The consumption of fashionable commodities is the key element whereby the Chinese new middle class creates new public spaces for the images of the Chinese new middle-class membership. The new public space is a consumer space of commoditised objects, services and information.

The Chinese new middle class are embracing the global marketplace as eager consumers. Consumption serves as a very important cultural aspect of class analysis in post-reform China. Consumer goods are the new social currency. For the new Chinese middle class, consumer goods are necessary both as an element of claim and as a new communicative medium. Consumption and trend-chasing are no longer options but are now necessities in China. Mutual tastes, lifestyles, and consumption practices form the new class boundary and the means of admission thereof. Consumption practices form a circle of class distinction by incorporating class privileges into the cultural spaces. However, as I have argued, this consumption ethos does not constitute a form of class consciousness in the Western sense and I have found no evidence of internal differentiations of distinction that are an important feature of Bourdieu's own account of class reproduction of the middle class.

## Contributions of the book

To be the author of an unusual study is something quite exciting. There are plenty of research studies about the Chinese new middle class but most are piecemeal efforts and not particularly well organised. Indeed, quite a number of people in China are inclined to think that there is no middle class in China, with society consisting of only the rulers and the ruled. The goals of this study were to provide a conceptual approach to theorising class analysis in post-reform China. I have chosen to rely more on first-hand field data and less on theoretical inferences from class-theoretic models. I have taken a sociocultural perspective to explain the whys and wherefores of that class because it is so patently obvious that the sociological literature on this particular class is in need of an alternative perspective. The current data on the middle class of China are overwhelmingly drawn from quantitative research methods. The data and findings of this study help to narrow the gap somewhat and provide an alternative approach for subsequent research on the middle class (or *classes*?) of China. The study of the Chinese middle class is welcome not only because of the rapid ascendancy of China in the world but also because the topic is still under-studied. Using ethnographic data, I make some perceptive observations about Chinese society. They include the claims that China is a low-trust society, thereby highlighting the growing importance of social capital in the society, and that the consumption patterns of the Chinese middle class are socially constructed by the ruling Chinese Communist party. This book stands a chance of being able to offer a fresh insight into this new social phenomenon in China under reform.

What are the roles of the Chinese new middle class in the foreseeable future? Undoubtedly, the Chinese new middle class is in the vanguard of consumption in urban China. At the same time, they are laggards in politics. They do not function as a bridge between the government and the citizenry or promote democracy and civil society. The present political set-up leaves little, if any, room for the new middle class to flex their political muscle. The chief reason is that the CCP puts economic performance as the top priority and that is given mass support and unlikely to change anytime soon. Indeed, the new middle class relies on and puts a great deal of trust in the party-state like nothing seen anywhere in the rest of the world. For that class, preserving status quo is paramount.

China is now at a crossroads on its road to modernity and prosperity. Present-day consumption in China sways between the traditional and modern ends of the consumption spectrum – that is to say, it is moderate and extravagant in the same breath. In terms of cultural and social identity, the new middle class mostly have yet to recognise themselves as a class. Compared with Western middle classes, the Chinese new middle class are nowhere near a Western level of formation. Yet cultural appreciation and a leisured life are what these people like the most about Western life. To many of them, the Western middle class appears the most blessed with internal assets like cultural capital nurtured and accumulated over time. The Western middle class appears to involve themselves with activities that carry a strong flavour of cultural appreciation and social etiquette. However, that is not the story for the Chinese new middle class. The Chinese class still lacks true middle-class values (So 2001). Politically very conservative, it is very ambitious and assertive about career-building prospects and economic status. Its unambiguously utilitarian and pragmatic traits may or may not cause it to have any commitments or missions regarding a civil society in China, depending perhaps on whether or not a civil society serves the needs and interests of that class. Still without a clear-cut class culture to define standards of ethical behaviour, the new Chinese middle class personifies the Chinese model as lacking the political motivation to sow the seeds of a civil society (Pearson 1997). While China is on the road to becoming a nation of middle-class people, the current state of politics in China hinders the Chinese new middle-class from forming the real and full-fledged middle-class culture.

The overall argument that the Chinese new middle class in this book is best defined through cultural markers, and that it is economically progressive but politically conservative, is original, important, and interesting. The 'thick description' of consumption practices and attitudes, and their role in producing a shared sentiment, is similarly novel, and potentially of interest to a more general type of readership curious to learn about contemporary China. I have pared down more to really bring these key arguments/distinctive issues to the core chapters (Chapters 2 to 5).

I discussed the emergence of the new middle class in post-reform China, distinguished two generations (old and young) in the Chinese new middle class and argued that Western class categories cannot be directly applied to the Chinese situation and that the Chinese new middle class is distinguished more by sociocultural than by economic factors. It is a typical qualitative study based on interviewing data. It would make an important addition to the literature. The rise of a middle class in China is a very hotly discussed issue at this moment.[1]

## The limitations of the book and future research themes

My research journey has come to an end for the time being. Other, hopefully just as exciting, journeys will come. The work here has truly turned out to be a learning process – about the subject matter and also the actual research work and, most certainly, the trials and tribulations of writing it. To paraphrase Ceglowski (1997: 188–201): If I could redo the study, I might well have done it differently – or not, as the case may be. Everything could be done differently on hindsight if I had more time and resources.

There is, however, a need to address some of the limitations of the research and future research themes. The research focused only on South China, but it will be more comprehensive to focus some samples in prosperous cities such as Shanghai, Beijing, and some coastal regions besides Guangdong to avoid homogenous findings. In addition, it is worthwhile to study the major differences between the old generation and the young generation. The individualisation of the Chinese new middle class will be more likely a good and viable topic for future research. Whilst research into China's nascent new middle class remains in an embryonic stage, there is a conspicuous hiatus surrounding the various paths of individualisation embodied by the disparate generation that comprise this variegated group. Through the development of a much-needed theoretically-led empirical expatiation of the emerging Chinese new middle-class milieu, their culture, careers and consumption, the future research may examine the critical role individualisation would play in the formation and reproduction of class in post-reform China. The coalescence of these two themes will contribute a perspicuous theoretical account for the rise of individual agency that appears to be at variance with – but remains nevertheless entangled in – the cosmopolitics of a collectivist culture widely perceived to be one that aggrandises society at the expense of the individual.

It is hoped that the completed work will offer a nuanced conceptual framework – and worthy succedaneum to Western classicist theories of class that are impervious to Chinese society's transition from state socialism to market socialism – for analysing class and individualisation in China.

# Appendix 1  Research Questions to Interview the Chinese New Middle Class

## A. The interviewee

A1.  Occupation of the target interviewee
A2.  Background information
A3.  Personal life experiences and encounters
A4.  Food
A5.  Clothing
A6.  Accommodation
A7.  Means of travel
A8.  Accommodation or residence
A9.  Model of mobile phone, mp3, other electronic/electrical devices
A10. Are you a frequent credit-card user? Which bank credit cards do you hold and why?
A11. Electronic products, PDAs, hi-fi system, etc.
A12. Engagements in investments, funds or real-estate dealings
A13. Purchases of investment portfolios for children
A14. Plans or arrangements made for children's education

## B. Places to go for shopping/Mode of consumption

B1.  What activities do you do after work or on a day off?
B2.  How do you spend your holidays?
B3.  What do you think about yourself?
B4.  Are you proud of being a member of the middle class in China?
B5.  Do you think you are in any way superior or more privileged than others?
B6.  How do you teach or instruct your children? Do you buy more books for them or take them to the library? Have you ever thought of sending them to international schools? Do they study abroad?
B7.  In your opinion, what roles will your children play in China's social mobility in future?

## C. Work partners

C1.  Who or what are your major work partners?
C2.  How do you keep in touch with your work partners? What factors do matter in your choices for work partners?
C3.  Do you have social connections with businessmen and professionals because of your job needs? How often do you change your work partners? What are the reasons for changing?

C4.   How do you form mutual trust relationships with others? What are those relationships based on – schoolmates, fellow villagers, shared experiences, collective memories or academic qualifications?

## D.  Changing work partners

D1.   How often do you change work partners?

D2.   How do you get new work partners?

D3.   How do you maintain your social connections with businessmen, professionals and self-employed individuals? By way of dinner gatherings? Entertainment activities? Have you had these experiences before?

D4.   Regarding academic qualifications, what do you think are the advantages of outstanding academic achievements?

D5.   In the social context of China, are social connections and political capital more important than academic achievements?

D6.   What is the significance of social connections?

D7.   What is the significance of being a government official or cadre?

D8.   What is the significance of studying at school?

D9.   Out of political, economic, academic and cultural factors, which one (and only one) do you think is the most important?

D10. What do you think about the current patterns of social mobility in China? Or what conclusion can you draw from your observation?

## E.  Globalisation, economic reforms and the WTO

E1.   To you, how significant are globalisation, economic reforms and China's accession to the World Trade Organisation?

E2.   More opportunities?

E3.   Is there more or less convenience or ease for social mobility?

E4.   What is the general pattern of the current social mobility? What is the impact on the next generation?

E5.   How do you pass social class status onto the next generation? What are your strategic plans for the well-being of your children?

E6.   As a member of the new middle class, what difficulties do you have in your daily life in China? What is your opinion about the government's plans and arrangements on medical service, education, social welfare and retirement schemes?

## F.  Parent-children relationship

F1.   How do you describe your relationship with your parents/children?

F2.   How do you keep in touch with parents/children?

F3.   How to communicate with your parents/children? Indicators? Examples?

## G.  Marriage pattern

G1.   By what criteria do you select your boyfriend/girlfriend? What are your expectations?

G2.   Do you find it difficult to find a boyfriend/girlfriend in Guangdong?

G3.   Do you think late marriage is common in Guangdong? Will you have the tendency to delay your marriage?

G4.   What do you think about the highly-educated men/women in Guangdong? Will you choose one of them as your boyfriend/girlfriend? Why or Why not?

G5.   Do you think men and women have great expectations for marriage in today's China?

G6.   Do you accept late marriage for men/women?

# Appendix 2 Detailed Profiles of the Chinese New Middle Class

**Old generation of regional cadres**

| Name (Pseudo) | Sex | Age[1] | Marital status | Education | Present job | Former job | Monthly income (¥RMB) | Other income or investment |
|---|---|---|---|---|---|---|---|---|
| Chan (Uncle) | M | 1948 60 | Married | University graduate | Professional at a state-owned enterprise (SOE) ('xíngzhèng gànbù' 行政干部) | Carpenter, worker and engineer | ¥5,000 or above for basic salary ONLY | Part-time jobs. Investment in elevator company, garment and air-conditioner company |
| Fang (Uncle) | M | 1959 49 | Married | Senior high school. He finished his bachelor's degree through part-time study | Administrative cadre ('xíngzhèng gànbù' 行政干部) | Cadre | ¥5,000 or above for basic salary ONLY | Part-time job. Investment in transportation, trading company and air-conditioner company |
| Hui (Uncle) | M | 1948 60 | Married | Senior high school | Administrative cadre ('xíngzhèng gànbù' 行政干部) | Cadre | ¥5,000 or above for basic salary ONLY | Part-time job. Lychee orchards, shares and funds, and property investment |
| Jane (Aunt) | F | 1968 40 | Married | University graduate | Doctor at a government hospital ('shìyè gànbù' 事业干部) | Cadre (doctor) | ¥8,000 or above for basic salary ONLY | Extra income from part-time job, partnership to run private clinics, medical consultant, shares and funds investment |
| Jennifer (Aunt) | F | 1955 53 | Married | Senior high school | Administrative cadre ('xíngzhèng gànbù' 行政干部) | Cadre | ¥5,000 for basic salary ONLY | Lychee orchards, shares and funds, special business like entertainment centres, travel agencies and property investment |

186

**Old generation of regional cadres** – *continued*

| Name (Pseudo) | Sex | Age[1] | Marital status | Education | Present job | Former job | Monthly income (¥RMB) | Other income or investment |
|---|---|---|---|---|---|---|---|---|
| Leung (Uncle) | M | 1968 48 | Married | Bachelor's degree and MBA through part-time study | Administrative cadre ('xíngzhèng gànbù' 行政干部) | Worker at a SOE | ¥5,000 for basic salary ONLY | Part-time job. Land and property tendering |
| Man (Uncle) | M | 1968 40 | Married | Senior high school | Lawyer ('shìyè gànbù' 事业干部) | Managerial position at a foreign venture enterprise | ¥9,000 | Part-time job. Shares, property investment |
| Monica (Aunt) | F | 1958 60 | Married | Senior high school | Business cadre ('shìyè gànbù' 事业干部) | Cadre | ¥5,000 for basic salary ONLY | Property investment |
| Tang (Uncle) | M | 1959 49 | Married | Senior high school | Business cadre ('shìyè gànbù' 事业干部) | Worker and vice director at a SOE or collectively owned enterprise | ¥5,000 for his basic salary | Investment in private property, hotel, entertainment centre, resort centre, massage saloon and karaoke lounge |
| Yip (Uncle) | M | 1960 48 | Married | Senior high school | Administrative cadre ('xíngzhèng gànbù' 行政干部) | Worker at a SOE | ¥5,000 for his basic salary | Investment in property, commercial building, entertainment centre and shopping mall |

[1] The base year for accounting age was 2008.
Total number of the old generation of regional cadres: 10.

**Young generation of regional cadres**

| Name (Pseudo) | Sex | Age | Marital status | Education | Present job | Former job | Monthly income (¥RMB) | Other income or investment |
|---|---|---|---|---|---|---|---|---|
| Raymond | M | 1978 30 | Single | University graduate | Doctor ('shìyè gànbù' 事业干部) | Nil | Around ¥8,000 (excluding bonus) | Shares and funds |

Total number of the young generation of regional cadre: 1.

**Old generation of entrepreneurs ('*getihu*' 个体户)**

| Name (Pseudo) | Sex | Age | Marital status | Education | Present job | Former job | Monthly income (¥RMB) | Other income or investment |
|---|---|---|---|---|---|---|---|---|
| Beck (Uncle) | M | 1952 56 | Married | Senior high school | Entrepreneur at an entertainment centre | Worker and vice director at a SOE | ¥30,000 or above | Land and property investment |
| Billy (Uncle) | M | 1952 56 | Married | Senior high school | Entrepreneur at a mobile phone company | Supervisor at a foreign venture enterprise, attempted different businesses | At least ¥100,000 | Land and property investment |
| Bryan (Uncle) | M | 1968 40 | Married | University graduate | Entrepreneur at a gold retailing company | Cadre, director at a SOE | At least ¥100,000 | Investment in gold and jade. Shares and property investment |
| Cheng (Uncle) | M | 1968 40 | Married | Senior high school | Entrepreneur at an embroidery company | Managerial position at a foreign venture enterprise | At least ¥40,000 | Land and property investment |
| Chris (Uncle) | M | 1959 49 | Married | Senior high school | Entrepreneur at a fabric factory | Worker at a SOE, sales and librarian | At least ¥50,000 | Land and property investment |
| Chung (Uncle) | M | 1952 56 | Married | Senior high school | Entrepreneur at a grocery shop | Worker and vice director at a collectively owned enterprise | ¥10,000 or above | Part-time job |

**Old generation of entrepreneurs (*getihu* 个体户) – *continued***

| Name (Pseudo) | Sex | Age | Marital status | Education | Present job | Former job | Monthly income (¥RMB) | Other income or investment |
|---|---|---|---|---|---|---|---|---|
| Fong (Uncle) | M | 1960 48 | Married | Senior high school | Entrepreneur at a garment factory, entertainment and resort centre, construction and building company, electronic and air-conditioner company | Worker at SOE. He was a butcher, salesman and teacher | At least ¥200,000 | Entertainment centres, air-conditioner company and resort centre. Land and property investment |
| Henry (Uncle) | M | 1958 50 | Married | Senior high school | Entrepreneur at a cement factory | Worker and vice director at a SOE/joint venture enterprise | At least ¥100,000 | Part-time job. Investment in commercial centre, land and property investment |
| Ho (Uncle) | M | 1959 49 | Married | Senior high school | Entrepreneur at a handbag factory | Worker at a SOE, teacher, attempted different businesses | At least ¥50,000 | Part-time job. Property investment |
| Jimmy (Uncle) | M | 1959 49 | Married | Senior high school | Entrepreneur at a multinational enterprise | Supervisor at a foreign venture or multinational enterprise | At least ¥50,000 | Shares and property investment |

**Old generation of entrepreneurs ('getihu' 个体户) – continued**

| Name (Pseudo) | Sex | Age | Marital status | Education | Present job | Former job | Monthly income (¥RMB) | Other income or investment |
|---|---|---|---|---|---|---|---|---|
| Kwok (Uncle) | M | 1968 40 | Married | Senior high school | Director at a property company | Manager at a foreign venture enterprise | At least ¥30,000 | Shares and funds |
| Lam (Uncle) | M | 1968 40 | Married | University graduate | Entrepreneur at a printing company | Cadre at a SOE and manager at a foreign venture enterprise | ¥30,000 or above | Property investment |
| Lee (Uncle) | M | 1968 40 | Married | University graduate | Entrepreneur at a garment factory | Worker at a SOE; farmer | At least ¥40,000 | Shares and property investment |
| Lisa (Aunt) | F | 1968 40 | Married | University graduate | Entrepreneur at a garment factory | Worker at a SOE | At least ¥100,000 | Shares and property investment |
| Moss (Uncle) | M | 1960 48 | Married | Senior high school | Entrepreneur at a garment factory | Cadre at a SOE. Worker at a collectively owned enterprise | ¥50,000 or above | Property investment |
| Pan (Uncle) | M | 1968 40 | Married | Senior high school | Entrepreneur at a property company | SOE worker and farmer | ¥50,000 | Shares and property investment |
| Robert (Uncle) | M | 1958 50 | Married | University graduate | Entrepreneur at a mobile phone company | Worker/manager at a SOE, accountant | ¥50,000 | Shares and property investment |
| Sam (Uncle) | M | 1959 49 | Married | Senior high school | Entrepreneur at an underwear factory | Cadre at a SOE | At least ¥10,000 | Shares and funds |

Old generation of entrepreneurs (*'getihu'* 个体户) – *continued*

| Name (Pseudo) | Sex | Age | Marital status | Education | Present job | Former job | Monthly income (¥RMB) | Other income or investment |
|---|---|---|---|---|---|---|---|---|
| Tony (Uncle) | M | 1958 50 | Married | Senior high school | Entrepreneur at an infrastructure company | Worker and vice director at a collectively owned enterprise | At least ¥100,000 | Investment in commercial centres and residential buildings |
| Victor (Uncle) | M | 1958 50 | Married | Bachelor's and MBA (part-time mode) | Entrepreneur at a listed garment company | Managerial position at a SOE, entrepreneur | At least ¥100,000 | Part-time job, land and property investment, shares and funds |
| Yuen (Uncle) | M | 1952 56 | Married | Senior high school | Entrepreneur at a machine factory | Worker at a joint or foreign venture enterprise and entrepreneur | At least ¥100,000 | Land and property investment |

Total number of the old generation of entrepreneurs: 21.

**Young generation of entrepreneurs (*'getihu'* 个体户)**

| Name (Pseudo) | Sex | Age | Marital status | Education | Present occupation | Former occupation | Estimated monthly income (¥RMB) | Other income or investment |
|---|---|---|---|---|---|---|---|---|
| Ada | F | 1976 32 | Married | University graduate | Entrepreneur at a garment factory | Manager at a foreign owned enterprise | At least ¥50,000 | Shares and funds, property investment |
| Ben | M | 1973 35 | Married | Bachelor's and MBA | Entrepreneur at an air-conditioning company | Manager at a multinational enterprise | At least ¥100,000 | Shares and property investment |
| Chiu | M | 1970 28 | Married | Senior high school | Entrepreneur at an automobile factory | Manager at a foreign venture enterprise | At least ¥10,000 | Shares and funds |
| Fai | M | 1980 28 | Married | University graduate | Entrepreneur at an embroidery factory | Customer service at a foreign venture enterprise | At least ¥20,000 | Shares |
| Ken | M | 1978 30 | Married | University graduate and MBA | Entrepreneur at an engineering company | Nil (student) | At least ¥50,000 | Part-time job. Shares and property investment |
| King | M | 1972 30 | Married | Senior high school | Entrepreneur at a garment factory | Manager at a foreign venture enterprise | At least ¥50,000 | Shares and property investment |
| Mark | M | 1973 35 | Married | University graduate | Entrepreneur at an automobile factory | Manager at a foreign venture enterprise | At least ¥30,000 | Shares and property investment |

**Young generation of entrepreneurs ('*getihu*' 个体户) – *continued***

| Name (Pseudo) | Sex | Age | Marital status | Education | Present occupation | Former occupation | Estimated monthly income (¥RMB) | Other income or investment |
|---|---|---|---|---|---|---|---|---|
| Peter | M | 1974 34 | Single | University graduate | Entrepreneur at a garment factory | Waiter, designer, bartender and worker at a private garment factory | About ¥80,000–¥90,000 | Shares, funds and property investment |
| Sunny | M | 1974 34 | Single | University graduate | Entrepreneur at a garment factory | Supervisor at a joint venture enterprise | ¥80,000–¥90,000 | Shares and property investment |
| Tsang | M | 1971 37 | Married | Senior high school | Entrepreneur at a garment company | Manager at a foreign venture enterprise | ¥60,000–¥70,000 | Shares and funds, property investment |

Total number of the young generation of entrepreneurs: 10.
Total no. of entrepreneurs: 31.

**Old generation of professionals**

| Name (Pseudo) | Sex | Age | Marital status | Education | Present job | Former job | Monthly income (¥RMB) | Other income or investment |
|---|---|---|---|---|---|---|---|---|
| Tom (Uncle) | M | 1963 45 | Married | University graduate | Managing director at a service company | Cadre, managerial position at a SOE | ¥80,000– ¥90,000 | Part-time job |
| Vicky (Uncle) | M | 1963 45 | Married | University graduate | Managerial director at a service company | Cadre and manager at a SOE | ¥80,000– ¥90,000 | Shares, funds and property investment |
| Wah (Uncle) | M | 1958 50 | Married | University graduate | Deputy director at a property company | Worker at a SOE, reporter, writer and editor | ¥70,000– ¥80,000 | Shares and property investment |
| Yang (Uncle) | M | 1968 40 | Married | PhD | Associate professor | Assistant professor | ¥15,000– ¥20,000 | Shares and property investment |

Total numbers of the old generation of professionals are 4.

**Young generation of professionals**

| Name (Pseudo) | Sex | Age | Marital status | Education | Present job | Former job | Monthly income (¥RMB) | Other income or investment |
|---|---|---|---|---|---|---|---|---|
| Alex | M | 1973 35 | Married | University graduate | Managerial position at a telecommunication company | Engineer | Around ¥7,000 | Part-time job, shares, funds, property investment |
| Andy | M | 1973 35 | Married | University graduate | Professional | Teacher and sport trainer | Around ¥30,000 | Property investment |
| Betty | F | 1978 30 | Single | Master's | Professional | Student | Around ¥8,000 | Shares |
| Dan | M | 1979 29 | Single | PhD | Professional | Student | Around ¥5,000 (part-time) | Shares and funds |
| Kong | M | 1978 30 | Single | University graduate | Website designer at a multinational enterprise | Fashion designer, secondary teacher | About ¥5,000 for his basic salary | Part-time jobs, shares, funds and property investment |
| Ivy | F | 1982 26 | Single | University graduate | Professional | Student | Around ¥9,000 | Shares |
| Jacky | M | 1978 30 | Married | University graduate | Taekwondo trainer | Teacher and sport trainer | Around ¥8,000 | Shares and funds |
| Jiang | M | 1977 31 | Married | PhD | Assistant Professor | Student | Around ¥15,000 | Shares |

**Young generation of professionals** – *continued*

| Name (Pseudo) | Sex | Age | Marital status | Education | Present job | Former job | Monthly income (¥RMB) | Other income or investment |
|---|---|---|---|---|---|---|---|---|
| Lily | F | 1978 30 | Married | Senior high school and technical school of Taekwondo | Taekwondo trainer | Teacher and sport trainer | Around ¥8,000 | Shares and funds |
| Mary | F | 1983 25 | Single | MBA | Accountant | Student in France | Around ¥9,000 | Shares and funds |
| Melody | F | 1980 28 | Single | Master's degree | Professional | Student | Around ¥8,000 | Shares |
| Sung | M | 1978 30 | Single | University graduate | Freelance designer | Professional | Around ¥8,000 | Shares and funds |
| Tong | M | 1976 32 | Single | University graduate | Engineer at a private company | Trainee | ¥8,000 above for his basic salary ONLY | Shares, funds, bonus and commission from his job |

Total numbers of the young generation are 13.
**Total of interviewees: 59.**
**Regional cadres: 11.**
**Entrepreneurs: 31.**
**Professionals: 17.**

# Appendix 3
# Casenotes of Chen Xitong (陈希同)

[Criminal; Corruption; Embezzlement; China]

## CASENOTES

### People's Republic of China v. Chen Xitong (陈希同) (1995)

Defendant was a city mayor and a well-connected Politburo member accused of corruption, embezzlement and dereliction of duty in an anti-corruption drive instigated by political rivals. His colleague, the vice-mayor, committed suicide in the wake of the corruption charges. D was sentenced to 16 years in prison but released after serving half the term. The small amount of money said to be involved in the embezzlement suggests that D's political downfall and removal from public office may have been politically inspired. D's downfall was not saved by his hardline political stance during the Tiananmen Square protests several years previously.

## FACTS:

(1)   Chen Xitong (simplified Chinese: 陳希同 ; traditional Chinese: 陳希同; pinyin: *Chén Xītóng*), born June 1930, was a member of the Politburo of the Communist Party of China and the Mayor of Beijing until he was removed from office on charges of corruption in 1995.

(2)   In 1995, Chen was removed from mayoral office on charges of corruption and dereliction of duty. It was later revealed that Chen had embezzled RMB¥5,000,000 (renminbi five million yuan).

(3)   Details not known or unreported: arrest date, place of questioning, formal charges, prosecuting body, trial dates, trial court, prosecution, defence and judges/adjudicators.

(4)   In 1998, Chen was given a 16-year prison sentence. Place of incarceration are not known or unreported.

(5)   In 2006, Chen was released early from prison, officially on reasons of ill health, after serving eight years of his 16-year sentence.

## UNRELATED FACTS:

(6)   His son, Chen Xiaotong, was also charged and sentenced contemporaneously.

(7)   Before the corruption charges, Beijing Vice Mayor Wang Baosen committed suicide in 1994.

(8)  A graduate of Peking University, Chen had close ties to Deng Xiaoping and his family. Chen was once considered a possible successor to Deng Xiaoping.

(9)  A one time rival to Jiang Zemin, Chen's downfall came in 1995 during an anti-corruption campaign led by Jiang's Shanghai clique. Clique members Zeng Qinghong and Jia Qinglin played key roles in the campaign that eventually led to Chen's arrest.

(10)  Some observers viewed Chen's fall as a political struggle between him and Jiang because it was only revealed later that Chen had embezzled RMB¥5,000,000 (five million yuan). Observers considered it to be a relatively small amount compared with the higher amounts of other corrupt cadres who were left unscathed in the anti-corruption campaign.

(11)  Beijing residents were apparently pleased to see Chen fall from grace. Chen was mayor of Beijing at the time of the Tiananmen protests. He was advocating use of force to quell protestors and was responsible for declaring martial law in the city that led to shootings of the protesters.

(12)  During the 1980s, Chen became a fan of American TV series *Hunter* when it was first aired in China. In his speeches, Chen made various references to the TV series.

(13)  In December 1996, a fictionalised account of the case was published in novel form and quickly banned in China. It was written from the point of an investigator and many pirate copies were printed or available.

> 'The Wrath of Heaven: The Anti-Corruption Bureau in Action'
> [天怒：反贪局在行动 *Tiān Nú: Fǎntānjú Zài Xíngdòng*]
> By Fang Wen [pseudonym]
> Published by Yuanfang Chubanshe of Hohhot, Inner Mongolia
> Year of publication: December 1996
> ISBN 7-80595-271-X/1 120
> Printed January 1997 (press run of 5,000 copies)

Hearsay source:
http://web.archive.org/web/20030308005126/http://www.usembassy-china.org.cn/sandt/wrath.htm

Casenote prepared on 1st September 2009

# Appendix 4
# Casenotes of Ching Cheong (程翔)

[Criminal; Espionage; China]

## CASENOTES

### People's Republic of China v. Ching Cheong (程翔) (2005)

## Full citation

People's Republic of China (Beijing People's Procuratorate Branch No. 2) v. Ching Cheong (程翔) [2005] 31 August 2006 *Reuters* (*Financial Times*) [Beijing Second Intermediate Court, Criminal Case No. 862]

Defendant (D) was the first Hong Kong journalist to be detained by China for espionage since the Hong Kong sovereignty handover. D accused of receiving a manuscript containing secret memoirs of Zhao Ziyang. Formally charged with passing state secrets to Taiwan for monetary reward over a five-year period. D alleged entrapment by authorities. Authorities regarded the Home Visit Permit on which D travelled into China was a form of Chinese citizenship. Sentenced to five years' imprisonment but released after having served half the term.

# Notes

## Introduction: China Engages a Middle-Class Society in the 21st Century?

1  All the exchange rate in this study is RMB1 = US$0.146 and RMB1 = £0.102. Retrieved www.xe.com on 25 May 2010.
2  'Collectively-owned enterprise' (*jiti suoyouzhi qiye* 集体所有制企业 ) is an economic unit (i.e. business) where the assets are owned collectively by the workers and/or managers of the unit (China Data Online 2008).
3  The notion of housing classes in Western sociology is associated in particular with the work of Peter Saunders (1984).
4  When I collected data in 2008, most of the Chinese new middle class prefer to belong to an urban *hukou* rather than a rural one. But from 2010, the Chinese government launched a campaign to attract more people to retain their rural *hukou* by giving more land to the holders of the rural *hukou*. This explains why most of the migrant workers prefer to preserve their rural *hukou*. This means that the urban *hukou* has lost its privileges since 2010.
5  This is learned from in-depth interviews with the Chinese new middle class.
6  Gifts should not be understood as bribery. The Chinese are at times highly sensitive about matters of social honour and sensibility ('face'), for instance, they are fond of comparing gift money from celebrations or even funerals to show which person has the most 'face'.

## Chapter 1    (Re) Framing Class Theories: Class Analysis in Post-Reform China

1  See Wang (2004) for further details about *hukou*. See Solinger (1999) for a vivid description and analysis of how *hukou* constrains the rights and life chances of urban and rural populations in China.
2  Those who have urban *hukou* in Guangdong can pay cheaper tuition fees, have special discounts or receive hospitalisation expenses and medical care. In addition, urban *hukou* holders are entitled to compensation if they have traffic accidents. If one pays tax approximately RMB80,000 for five consecutive years, one is entitled to an urban *hukou* in Guangdong (Chan 2009; in-depth interviews 2008). Though buying a house in Guangdong does not automatically entitle one to an urban *hukou* in today's China, many of the Chinese new middle class still have their advantages in gaining their urban *hukou*, in contrast to some migrant workers.
3  For the benefit of legally minded readers, the Chinese meaning of freehold is analogous to the English legal term 'fee simple absolute in possession'. Thus, freehold ownership is not liable to end upon the death of any person, where

ownership rights are not conditional or liable to terminate on the occurrence of any event, and that owner's rights are immediate but need not imply physical occupation of the property.

## Chapter 2    Class Boundaries of the Old Generation of the Chinese New Middle Class

1   As children, the first generation lived through the famine at the time of the Great Leap Forward in 1958 (Yang 1996). With the disruption of their education, the government carried out a 'send-down' policy intended to lower the rate of urban unemployment and build up rural development. Millions of urban youth were 'mobilised' and sent 'up the mountains and down to the villages' (上山下乡运动 *shangshan xiaxiang*) (Bernstein 1977). Secondary school graduates at the outbreak of the Cultural Revolution are later dubbed *laosanjie* (老三届 the 'three old classes') in the reform years. Many married couples during the Cultural Revolution lived apart in different cities for years at a time. The experience of the first generation of having a peaceful life only began when Deng Xiaoping launched the economic reforms in 1978. Therefore, major nationwide socialist campaigns to re-engineer everyday life define the first generation (Hung & Chiu 2003: 210).

2   For details of the research samples see the Appendices at the end of the book.

3   'Smuggling' (*zousi* 走私) has a somewhat different meaning in Chinese. Normally speaking, smuggling has a negative meaning in Chinese. The Chinese meaning can cover illegal stowaway (*toudu* 偷渡). In addition, the legal meaning of smuggling is 'the offence of importing or exporting specified goods that are subject to customs or excise duties without having paid the requisite duties' (*Oxford Dictionary of Law*, 4th edition, 1997: 434). But the normal English meaning is to bring into or take out of the country secretly under illegal conditions.

4   That may variously be Standard Cantonese *vs.* any other kind of Cantonese, or Cantonese *vs.* the dialects of other provinces or regions, or Cantonese *vs.* Putonghua or even Putonghua spoken in Guangdong *vs.* Putonghua spoken in other regions.

5   I interviewed those members of the Chinese new middle class in 2008. All ages of the Chinese new middle class are as at the year 2008. In 2008, the old generation sorted out any opportunities arising from the World Expo to be held in Shanghai in 2010.

6   *Wuliangye* 五粮液 ('The Five Nights') and *Xiaohutuxin* 小葫涂仙 ('Fairy of the Little Lake') are top-selling brands of alcohol in China. *Xiaohutuxin* in particular is a favourite among the older new middle class in Guangdong. The name *Xiaohutuxin* apparently means something along the lines of 'to soothe annoyance and anxiety', so to serve this brand at gatherings is to suggest that annoyance or disappointment would become lessened.

7   *Hongtashan* (红塔山 'Red Pagoda Mountain') is a domestic brand of cigarettes from the southwestern part of Yunnan and highly popular in Guangdong. Most domestic cigarettes come in soft packs but *Hongtashan* comes in a crushproof packet and costs around RMB15 (US$2 or £1.3) a packet, much higher than the price of foreign brands. In fact, *Hongtashan* is considered the archetypal brand-name cigarette in Guangdong. Also popular are

imported and foreign-branded cigarettes. Back in the 1990s, Good Companion 良友 (*Liang You*), a Hong Kong-made premium brand made from blended American tobacco and priced around RMB5 (less than £1) a packet, was popular with entrepreneurs. Today, the most popular foreign brands are the so-called *laopaizi* (老牌子 'the old brands'): Kent, followed by Winston, Marlboro and other brands such as 555 (Davis 2000a: 275). The 555 in particular evoke images of 'old money' business family heritage within the Guangdong business community and connote an aura of good breeding, reliability and professionalism. The average price of foreign cigarettes is RMB12 (£1) a packet. The state heavily regulates and taxes cigarette imports.

8 The people of Shanghai, Nanjing and Hangzhou are far more fashion conscious than the Cantonese, and they place a considerable amount of cachet on what to wear and how to wear for different occasions. Indeed, they are relatively sophisticated dressers and are very attracted to clothes that are branded and of good construction using quality materials.

## Chapter 3   Generational Effects in the Chinese New Middle Class

1 The name *Huang-rong* comes from (射鵰英雄传 *shediao yingxiongzhuan*). *Limochou* comes from (神雕侠侣 *shendiao xialü*) and *miejueshitai* comes from (倚天屠龙记 *yitian tulong ji*). All are the major characters from the martial arts novel or *gongfu* novel from Jinyong (金庸), a very famous Chinese *gongfu* (功夫) novel writer in Hong Kong and China.

2 Chongqing Commercial Newspaper interviewed 500 single women, their ages range from 28 or over. This research shows about 83.56% have their own houses, 29.16% have cars, 75.46% have a monthly salary of more than RMB4000 (the mean salary in Chongqing was around RMB2248.5 in 2008). ('More you have, more difficult to get married, increases the number of 3S women' ('条件愈好愈难嫁, 3S女日增', *Chinese Daily*, A16, 20 February 2010)). This story predicts what is to happen in Guangdong as well.

3 The Chinese sociologist Li Peilin (2005) finds that the cumulative direct cost of raising children in China from birth to sixteen years is no less than RMB250,000 (US$35,000 or £17,500). Tuition fees for secondary education alone could total as much as RMB48,000. Tertiary education is a major cause of the rising school costs. Most Chinese parents are exceptionally demanding in relation to their children's education, and many are desperate that their children should be fluent in as many as eight languages. Even while the income levels of the Chinese new middle class are constantly rising, they are not keeping pace with the sky-rocketing costs of living (Xiao, Fen 2007).

## Chapter 4   *Guanxi* Networks and the Chinese New Middle Class

1 'Red packets' (*hongbao* 红包) are a uniquely Chinese feature in the exchange of gifts and gift money during times of festivities and celebrations. The practice of giving and receiving red packets is called *song hongbao* (送红包) in Putonghua. 'Red packet' is known in Hong Kong and the rest of the world by its more familiar Cantonese name of *laisee* (利是).

2  That is, to wait around for and solicit customers or be solicited by them with a view to being paid for sex.
3  This is a very well-known private housing estate in China, and particularly in Guangdong province.

## Chapter 5   Class Formation and Political Development

1  Tocqueville (1862/1988).
2  Lipset (1959); Almond & Verba (1963); Inglehart (1997); Diamond (1999).
3  Aspinall (2004).
4  Alagappa (2004).
5  Some authoritarian countries are prosperous in economic development but they do not have strong civil societies. See Przeworski & Limongi (1997); Burhart and Lewis-Beck (1994); Chen & Dickson (2008).
6  Malloy (1974); Newton (1974); Lehmbruch (1977); Spires (2011).
7  For more findings see Tsang & Lee (2013).
8  Unger (2008).
9  Woju (蝸居) or huoguiwu (货柜屋). This means a tiny house like a container. This is a very popular phenomenon in Guangdong. Most of the university graduates struggle to find employment and when they do so, the job is low-paid. It is very difficult for them to maintain high living standards in Guangdong. They rent the house, called a container house, which costs around RMB6 per day. Details refer to http://www.cna.com.tw (大陸底層工蟻抗漲深圳打工族「蝸居」) 8 March 2010. Retrieved 21 April 2010.
10  Ching Cheong was a China-based journalist for *The Straits Times* of Singapore. In 2005, he was arrested in Guangzhou and held almost incommunicado for several years for reporting on 'state secrets'. He was released in 2007 on health reasons and with the help of the Hong Kong SAR government. See the casenotes in Appendix 4 for details.
11  Zhu Rongji (朱镕基) was a vice-premier of the State Council in 1993–98. He was then promoted to the fifth Premier of the People's Republic of China, serving from March 1998 to March 2003.

## Conclusion: A China in the Making with a New Middle Class?

1  Just in 2010, at least two books were published on this issue: Zhang 2010 and Li 2010.

# Bibliography and Citations

*Note*: For legal citations, simplified Chinese characters are used by default unless otherwise indicated. Traditional Chinese characters are in round brackets.

## Caselaw

People's Republic of China *v.* Chen Xitong 陳希同 (1995).

## Statutes, Legislation, and Treaties

Basic Law of the Hong Kong Special Administrative Region of the People's Republic of China (中华人民共和国香港特别行政区基本法) [1 July 1997].

City Planning Law of the People's Republic of China 中华人民共和国城市规划法 [1989], promulgated 26 December 1989; HTML document at http://english.mep. gov.cn/Policies_Regulations/laws/envirelatedlaws/200710/t20071009_109927.htm.

Employment Promotion Law 中华人民共和国就业促进法 [2007] (passed 30 August 2007, entered into force 1 January 2008).

Individual Visit Scheme (自由行) (entered into force 28 July 2008; PRC: 个人游)

Labour Contract Law 中华人民共和国劳动合同法 [2008] (in force January 2008).

Mainland and Hong Kong Closer Economic Partnership Arrangement (内地与香港关于建立更紧密经贸关系的安排) [2003].

Property Law of the People's Republic of China 中华人民共和国物权法 [2007], promulgated 16 March 2007; HTML document at http://big5.xinhuanet.com/gate/ big5/news.xinhuanet.com/legal/2007-03/26/content_5898343.htm.

Regulations on *Hukou* Registration of the People's Republic of China 中华人民共和国户口登记条例 [January 1958], issued by the Standing Committee of the National People's Congress.

State Constitution of the People's Republic of China 中华人民共和国宪法 [1982].

## Bibliography

Acciaioli, G. L. (1981). Knowing What You're Doing? A Review of Pierre Bourdieu's Outline of a Theory of Practice. *Canberra Anthropology*, IV, **1**, 23–51.

Alagappa, M. (2004). Civil Society and Political Change: An Analytical Framework. In M. Alagappa (ed.), *Civil Society and Political Change in Asia: Expanding and Contracting Democratic Space* (pp. 25–60). Stanford, CA: Stanford University Press.

Aldridge, A. (2003). *Consumption*. London: Polity Press.

Almond, G. A. & Verba, S. (1963). *The Civic Culture: Political Attitudes and Democracy in Five Nations*. Princeton: Princeton University Press.

Anagnost, A. (2008). From Class to Social Strata: Grasping the Social Totality in Reform-Era China. *Third World Quarterly*, **29**(3): 497–519.

Anderson, A. R. & Lee, Y. C. (2008). From Tradition to Modern: Attitudes and Applications of *Guanxi* in Chinese Entrepreneurship. *Journal of Small Business and Enterprise Development*, **15**(4): 775–787.

Andreas, J. (2009). *Rise of the Red Engineers. The Cultural Revolution and the Origins of China's New Class*. Stanford, CA: Stanford University Press.

Arbam, L. H. (ed.) (1989). *Race, Radicalism, and Reform*; with an Introduction by W. J. Darity. NJ: Transaction Publishers.

Ashley, D. & Orenstein, D. M. (2005). *Sociological Theory: Classical Statements*. NJ: Pearson.

Aspinall, E. (2004). Indonesia: Transformation of Civil Society and Democratic Breakthrough. In M. Alagappa (ed.) *Civil Society and Political Change in Asia: Expanding and Contracting Democratic Space* (p. 62). Stanford, CA: Stanford University Press.

Barnard, M. (1996). *Fashion as Communication*. London: Routledge.

Baron, S., Field, J. & Schuller, T. (ed.) (2000). *Social Capital: Critical Perspectives*. Oxford: Oxford University Press.

Baudrillard, J. (1998). *The Consumer Society: Myths and Structure*. London: Sage.

Beck, U. (1992). *World Risk Society: Towards a New Modernity*. London: Sage.

Beck, U. & Beck-Gernsheim, E. (2002). *Individualization: Institutionalized Individualism and its Social and Political Consequences*. London: Sage.

Belk, R. W. (1988). Possessions and the Extended Self. *Journal of Consumer Research*, **15**(2): 139–168.

Belk, R. W. (1991). Possessions and the Sense of Past. In R. W. Belk (ed.), *Highways and Buyways: Naturalistic Research from the Consumer Behaviour Odyssey, Association for Consumer Research* (pp. 114–130). Valdosta, GA.

Bernstein, T. P. (1977). *Up to the Mountains and Down to the Villages: The Transfer of Youth from Urban to Rural China*. New Haven, CT: Yale University Press.

Bestor, T. C. (2005). How Sushi Went Global. In James L. Watson and Melissa L. Caldwell (eds), *The Cultural Politics of Food and Eating: A Reader* (pp. 13–20). Malden, MA: Blackwell.

Bian, Yanjie (1994). *Work and Inequality in Urban China*. Albany, New York: State University of New York Press.

Bian, Yanjie (2002a). Chinese Social Stratification and Social Mobility. *Annual Review of Sociology*, **28**, 91–116.

Bian, Yanjie (2002b). Sociological Research on Reform-Era China. *Issues and Studies*, **38**(9): 139–174.

Bian, Yanjie, Breiger, R., Davis, D. S. *et al.* (2005). Occupation, Class, and Social Networks in Urban China. *Social Forces*, **83**(4): 1443–1468.

Bian, Yanjie, Logan, J. R. *et al.* (1997). Work Units and Housing Reform in Two Chinese Cities. In X. Lu & E. Perry (eds), *Danwei: The Chinese Work Unit in Historical and Comparative Perspective* (pp. 223–250). New York: M. E. Sharpe.

Bloomberg News (2009). *Morning Call*, Television Programme Broadcast 6 a.m. December 3, Hong Kong: Bloomberg Television.

Bourdieu, P. (1977). *Outline of a Theory of Practice*. Cambridge: Cambridge University Press.

Bourdieu, P. (1979). *Distinction: A Social Critique of the Judgement of Taste*. Cambridge, MA: Harvard University Press.

Bourdieu, P. (1982). Introduction. In J. B. Thompson, *Language and Symbolic Power* (pp. 105–162). Cambridge: Polity Press.

Bourdieu, P. (1984). *Distinction: A Social Critique of the Judgment of Taste* (Nice, R. Trans). London: Routledge & Kegan Paul.

Bourdieu, P. (1986). The Forms of Capital. In J. G. Richardson (eds), *Handbook of Theory and Research for the Sociology of Education* (pp. 241–258). New York: Greenwood Press.

Bourdieu, P. (1989). *Distinction: A Social Critique of the Judgement of Taste.* Cambridge, MA: Harvard University Press.

Bourdieu, P. (1990). *In Other Words: Essays Towards a Reflexive Sociology.* Cambridge: Polity Press.

Bourdieu, P. (1991). *Language and Symbolic Power* (Adamson, M. & Adamson, R. Trans). Cambridge, MA: Harvard University Press.

Bourdieu, P. (1996). *The Rules of Art: Genesis and Structure of the Literary Field* (Introduction). Cambridge: Polity Press.

Bourdieu, P. *et al.* (1999). *The Weight of the World: Social Suffering in Contemporary Society.* Cambridge: Polity Press.

Bourdieu, P. & Passeron, J. C. (1979). *The Inheritors: French Students and Their Relation to Culture* (Nice, R. Trans). Chicago: University of Chicago Press.

Bourdieu, P. & Wacquant, L. (1992). *An Invitation to Reflexive Sociology.* Chicago: University of Chicago Press [and] Cambridge: Polity Press.

Bourdieu, P., Wacquant, Loïc J. D. (1992). *An Invitation to Reflexive Sociology.* Chicago: University of Chicago Press.

Breen, R. & Rottman, D. B. (1995). *Class Stratification. A Comparative Perspective.* London: Harvester Wheatsheaf.

Breslin, S. (2000). Decentralization, Globalization and China's Partial Re-Engagement with the Global Economy. *New Political Economy*, 5(2): 205–226.

British Broadcasting Corporation (BBC) (1999, September 9). *Special Report: China's Iron Rice Bowl.* Retrieved June 3, 2009, from http://news.bbc.co.uk/hi/english/static/special_report/1999/09/99/china_50/iron.htm

Brown, P. (2003). The Opportunity Trip: Education and Employment in a Global Economy. *European Educational Research Journal*, 2(1): 141–179.

Bruner, J. (1987). Life as Narrative. *Social Research*, 54(1): 11–32.

Burhart, R. E. & Lewis-Beck, M. (1994). Comparative Democracy: The Economic Development Thesis. *American Political Science Review*, 88(4): 903–910.

Calhoun, C. (2007). Pierre Bourdieu and Social Transformation: Lessons from Algeria. *Development and Change*, 37(6): 1403–1415.

Cao, Y. (2001). Career Inside Organizations: A Comparatively Study of Promotion Determination in Reforming China. *Social Force*, 80: 1–29.

Ceglowski, D. (1997). That's a Good Story, but is it Really Research? *Qualitative Inquiry*, 3(2): 188–201.

Chadha, R. & Husband, P. (2006). *The Cult of the Luxury Brand: Inside Asia's Love Affair with Luxury.* London & Boston: Nicholas Brealey International.

Chambell, C. (1995). The Sociology of Consumption. In D. Miller (ed.), *Acknowledging Consumption: A Review of New Studies* (pp. 96–126). London: Edward Arnold.

Chan, K. W. (2009). The Chinese *Hukou* System at 50. *Eurasian Geography and Economics*, 50(2): 197–221.

Chan, K. W. & Buckingham, W. (2008). Is China Abolishing the *Hukou* System? *The China Quarterly*, 195, 582–606.

Chan, S. C. (2003). Memory Making, Identity Building: The Dynamics of Economics and Politics in the New Territories of Hong Kong. *China Information*, 17, 660–691.

Chaney, D. C. (1994). *The Cultural Turn: Scene-Setting Essays on Contemporary Cultural History*. London: Routledge.

Chaney, D. C. (1996). *Lifestyles: Key Ideas*. London & New York: Routledge.

Chen, A. (2003). China's Changing of the Guard: The New Inequality. *Journal of Democracy*, **14**(1): 51–59.

Chen, C. J. (2006). Elite Mobility in Post-Reform Rural China. *Issues and Studies*, **42**(2): 53–83.

Chen, J. & Dickson, B. J. (2008). Allies of the State: Democratic Support and Regime Support among China's Private Entrepreneurs. *The China Quarterly*, 196 (December), 780–804.

Chen, J. & Lu, C. L. (2005). Social Capital in Urban China: Attitudinal and Behaviour. *Social Science Quarterly*, **88**(2): 422–442.

Chen, X. M. & Sun, J. M. (2006). Sociological Perspectives on Urban China: From Familiar Territories to Complex Terrains. *China Information*, **20**, 519–551.

Cheng, Y. S. (ed.) (2000). *Guangdong in the Twenty-First Century: Stagnation or Second Take-Off?* Hong Kong: City University of Hong Kong Press.

Cheng, Y. S. (ed.) (2007). *Challenges and Policy Programmes of China's New Leadership*. Hong Kong: City University of Hong Kong Press.

Cherrington, R. (1997). Generational Issues in China: A Case Study of the 1980s Generation of Young Intellectuals. *The British Journal of Sociology*, **48**(2): 302–320.

*China Daily* (2005, December 6). First Book on Rural Enterprises, *Xinhuanet*. Retrieved September 9, 2008 from http://news.xinhuanet.com/english/2005-12/06/content_3883231.htm.

China Data Online (2008). All China Data Centre. Retrieved February 2, 2009 from http://chinadataonline.org/info/yearly02.asp.

China Map. Retrieved November 1, 2008 from http://www.travelChinaguide.com/cityguides/guangdong/Dongguan.

China Map. Retrieved February 5, 2009 from http://www.sacu.org/provmap.html.

Chinese Academy of Social Sciences (CASS) (2002). *Dangdai Zhongguo Shehui Jieceng Yanjiu Baogao* (Research Report on Contemporary Chinese Social Strata). Beijing: Shehui Kexue Wenxian Chubanshe.

Chinese Academy of Social Sciences (CASS) (2007). The Average Individual Monthly Salary Level of White-Collar Class in Major Cities in 2007. *Salary Index for the White-Collars: The Anxiety of Social Positioning Behind the Fictitious Criteria*. CBN, A06, P1. Retrieved November 14, 2007 from http://www.univiu.org/research/ten/projects/cass. [In Chinese]

Clark, T. N. & Lipset, S. M. (eds) (2004). *The Breakdown of Class Politics: A Debate on Post Industrial Stratification*. Baltimore: Johns Hopkins University Press.

CNA News (2010, March 18). 大陆底层工蚁抗涨深圳打工族「蜗居」 *CNA News*. Retrieved April 21, 2010 from http://www.cna.com.tw.

Coleman, J. S. (1988). Social Capital in the Creation of Human Capital. *American Journal of Sociology*, Vol. 94, 95–120.

Coleman, J. S. (1990). *Foundations of Social Theory*. Cambridge, MA: Harvard University Press.

Davis, D. S. (1990). Urban Job Mobility. In D. Davis & E. F. Vogel (eds), *Chinese Society on the Eve of Tiananmen* (pp. 85–108). Cambridge, MA: Harvard University Press.

Davis, D. S. (1992a). Job Motility in Post-Mao Cities: Increases on the Margins. *China Quarterly*, **48**, 1062–1085.

Davis, D. S. (1992b). Skidding: Downward Mobility among Children of the Maoist Middle Class. *Modern China*, **18**(4): 410–437.

Davis, D. S. (2000a). Social Class Transformation in Urban China: Training, Hiring and Promoting Urban Professionals and Mangers After 1949. *Modern China*, **26**(3): 251–275.

Davis, D. S. (ed.) (2000b). *The Consumer Revolution in Urban China*. Berkeley: University of California Press.

Davis, D. S. (2003). From Welfare Benefit to Capitalized Asset: The Recommodification of Residential Space in Urban China. In R. Forrest & L. James (eds), *Housing and Social Change: East-West Perspectives* (pp. 183–198). London: Routledge.

Deng, Z. & Treiman, D. J. (1997). The Impact of the Cultural Revolution of Trends in Educational Attainment in the People's Republic of China. *American Journal of Sociology*, **103**, 391–428.

Devine, F. (2005). *Class Practice: How Parents Help Their Children Get Good Jobs*. Cambridge: Cambridge University Press.

Devine, F., Savage, M. & *et al.* (2005). *Rethinking Class Culture, Identities and Lifestyle*. London: Palgrave Macmillan.

Diamond, L. (1999). *Developing Democracy: Toward Consolidation*. Baltimore, MD: The Johns Hopkins University Press.

Dickson, B. J. (2003). *Red Capitalists in China: The Party, Private Entrepreneurs, and Prospects for Political Change*. Cambridge: Cambridge University Press.

Dickson, B. J. (2004). Dilemmas of Party Adaptation: The CCP's Strategies for Survival. In P. H. Gries and S. Rosen (eds), *State and Society in 21st Century China: Crisis, Contention and Legitimation* (pp. 141–158). New York: RoutledgeCurzon.

Dickson, B. J. (2006). The Future of the Chinese Communist Party: Strategies of Survival and Prospects for Change. In J. H. Chung (ed.), *Charting China's Future* (pp. 21–49). Lanham, MD: Rowman & Littlefield.

Dickson, B. J. (2007). Integrating Wealth and Power in China: The Communist Party's Embrace of the Private Section. *China Quarterly*, **192**, 827–854.

Ding, X. L. (1999). Who Gets What, How? When Chinese State-Owned Enterprises Become Shareholding Companies? *Problems of Post-Communism*, **46**(3): 32–41.

Ding, X. L. (2000a). The Illicit Asset Stripping of China State Firms. *The China Journal*, **43**, 1–28.

Ding, X. L. (2000b). Systematic Irregularities and Spontaneous Property Transformation in the Chinese Financial System. *The China Quarterly*, **163**, 655–676.

Djilas, M. (1957). *The New Class: An Analysis of the Communist System*. New York: Frederick A. Praeger.

Douglas, M. & Isherwood, B. (1996). *The World of Goods*. London: Routledge.

Duara, P. (1988). *Culture, Power, and the State: Rural North China, 1900–1942*. Stanford, CA: Stanford University Press.

*Economic Daily* (Jingji Ribao) (2010). 'More You Have, Difficult to Get Married, Increasing the Number of 3S Women' (条件愈好愈难嫁，3S女日增), February 20, A16.

*Economist*, The (2006, August 3). An Old Friend Comes Back. Retrieved June 4, 2009 from http://www.economist.com/world/europe/displaystory.cfm? story_id=7252974.

Fan, C. C. (2002). The Elite, the Natives, and the Outsiders: Migration and Labour Market Segmentation in Urban China. *Annals of the Association of American Geographers*, **92**(1): 103–124.

Farrer, J. (2000). Dancing through the Market Transition: Disco and Dance Hall Sociability in Shanghai. In D. S. Davis (ed.), *The Consumer Revolution in Urban China* (pp. 25–53). Berkeley: University of California Press.

Faure, G. O. (2008). Chinese Society and Its New Emerging Culture. *Journal of Contemporary China*, **17**(56): 469–491.

Featherstone, M. (1991). *Consumer Culture and Postmodernism*. London: Sage.

Fewsmith, J. (2007). The Political Implications of China's Growing Middle Class. *China Leadership Monitor*, **21**, 1–8.

Fladrich, A. M. (2006). Graduate Employment in China: The Case of Jiujiang Financial and Economic College in Jiangxi. *China Information*, **20**, 201–235.

Flew, T. (2006). The New Middle Class Meets the Creative Class: The Masters of Business Administration (MBA) and Creative Innovation in 21st Century China. *International Journal of Cultural Studies*, **9**(3): 419–429.

Fraser, D. (2000). Inventing Oasis: Luxury Housing Advertisements and Reconfiguring Domestic Space in Shanghai. In D. S. Davis (ed.), *The Consumer Revolution in Urban China* (pp. 25–53). Berkeley: University of California Press.

Friedmann, D. D. (1985). Intergenerational Inequalities and the Chinese Revolution. *Modern China*, **2**(April), 177–201.

Friedmann, J. (2005). *China's Urban Transition*. Minneapolis: University of Minnesota Press.

Fung, A. (2005). Music and Youth Culture: From Leisure Consumption to Intervention. *Journal of Youth Studies*, **8**(1): 12–20.

Fung, A. (2009). Fandom, Youth and Consumption in China. *European Journal of Cultural Studies*, **12**(3): 285–303.

Furlong, A. & Cartmel, F. (1997). *Young People and Social Change: Individualisation and Rise in Late Modernity*. Buckingham, England: The Open University Press.

Gallagher, M. (2005). *Contagious Capitalism: Globalization and the Politics of Labour in China*. Princeton, NJ: Princeton University Press.

Gay, D. P. (1996). *Consumption and Identity at Work*. London: Sage.

Gerber, T. P. & Hout, M. (2004). Tightening Up: Declining Class Mobility During Russia's Market Transition. *American Sociological Review*, **69**(5): 677–703.

Giddens, A. (1990). *The Consequences of Modernity*. Stanford, CA: Stanford University Press.

Giddens, A. (1991). *Modernity and Self-Identity: Self and Society in the Late Modern Age*. Cambridge: Polity Press.

Gilbert, N. (eds) (1993). *Research Social Life*. London: Sage.

Gilley, B. (2008). Legitimacy and Institutional Change. *Comparative Political Studies*, **41**(3): 259–284.

Gladney, D. C. (2000). China's National Insecurity: Old Challenges at the Dawn of the New Millennium. *Asian Perspectives on the Challenges of China*. Washington DC: Institute for National Security Studies, National Defence University. Retrieved March 10, 2009 from http://www.comw.org/cmp/full-text/0003gladney.htm.

Gold, T., Guthrie, D. *et al.* (2002). *Social Connections in China: Institution, Cultures, and the Changing Nature of Guanxi*. Cambridge: Cambridge University Press.

Goldman, M. (2005). *From Comrade to Citizen: The Struggle for Political Rights in China*. Cambridge, MA: Harvard University Press.

Goldthorpe, J. H. (1980). *Social Mobility and Class Structure in Modern Britain*. Oxford: Clarendon Press.

Goldthorpe, J. H. (1982). On the Service Class: Its Formation and Future. In A. Giddens & G. Mackenzie (eds), *Social Class and the Division of Labour* (pp. 162–185). London: Cambridge University Press.

Goldthorpe, J. H. & Lockwood, D. (1969). The Affluent Worker: Industrial Attitudes and Behaviour. Cambridge Studies in Sociology. *The Economic Journal*, **79**(313): 167–169.

Goldthorpe, J. H., Lockwood, D. *et al.* (1968). *The Affluent Worker: Industrial Attitudes and Behaviour*. Cambridge: Cambridge University Press.

Goodman, D. S. G. (1996). The People's Republic of China: The Party-State, Capitalist Revolution and New Entrepreneurs. In R. Robison & D. S. G. Goodman (eds), *The New Rich in Asia* (pp. 225–242). London: Routledge.

Goodman, D. S. G. (1998). In Search of China's New Middle Classes: The Creation of Wealth and Diversity in Shaanxi during the 1990s. *Asian Studies Review*, **22**(1): 39–62.

Goodman, D. S. G. (1999). The New Middle Class. In M. Goldman & R. MacFarquhar (eds), *The Paradox of Post-Mao Reforms* (pp. 241–261). Cambridge, MA: Harvard University Press.

Goodman, D. S. G. (ed.) (2008). *The New Rich in China: Future Rulers, Present Lives*. London & New York: Routledge.

Gouldner, A. W. (1979). *The Future of Intellectuals and the Rise of the New Class*. London: Macmillan.

Guangdong Provincial Statistical Bureau (GPBS) (2001–2009). *Guangdong Statistical Yearbook*. Beijing: China Statistics Press.

Guthrie, D. (1998). The Declining Significance of *Guanxi* in China's Economic Transition. *The China Quarterly*, **9**, 254–282.

Hannum, E. (2005). Market Transition, Educational Disparities, and Family Strategies in Rural China: New Evidence on Gender Stratification and Development. *Demography*, **42**(2): 257–299.

Hasan, S. (2005). Social Capital and Social Entrepreneurship in Asia: Analyzing the Links. *Asia Pacific Journal of Public Administration*, **27**(1): 1–17.

Heberer, T. (2007). *Doing Business in Rural China: Liangshan's New Ethnic Entrepreneurs*. Seattle, WA: University of Washington Press.

Held, D. & McGrew, A. (2002). *Globalization/Antiglobalization*. Cambridge: Polity Press.

Held, D. & McGrew, A. (eds) (2003). *The Global Transformations Reader*. Cambridge: Polity Press.

Hewitt, D. (2007). *Getting Rich First: Life in A Changing China*. New York: Vintage.

Ho, P. (2001). Who Owns China's Land? Politics, Property Rights and Deliberate Institutional Ambiguity. *The China Quarterly*, **2001**, 394–421.

Hoffman, L. (2006). Autonomous Choices and Patriotic Professionalism: On Governmentality in Late-Socialist China. *Economy and Society*, **34**(5): 550–570.

Holmwood, J. (2007). Only Connect: The Challenge of Globalization for the Social Sciences. *21st Century Society*, **2**(1): 79–93.

Hsu, C. L. (2005). A Taste of 'Modernity': Working in a Western Restaurant in Market Socialist China. *Ethnography*, **6**(4): 543–565.

Huang, X. B. (2008). *Guanxi* Networks and Job Searchers in China's Emerging Labour Market: A Qualitative Investigation. *Work Employment Society*, **22**, 467–484.

Hubacek, K., Guan, D. & *et al.* (2007). Changing Lifestyles and Consumption Patterns in Developing Countries: A Scenario Analysis for China and India. *Futures*, **39**, 1084–1096.

Hughes, N. C. (1998). Smashing the Iron Rice Bowl. *Foreign Affairs*, July/August. Palm Coast, FL: Council on Foreign Relations. Retrieved June 3, 2009 from http://www.foreignaffairs.com/articles/54211/neil-c-hughes/ smashing-the-iron-rice-bowl.

Hui, C. H. (1988). Measurement of Individualism-Collectivism. *Journal of Research in Personality*, **22**, 17–36.

Hung, K. H., Fang F. G. *et al.* (2007). A Social Institutional Approach to Identifying Generation Cohorts in China with a Compassion with American Consumers. *Journal of International Business Studies*, **38**, 836–853.

Hung, P. W. & Chiu, W. K. (2003). The Lost Generation: Life Course Dynamics and Xiagang in China. *Modern China*, **29**(2): 204–236.

Hurst, W. (2006). The City as the Focus: The Analysis of Contemporary Chinese Urban Politics. *China Information*, **20**, 457–479.

Inglehart, R. (1977). *The Silent Revolution: Changing Values and Political Styles Among Western Publics*. Princeton, NJ: Princeton University Press.

Inglehart, R. (1990). *Culture Shift in Advanced Industrial Society*. Princeton, NJ: Princeton University Press.

Inglehart, R. (1997). *Modernization and Postmodernization: Cultural, Economic, and Political Change in 43 Societies*. Princeton, NJ: Princeton University Press.

Inglehart, R. & Norris, P. (2003). *Rising Ride: Gender Equality and Cultural Change Around the World*. Cambridge: Cambridge University Press.

Institute of Economy, National Development and Reform Commission (IENDRC) (2007). Retrieved January 2, 2008 from http://en.ndrc.gov.cn/.

Jacksons, P. (2008). Pierre Bourdieu: The Cultural Turn and the Practice of International History. *Review of International Studies*, **34**, 155–181.

Jacques, M. N. (2009). *When China Rules the World: The Rise of the Middle Kingdom and the End of the Western World*. London: Penguin Books.

Jayne, M. (2006). *Cites and Consumption*. London & New York: Routledge.

Ji, J. (2003). An Assessment of the Demographic Transition in China. *Journal of Developing Societies*, **19**(1): 1–25.

Jim, C. Y. & Chen, W. Y. (2009). Leisure Participation Pattern of Residents in a New Chinese City. *Annals of the Association of American Geographers*, **99**(4): 657–673.

Josselson, R. & Lieblich, A. (eds) (1999). *Making Meaning of Narratives in the Narrative Study of Lives*. Thousand Oaks, CA: Sage.

Jussaume, R. (2001). Factors Associated with Modern Urban Chinese Food Consumption Patterns. *Journal of Contemporary China*, **10**(27): 219–232.

Konrad, G. & Szelenyi, I. (1979). *Intellectuals on the Road to Power: A Sociological Study of the Role of the Intelligentsia in Socialism*. New York: Harcourt Brace Jovanovich.

Kraus, R. C. (1981). *Class Conflict in Chinese Socialism*. New York: Columbia University Press.

Kung, K. S. & Lin, Y. M. (2007). The Decline of Township-and-Village Enterprises in China's Economic Transition. *World Development*, **35**(4): 569–584.

Kwong, W. M. (2001). *Constructing Social Work, Stories of the Developing Social Worker*. Unpublished dissertation submitted to the University of Bristol. United Kingdom.

Laliberte, A. & Lanteigne, M. (eds) (2008). *The Chinese Party-State in the 21st Century: Adaptation and the Reinvention of Legitimacy*. London & New York: Routledge.

Lamont, M. (1989). Social Space and Symbolic Power. *Sociological Theory*, 7(1): 14–25.

Lamont, M. (1992). *Money, Morals and Manners: The Culture of the French and American Upper-Middle Class*. Chicago & London: The University of Chicago Press.

Lamont, M. & Fournier, M. (1992). *Cultivating Differences: Symbolic Boundaries and the Making of Inequality*. Chicago & London: University of Chicago Press.

Lamont, M. & Lareau, A. (1988). Cultural Capital: Allusions, Gaps and Glissandos in Recent Theoretical Developments. *Sociological Theory*, 6(3): 153–168.

Latham, K., Thompson, S. *et al.* (2006). *Consuming China: Approaches to Cultural Change in Contemporary China*. London & New York: Routledge.

Lau, P. Y. (2002). Symbolic Boundaries and Domains of Social Relationship: A Preliminary Study of the Normative Formation of the Hong Kong Middle Classes. *E-Journal on Hong Kong Cultural and Social Studies*, 1(2): 247–266.

Lee, C. & Shen, Y. (2009). China: The Paradox and Possibility of a Public Sociology of Labour. *Work and Occupations*, 36(2): 110–125.

Lee, C. K. (2000). The Revenge of History: Collective Memories and Labour Protests in North-Eastern China. *Ethnography*, 1(2): 217–237.

Lee, C. K. (2005). *Livelihood Struggles and Market Reform: (Un)making Chinese Labor After State Socialism*. Geneva: United Nations Research Institute for Social Development, Occasional Paper.

Lee, C. K. & Yang, G. B. (eds) (2007). *Re-envisioning the Chinese Revolution: The Politics and Poetics of Collective Memories in Reform China*. Washington DC: Woodrow Wilson Center Press.

Lee, J. & Zhu, Y. P. (2009). Neoliberalizing Chinese Cities: Housing Reform and Urbanization. In C. L. Li (eds), *The Chinese State in Transition Processes and Contests in Local China* (pp. 36–54). London & New York: Routledge.

Lehmbruch, G. (1977). Liberal Corporatism and Party Government. *Comparative Political Studies*, 10, 91–126.

Li, C. (ed.) (2010). *China's Emerging Middle Class Beyond Economic Transformation*. Washington DC: Brookings Institution Press.

Li, C. L. (ed.) (2009). *The Chinese State in Transition Processes and Contests in Local China*. London & New York: Routledge.

Li, H. (2003). Middle Class: Friends or Foes to Beijing's New Leadership. *Journal of Chinese Political Science*, 8(1&2), Fall 2003, 87–100.

Li, H. (2006). Emergence of the Chinese Middle Class and Its Implications. *Asian Affairs*, 33(2): 67–83.

Li, H. B., Meng, L. S. & Zheng, J. S. (2006). Why Do Entrepreneurs Enter Politics? Evidence From China. *Economic Inquiry*, 44(3): 559–578.

Li, Z. (2001). Migration & Privation of Space and Power in Late Socialist China. *American Ethnologist*, February, 28(1): 179–205.

Li, Z. (2010). *China's Emerging Middle Class Beyond Economic Transformation*. Washington DC: Brookings Institution Press.

Liechty, M. (2003). *Suitably Modern: Making Middle Class Culture in a New Consumer Society*. Princeton & Oxford: Princeton University Press.

Lin, N. (1982). Social Resources and Instrumental Action. In P. V. Marsden & N. Lin (eds), *Social Structure and Network Analysis* (pp. 131–145). Beverly Hills, CA: Sage.

Lin, N. (1995a). Les Resources Sociales: Une Theorie Du Capital Social. *Revue Francaise*, XXXVI, **4**, 685–704.

Lin, N. (1995b). Local Market Socialism: Local Corporatism in Action in Rural China. *Theory and Society*, **24**, 301–354.

Lin, N. (1999). Building a Network Theory of Social Capital. *Connections*, **22**(1): 28–51.

Lin, N. (2000). 'Social Capital: Social Networks, Civic Engagement, or Trust?' in the proceedings of the Second Annual Meeting of the Hong Kong Sociological Association (pp. 1–52), 25 November.

Lin, N. (2001). *Social Capital: A Theory of Structure and Action*. Cambridge: Cambridge University Press.

Lingle, C. (1997). *The Rise and Decline of the Asian Century*. London: IB Tauris.

Lipset, S. M. (1959). Some Social Requisites of Democracy: Economic Development and Political Legitimacy. *American Political Science Review*, **53**, 69–105.

Lipsitz, G. (1990). *Time Passages: Collective Memory and American Popular Culture*. Minneapolis, MN: University of Minnesota Press.

Liu, B. Y. (1983). People or Monsters? In P. Link (ed.), *People or Monsters? And Other Stories and Reportage from China After Mao* (pp. 11–68). Bloomington, IN: Indiana University Press.

Liu, F. S. (2008). Constructing the Autonomous Middle-Class Self in Today's China: The Case of Young-Adult Only-Children University Students. *Journal of Youth Studies*, **11**(2): 193–212.

Liu, S. (2003). Cultures Within Culture: Unity and Diversity of Two Generations of Employees in State-Owned Enterprise. *Human Relations*, **56**(4): 387–417.

Louis, M. R. (1980). Surprise and Sense-Making: What Newcomers Experience in Entering Unfamiliar Organizational Settings. *Administrative Science Quarterly*, **25**, 226–251.

Lu, X. B. & Perry, J. E. (eds) (1997). *Danwei: The Changing Chinese Workplace in Historical and Comparative Perspective*. Armonk, NY: M. E. Sharpe.

Lu, X. Y. (ed.) (2002). *Dangdai Zhongguo Shehui Jieceng Yanjiu Baogao* [Research Report on Contemporary Chinese Social Stratification]. Beijing: Shehu Kexue Wenxian Chubanshe.

Ma, J. C. & Wu, Fulong (eds) (2005). *Restructuring the Chinese City: Changing Society, Economy and Space*. London & New York: RoutledgeCurzon.

Ma, K. W. (2006). 酒吧工厂，南中国城市文化研究 [Bar Factory: Cultural Studies in South China]. Nanjing: Jiangsu renmin chubanshe.

Macuse, P. (1996). Privatisation and Its Discontents Property Rights in Land and Housing in the Transition in Eastern Europe. In G. Andrusz., M. Harloe *et al.* (eds), *Cities After Socialism: Urban and Regional Change and Conflict in Post-Socialist Societies* (pp. 119–191). Oxford: Oxford University Press.

Malloy, J. M. (1974). Authoritarianism, Corporatism and Mobilization in Peru. *Review of Politics*, **36**(1): 52–84.

Martin, J. (1992). *Cultures in Organizations: Three Perspectives*. New York: Oxford University Press.

Mayer, K. & Muller, W. (1986). The State and the Structure of the Life Course. In Sorensen, F., Weinert, E. *et al.* (eds), *Human Development and the Life Course: Multidisciplinary Perspectives* (pp. 217–245). Hillsdale, NJ: Erlbaum.

Mayer, K. U. & Schoepflin, U. (1989). The State and the Life Course. *Annual Review of Sociology*, **15**, 187–209.

Meiksins, W. E. (1998). *The Retreat from Class. A New 'True' Socialism*. London: Verso.

Meisner, M. (1999). *Mao's China and After: A History of the People's Republic*. New York: The Free Press.

Mendez, M. L. (2008). Middle Class Identities in a Neoliberal Age: Tensions between Contested Authenticities. *Sociological Review*, **56**(2): 220–237.

Michelson, E. (2007). Lawyers, Political Embeddedness and Institutional Continuity in China's Transition from Socialism. *American Journal of Sociology*, **113**(2): 352–414.

Migone, A. (2007). Hedonistic Consumerism: Patterns of Consumption in Contemporary Capitalism. *Review of Radical Political Economics*, **39**(2): 173–200.

*Ming Pao Daily* (2008). Fire Incident in Karaoke Lounge. September 22.

Moore, R. L. (2005). Generation Ku: Individualism and China's Millennial Youth. *Ethnology*, **44**(4): 357–376.

Muhlhahn, K. (2004). Remembering a Bitter Past: The Trauma of China's Labour Camps, 1949–1978. *History and Memory*, **16**(2): 108–139.

Nee, V. (1989). A Theory of Market Transition: From Redistribution to Markets in State Socialism. *American Sociological Review*, **54**(5): 663–681.

Nee, V. (1991). Social Inequality in Reforming State Socialism: Between Redistribution and Markets in China. *American Sociological Review*, **56**, 267–281.

Nee, V. (1996). The Emergence of a Market Society: Changing Mechanisms of Stratification in China. *American Journal of Sociology*, **101**, 908–949.

Newton, R. C. (1974) Natural Corporatism and the Passing of Populism in Spanish America. *Review of Politics*, **36**(1): 34–51.

Oi, J. C. (1991). Partial Market Reform and Corruption in Rural China. In R. Baum (ed.), *Reform and Reaction in Post-Mao China: The Road to Tiananmen* (pp. 143–161). New York: Routledge.

Oi, J. C. (1992). Fiscal Reform and the Economic Foundations of Local State Corporatism in China. *World Politics*, **45**, 99–126.

Ong, A. (1999). *Flexible Citizenship: The Cultural Logics of Transnationality*. Durham, NC: Duke University Press.

Otis, E. M. (2003). Reinstating the Family: Gender and the State-Formed Foundations of China's Flexible Labor Force. In L. Haney, S. Michel & L. Pollard (eds), *Families of a New World: Gender, Politics, and State Development in a Global Context* (pp. 196–216). New York: Routledge.

*Oxford Dictionary of Law* (1997). Oxford: Oxford University Press.

Parish, W. L. (1984). Destratification in China. In J. Watson (eds), *Class and Social Stratification in Post-Revolution China* (pp. 84–120). New York: Cambridge University Press.

Park, A. & Shen, M. G. (2003). Joint Liability Lending and the Rise and Fall of China's Township and Village Enterprises. *Journal of Development Economics*, **71**(2): 497–531.

Pearson, M. (1997). *China's New Business Elite: Political Consequences of Economic Reform*. Berkeley, CA: University of California Press.

Pinches, M. D. (ed.) (1999). *Culture and Privilege in Capitalist Asia*. London: Routledge.

Poulantzas, N. (1973). *Political Power and Social Classes*, translated by T. O. Hagan. London: NLB.

Poulantzas, N. (1975). *Classes in Contemporary Capitalism*, translated by D. Fernbach. London: NLB.

Poulantzas, N. (1978). *State, Power, Socialism*, translated by P. Camiller. London: NLB.

Poulantzas, N. (1982). On Social Classes. In A. Giddens & D. Held (eds), *Classes, Power and Conflict: Classical and Contemporary Debates* (pp. 101–111). Berkeley, CA: University of California Press.

Przeworski, A. & Limongi, F. (1997). Modernization: Theories and Facts. *World Politics*, **49**(2): 155–183.

Pun, N. (2003). Subsumption or Consumption? The Phantom of Consumer Revolution in Globalizing China. *Cultural Anthropology*, **18**(4): 469–492.

Pun, N. (2005). *Made in China: Subject, Power and Resistance in a Global Workplace*. Durham, NC: Duke University Press.

Pye, L. W. (1999). Civility, Social Capital, and Civil Society: Three Powerful Concepts for Explaining Asia. *Journal of Interdisciplinary History*, **XXIX**(4): 763–782.

Qiao, Jian & Jiang, Ying (2005). An Analysis of Labour Demonstrations. In Xin Yu, Xueyi Lu *et al.* (eds), *Analysis and Forecast on China's Social Development*. Beijing: Social Science Academic Press.

Raynor, J. (1969). *The Middle Class*. London & Harlow: Longmans, Green & Co. Ltd.

Ritzer, G. (2001). *Explorations in the Sociology of Consumption, Fast Food, Credit Cards and Casinos*. London and New Delhi: Sage.

Robbins, D. (2000). *Bourdieu and Culture*. London: Sage.

Roberts, D. *et al.* (1999). China's New Capitalism. *Business Week Online*, September 27. Retrieved May 27, 2009 from http://www.businessweek.com.

Roberts, H. (eds) (1981). *Doing Feminist Research*. London: Routledge & Kegan Paul.

Robinson, R. & Goodman, D. S. G. (eds) (1996). *The New Rich in Asia: Mobile Phones, McDonalds and Middle-Class Revolution*. London: Routledge.

Ryan, M. & Musiol, H. (eds) (2008). *Cultural Studies: An Anthology*. Oxford: Blackwell Publishing.

Saich, T. (2001). *Governance and Politics of China*. New York: Palgrave.

Sassatelli, R. (2000). From Value to Consumption. A Social Theoretical Perspective on Simmel's Philosophie des Geldes. *Acta Sociologica*, **43**(3): 207–218.

Saunders, P. (1984). Beyond Housing Classes: The Sociological Significance of Private Property Rights of Means of Consumption. *International Journal of Urban and Regional Sciences*, 8: 202–227.

Saunders, P. (1990). *Social Class and Stratification*. London: Routledge.

Scott, J. (1994). Class Analysis: Back to the Future. *Sociology*, **28**: 933–942.

Shantou Statistics Bureau (2000). *Shantou Statistical Yearbook*. Beijing: Statistics Press.

Sheng, X. W. & Settles, B. H. (2006). Intergenerational Relationships and Elderly Care in China: A Global Perspective. *Current Sociology*, **54**(2): 293–313.

Shirk, S. L. (1984). The Evolution of Chinese Education: Stratification and Meritocracy in the 1980s. In N. Ginsburg & B. Lalor (eds), *China: The 80s Era* (pp. 245–272). Boulder, CO: Westview Press.

Shirk, S. L. (1993). *The Political Logic of Economic Reform in China*. Berkeley and Los Angeles, CA: University of California Press.

Shu, Xiaoling (2004). Education and Gender Egalitarianism: The Case of China. *Sociology of Education*, **77** (October), 311–336.

Silver, A. (1990). Friendship in Commercial Society: Eighteenth-Century Social Theory and Modern Sociology. *American Journal of Sociology*, **95**(6): 1474–1504.

Simmel, G. (2004) *The Philosophy of Money*. London: Routledge.

Sitnikov, A. (2000). Is a 'Middle Class' Forming? *Russian Social Science Review*, **41**(6): 66–80.

Skeggs, B. (2004). *Class, Self, Culture*. London: Routledge.

Smart, A. & Li, Zhang (2006). From the Mountains and the Fields: The Urban Transition in the Anthropology of China. *China Information*, **20**, 481–518.

Smart, A. & Smart, J. (2003). Urbanization and the Global Perspective. *Annual Review of Anthropology*, **32**, 263–285.

So, A. (2001). The State, Economic Development, and the Changing Patterns of Classes and Class Conflict in China. Paper presented in *International Conference on Money, Growth, and Distribution*, September, Taipei, Taiwan.

So, A. (ed.) (2003). *China's Developmental Miracle: Origins, Transformations, and Challenges*. Armonk, NY: M. E. Sharpe.

Solinger, D. (1999). China's Floating Population: Implications for State and Society. In M. Goldman & R. MacFarquhar (eds), *The Paradox of China's Post-Mao Reforms* (pp. 220–240). Cambridge, MA: Harvard University Press.

Spires, A. J. (2011). Contingent Symbiosis and Civil Society in an Authoritarian State: Understanding the Survival of China's Grassroots NGOs. *American Journal of Sociology*, **117**(1): 1–45.

State Bureau of Statistics (SBS) (2001). *China Statistical Yearbook 2001*. Beijing, China: China Statistics Press. [Bilingual]

State Bureau of Statistics (SBS) (2002). *China Statistical Yearbook 2002*. Beijing, China: China Statistics Press. [Bilingual]

Steier, F. (1991). Introduction: Research as Self-Reflexivity, Self-Reflexivity as Social Process. In F. Steier (ed.), *Research and Reflexivity* (pp. 1–10). London: Sage.

Stockman, N. (1992). *Chinese Politics and Society: An Introduction*. London: Prentice Hall.

Stockman, N. (1994). Gender Inequality and Social Structure in Urban China. *Sociology*, **28**(3): 759–777.

Stockman, N. (2000). *Understanding Chinese Society*. Cambridge: Polity.

Storey, J. (1999). *Cultural Consumption and Everyday Life*. London: Edward Arnold.

Sulkunen, P. & Holmwood, J. (1997). *Constructing the New Consumer Society*. New York: St. Martin's Press.

Sun, L. P. (2004). *Transition and Segmentation: Changing Social Structure in Reform China*. Beijing: Tsinghua University Press. [In Chinese]

Szelenyi, I. (1978). Social Inequalities in State Socialist Redistributive Economies. *International Journal Comparative Sociology*, **19**, 63–87.

Szelenyi, I. (1982). The Intelligentsia in the Class Structure of State-Socialist Societies. *The American Journal of Sociology*, Supplement: Marxist Inquiries: Studies of Labour, Class, and States, **88**, S287–S326.

Szelenyi, I., Eyal, G. & Twonsley, E. (1998). *Making Capitalism Without Capitalists: The New Ruling Elites in Eastern Europe*. London: Verso.

Tan, A. (2007). Hong Kong 10 Years On. *Asia Times Online*, July 14. Retrieved May 29, 2009 from http://www.atimes.com/atimes/china/if14ad01.html.

Ting, K. F. & Chiu, C. H. (2000). Materialistic Values in Hong Kong and Guangzhou: A Comparative Analysis of Two Chinese Societies. *Sociological Spectrum*, **20**, 15–40.

Ting, K. F., Chiu, C. H. *et al.* (1998). A Comparison of Occupational Values between Capitalist Hong Kong and Socialist Guangzhou. *Economic Development and Cultural Change*, **46**(4): 749–770.

Tocqueville, A. D. (1862/1988). *Democracy in America*. New York: Harper Perennial.

Tomlinson, A. (ed.) (1990). *Consumption, Identity and Style: Marketing, Meaning, and the Packaging of Pleasure*. New York: Routledge.

Tomlinson, J. (1999). *Globalisation and Culture*. Cambridge: Polity Press.

Tsai, K. S. (2005). Capitalists Without a Class: Political Diversity Among Private Entrepreneurs in China. *Comparative Political Studies*, **38**(9): 1130–1158.

Tsai, K. S. (2007). *Capitalism Without Democracy: The Private Sector in Contemporary China*. Ithaca, NY: Cornell University Press.

Tsang, E. Y. H. & Lee, P. K. (2013). Vanguard of *Guanxi* (Connections) Seeking, Laggard in Promoting Social Causes: The Chinese New Middle Class and Green NGOs in South China. *China: An International Journal* 11 (August).

Tsui, A. S., Bian, Y. J. & *et al.* (2006). *China's Domestic Private Firms: Multidisciplinary Perspectives on Management and Performance*. New York: M. E. Sharpe.

TVB Pearl News (2009). *News at 7.30*. December 4, Hong Kong: Television Broadcasts Limited.

Unger, J. (2008). Chinese Associations, Civil Society, and State Corporatism: Disputed Terrain. In J. Unger (eds), *Associations and the Chinese State: Contested Spaces* (pp. 1–13). New York: M. E. Sharpe.

Urry, J. (1995). *Consuming Places*. London: Routledge.

Veeck, A. (2000). The Revitalization of the Marketplace: Food Markets of Nanjing. In D. S. Davis (ed.), *The Consumer Revolution in Urban China* (pp. 107–123). Berkeley, CA: University of California Press.

Walder, A. G. (1986). *Communist Neo-Traditionalism: Work and Authority in Chinese Industry*. Berkeley, CA: University of California Press.

Walder, A. G. (1989). Social Change in Post-Revolution China. *Annual Review of Sociology*, 1(18): 405–424.

Walder, A. G. (1992). Local Bargaining Relationships and Urban Industrial Finances. In K. G. Lieberthal & M. Oskenberg (eds), *Bureaucracy, Politics, and Decisions Making in Post-Mao China* (pp. 308–333). Berkeley, CA: University of California Press.

Walder, A. G. (1994a). The Decline of Communist Power: Elements of a Theory of Institutional Change. *Theory and Society*, **23**, 297–323.

Walder, A. G. (1994b). Corporate Organization and Local Government Property Rights in China. In V. Milor (ed.), *Changing Political Economies: Privatization in Post-Communist and Reforming Communist States* (pp. 53–66). Boulder, CO: Lynne Rienner.

Walder, A. G. (1995a). Career Mobility and the Communist Political Order. *American Sociological Review*, **60**, 309–328.

Walder, A. G. (1995b). China's Transitional Economy: Interpreting Its Significance. *China Quarterly*, **144**, 963–979.

Walder, A. G. (ed.) (1995c). *The Waning of the Communist State Economic Origins of Political Decline in China and Hungary*. Berkeley & Los Angeles: University of California Press.

Wallace, R. A. (2006) *Contemporary Sociological Theory*. New Jersey: Pearson Education.

Wallace, R. A. & Wolf, A. (2006). *Contemporary Sociological Theory: Expanding the Classical Tradition*. London: Pearson.

Wang, F. L. (2004). Reformed Migration Control and New Targeted People: China's *Hukou* System in the 2000s. *China Quarterly*, **177**, 115–132.

Wang, Q. (2008). Sex, Money, Social Status-Chinese Men and Women in the Whirlwind of Modernization and Market Economy. *NIAS NYTT*, 1: 12–14.

Wang, S. G., Davis, D. S. *et al.* (2006). The Uneven Distribution of Cultural Capital: Book Reading In Urban China. *Modern China*, **32**(3): 315–348.

Wang, X. (2008). Divergent Identities, Convergent Interest: The Rising Middle-Income Stratum in China and Its Civic Awareness. *Journal of Contemporary China*, **17**(54): 53–69.

Wang, X. Y. (2002). The Post-Communist Personality: The Spectre of China's Capitalist Market Reforms. *The China Journal*, **47**, 1–18.

Wank, D. L. (1995). Bureaucratic Patronage and Private Business: Changing Networks of Power in Urban China. In A. G. Walder (ed.), *The Waning of the Communist State: Economic Origins of Political Decline in China and Hungary* (pp. 153–183). Berkeley, CA: University of California Press.

Wank, D. L. (1999). *Commodifying Communism: Business, Trust, and Politics in a Chinese City*. Cambridge, MA: Harvard University Press.

Warde, A. (1997). *Consumption, Food and Taste*. London: Sage.

Watson, J. (2007). 饮食全球化 *[Food Globalization]*. Taipei, Taiwan: 早安财经文化出版. [In Chinese]

Watson, J. L. & Caldwell, M. L. & *et al.* (2005). *The Cultural Politics of Food and Eating: A Reader*. London: Blackwell Publishing.

Webb, J., Schirato, T. & Danaher, G. (2002). *Understanding Bourdieu*. London: Sage.

Weber, M. (1946). Religious Rejections of the World and Their Directions. In M. Weber, *Essays in Sociology*; translated, edited and with an introduction by H. H. Gerth & C. W. Mills (pp. 323–359). New York: Oxford University Press.

Weber, M. (1947). *The Theory of Social and Economic Organization*, edited by A. M. Henderson & T. Parsons. New York: Free Press.

Weber, M. (1951). *The Religion of China: Confucianism and Taoism*. New York: The Free Press.

Welzel, C. (2006). Democratization as an Emancipative Process: The Neglected Role of Mass Motivations. *European Journal of Political Research*, **45**(6): 871–891.

Wright, E. O. (1979). *Class Structure and Income Determination*. New York & London: Academic Press.

Wright, E. O. (1985a). *Approaches to Class Analysis*. Cambridge: Cambridge University Press.

Wright, E. O. (1985b). *Classes*. London: Verso.

Wright, E. O. (1994). *Interrogating Inequality: Essays on Class Analysis, Socialism, and Marxism*. London & New York: Verso.

Wright, E. O. (1997). *Class Counts: Comparative Studies in Class Analysis*. New York: Cambridge University Press.

Wright, E. O. *et al.* (1999). *The Debate on Classes*. London & New York: Verso.

Wu, Fulong (2002). China's Changing Urban Governance in the Transition Towards a More Market-Oriented Economy. *Urban Studies*, **39**(7): 1071–1093.

Wynne, D. (1998). *Leisure, Lifestyle and the New Middle Class: A Case Study.* London & New York: Routledge.

Xiao, F. (2007). Ten Features of the Anxiety Disorders in the Chinese New Middle Class. http://www.cnr.cn. [In Chinese] [Retrieved 28 November 2007].

Xu, H. (2007). Brand-New Lifestyle: Consumer-Oriented Programmes on Chinese Television. *Media, Culture and Society*, 29(3): 363–376.

Yan, Y. X. (2002). Managed Globalization, State Power and Cultural Transition in Contemporary China. In Peter L. Berger and Samuel P. Huntington (eds), *Many Globalizations Cultural Diversity in the Contemporary World* (pp. 19–47). New York: Oxford University Press.

Yan, Y. X. (2006). Girl Power: Young Women and the Waning of Patriarchy in Rural North China. *Ethnology*, 45(2): 105–123.

Yan, Y. X. (2009). *The Individualization of Chinese Society.* Oxford & New York: Berg.

Yan, Y. X. (2010). The Chinese Path to Individualization. *British Journal of Sociology*, 61(3): 489–512.

Yang, G. B. (2003). China's Zhiqing Generation: Nostalgia, Identity, and Cultural Resistance in the 1990s. *Modern China*, 29(3): 267–296.

Yang, M. H. (1989). Between State and Society: The Construction of Corporateness in a Chinese Socialist Factory. *Australian Journal of Chinese Affairs*, 22, 31–60.

Yang, M. H. (1994). *Gifts, Favours and Banquets: The Art to Social Relationships in China.* Ithaca, NY: Cornell University Press.

Yau, H. M. (1994). *Consumer Behaviour in China: Customer Satisfaction and Cultural Values.* London & New York: Routledge.

Yu, F. (2005). 19 世纪末以来中国中产阶层的消费文化变迁与特征 [The Consumption Practice And Changes For Chinese Middle Class Since the 19th Century]. *Academic Research*, 7. [In Chinese]

Yuan, F. (1987). The Status and Role of the Chinese Elderly in Families and Society. In J. H. Schulz. & D. Friedman (eds), *Aging China: Family, Economics, and Government Policies in Transition* (pp. 36–46). Washington, DC: The Gerontological Society of America.

Zang, X. W. (2006). Social Resources, Class Habitus, and Friendship Ties in Urban China. *Journal of Sociology*, 42(1): 79–92.

Zang, X. W. (2008a). Market Transition, Wealth and Status Claims. In D. S. G. Goodman, *The New Rich in China: Future Rulers, Present Lives* (pp. 53–70). London & New York: Routledge.

Zang, X. W. (2008b). Gender and Ethnic Variation in Arranged Marriages in a Chinese City. *Journal of Family Issues*, 29(5): 615–638.

Zhang, H. Y. *et al.* (1999). 中国私营企业发展报告 (*Zhongguo siying qiye fazhan baogao*) [Report on the Development of China Private Enterprises 1978–1998]). Beijing, China: Zhehui Kexue Wenxian Chubanshe. [In Chinese]

Zhang, J. J. (2007). Marketization, Class Structure, and Democracy in China: Contrasting Regional Experiences. *Democratization*, 14(3): 425–445.

Zhang, L. (2010). *In Search of Paradise: Middle Class Living in a Chinese Metropolis.* Ithaca, NY: Cornell University Press.

Zhang, N. J. (2006). Gender Role Egalitarian Attitudes among Chinese College Students. *Sex Roles*, 55, 545–553.

Zhang, W. L. (2000). Zhongguo shehui jieji jieceng yanjiu ershinian (Twenty Years of Research on Chinese Class and Strata). *Shehuixue yanjiu [Sociological Research]*, 1, 24–39.

Zhang, W. W. (2000). *Transforming China: Economic Reform and its Political Implications.* Basingstoke: Macmillan Press.

Zhang, Z. (1988). 'Jia juai zhu fang huo bi fen pei ji zhi zhu huan, pei yu zhu fang jian she xin xde jing ji zeng zhang dian I' [speed up the transformation of the mechanism of monetary distribution and build up a new economic growth pole of housing construction (part one)], in *Zhongguo fangdichan [China real estate 中国房地产 ]*, 209(5): 4–10.

Zheng, S. (2003). Leadership Change, Legitimacy, and Party Transition in China. *Journal of Chinese Political Science*, 8(1/2): 47–63.

Zheng, T. T. (2005). From Peasant Women to Bar Hostesses: An Ethnography of China's Karaoke Sex Industry. In C. K. Lee (ed.), *Working in China: Ethnographies of Labour and Workplace Transformation* (pp. 124–144). London & New York: Routledge.

Zheng, Y. N. (2004). *Globalization and State Transformation in China.* Cambridge: Cambridge University Press.

Zheng, Y. N. & Fewsmith, J. (eds) (2005). *China's Open Society: The Non-State Sector and Governance.* London & New York: Routledge.

Zhou, X. (1996). *How the Farmers Changed China: Power of the People.* Boulder, CO: Westview Press.

Zhou, X. G. & Brandon, N. (1997). Institutional Change and Job-Shift Pattern in Urban China, 1949–1994. *American Sociological Review*, 62, 339–365.

Zhou, X. G. & Hou, L. R. (1999). Children of the Cultural Revolution: The State and the Life Course in the People's Republic of China. *American Sociological Review*, 64(1): 12–36.

Zhou, X. G. & Pei, X. M. (1997). Chinese Sociology in a Transitional Society. *Contemporary Sociology*, 26, 569–572.

Zhou, X. H. (2005). *Quanqiu Zhongchan Jieji Baogao* (全球中产阶级报告 [Report on the global middle classes]). Beijing, China: Shehui Kexue Wenxian Chubanshe (社会科学文献出版社). [In Chinese]

Zhu, J. M. (1999). Local Growth Coalition, the Context and Implication of China's Gradualist Urban Land Reforms. *International Journal of Urban and Regional Research*, 25, 534–548.

Zhu, J. M. (2002). Urban Development Under Ambiguous Property Right: A Case of China's Transition Economy. *International Journal of Urban and Regional Research*, 26(1): 41–57.

Zhu, J. M. (2005). A Transitional Institution for the Emerging Land Market in Urban China. *Urban Studies*, 42(8): 1369–1390.

Zweig, D. & Chen, Z. M. (eds) (2007). *China's Reforms and International Political Economy.* London & New York: Routledge.

## Organizations

Brookings Institute (2009). http://gigaom.com/2009/09/15/brookings-institution-open-networks-a-win-win/ [Retrieved 14 November 2009].

University of Birmingham (2010). Code of conduct for research website. http://www.ppd.bham.ac.uk/cop/code8.htm [Retrieved 27 January 2010].

University of Birmingham Research & Enterprise (2010). Governance, Management, Conduct and Ethics. http://www.res.bham.ac.uk/information/ethics.pdf [Retrieved 27 January 2010].

World Bank (2001–2009). The World Bank Annual Report. http://www.world-bank.org/html/extpb/2001/content.htm [Retrieved 2 January 2009].

World Trade Organisation. http://www.wto.int. [Retrieved 1 September 2009]. Exchange rate at www.xe.com on 25 May 2010 [Retrieved 28 May 2009].

# Index

Printed and bound in the United States of America